Follow]

Risking it all fo

Tesla
Elon musk

Frances Lawson

Printed by CreateSpace
Cover design by BespokeBookCovers
Editor: Michael Garrett
Book Layout © 2014 BookDesignTemplates.co
Photography by Frances Lawson
Available from Amazon.com and other retail outlets

Follow My Heart/ Frances Lawson. -- 1st Ed.
ISBN-13: 978-1496053749
ISBN-10: 1496053745

Dedication

To all who've struggled to realize a dream which later became
a goal,
To all who've found that goal much harder to achieve than
they could ever have imagined, and then questioned their
sanity for even attempting it,
For those of you who've wondered if you have crossed the
line from perseverance to recklessness but are still hanging
on, moved by glimpses of what could be …
This is for you.

"You never know how strong you are, until being strong is
your only choice."
—BOB MARLEY

CONTENTS

Acknowledgments

There are special people who have made a contribution to this memoir and I thank them wholeheartedly. Liz Mahoney was the first person to read a partial draft and offer a suggestion. Warren Judd gave me my first opportunity to be published in print and has continued to be supportive with this book, giving permission to include his personal comment. My editor Michael Garrett has helped me lift my writing to where I feel confident in offering a quality product. My daughter Laura sacrificed daily contact with me so I could head off to the other end of the earth and experience the material for this book. I'd especially like to thank my friend Jean-François who has contributed some photos and been my rock when I was all at sea.

To all the people who feature in this book, directly and indirectly, you are a part of its success. Thank you.

Stirrings

When people ask why I've had such a strong interest in France it's difficult to put my finger on it. It's simply a feeling, an urge that grew over the years. This strong yearning often went into hibernation when I was busy with my young daughter or in an abusive or unhappy relationship but it always resurfaced. When the new millennium approached it was natural for me to reassess what I wanted, so France popped into my head more and more frequently, yet I didn't have any particular plans or goals defined, so it sat there, biding its time.

There came a day when I decided to stop looking at the obstacles and put my dream up in front of me. Maybe I could make it happen that way. I told my daughter who was around eight at the time that when she finished the seventh form (year five of high school) we would take six months off and wander around Europe, but mostly France and Italy, just the two of us together on a holiday, living as cheaply as we could, with one exception. I wanted to hire a red Ferrari for a weekend and drive along the Mediterranean coast. There we'd be, two girls from New Zealand; the wind in our hair, sunglasses propped firmly on our noses, sun and smells of the ocean, cruising in style between Italy and France.

I put a picture of a red Ferrari above my home desk and it stayed there for years, for inspiration. I figured I'd have my house paid off by then by leading my usual austere lifestyle; but when I married again in 2001 I found myself not in control of my financial situation. My tiny savings disappeared in trying to keep the family going. My well-thought through financial plan could no longer be implemented and my mortgage interest rates increased.

It wasn't possible to do anything about a trip to France during my last marriage because my husband was the one doing all the travelling and everything seemed to revolve around what he wanted to do with his life. We were in debt. I had no money. France wasn't on his list of priorities for a visit even if we'd been able to afford it, but after we separated I gave myself permission to think about myself and what I wanted. Still, I couldn't see how to make it work. I was a solo mother again with no financial resources.

Once again I needed to stop looking at the obstacles and focus again on what I wanted. This time the want was a need. I decided that somehow I must find a way to visit France in 2010, alone, just for a few weeks, then maybe this yearning would sleep again. I realized it wouldn't be ideal experiencing France completely on my own with no one to share it with, so I decided to find someone or someones to share sectors of it along the way, and the best people to do that with would be French men.

CHAPTER ONE

Hope is born

Internet dating hadn't been working for me. I'd been online for a year via two dating sites, Find Someone, which had yielded a few coffee meetings with uninteresting or unsuitable Kiwi guys, and Match.com, which didn't seem to be offering anything better. I'd spent many hours in front of my computer, filling in profiles and answering queries; effort and expense in presenting myself attractively at initial meetings.

Few guys my age were good looking, in my opinion. They tended to be balding, overweight, unfit, florid or pasty, just not attractive to the eye, yet they expected to attract young and good-looking women. The guys who caught my eye were rare and usually younger than me. I needed to spread my search farther than New Zealand. I'd met Warren, a magazine editor and scientist, and Kevin, who was an ex anti-nuclear activist and photographer and Phillip who was a property manager. Each of these men had been interested in me, but were just not a good match. They all became friends by various degrees.

I'd always had a passion for France. It's in my blood, it's in my heart and soul, and it had been in my thoughts now for the past few years. A yearning to visit France before I got too much older had been swelling within me, so I thought perhaps I could make contact with some French men. That way I might have developed some friendships before I left for my trip and could meet up with some for shared experiences, and a less lonely travel experience. I made a commitment to myself to visit France in 2010, hang the cost.

I began again, filling in a French profile on the French version of the Match site which was free for women; quite a bonus. As I trawled through the photos and profiles of French guys in various parts of France that I wanted to visit, I was struck by how many more attractive men there seemed to be in France, but I received few 'nibbles'. I had to do the chasing because the men weren't interested in looking for a woman at the end of the earth.

There was Guy-Ange who lived in Marseilles, but who spent a lot of time as an occasional chef in Los Angeles. He started off with some enthusiasm, even offering to correct my French, but he quickly lost interest and seemed to have quite an ego, explaining he'd written a book on his life and been on a TV chat show. Alain lived near Marseilles. He was a retired navy man who communicated with me for a few weeks but then he ran out of steam. There were Pascal, Adrian, Jean-Paul, Jean-Marc and others, but no one wanted to create a real online relationship with me. I could understand it, but it still disappointed me.

On the fourteenth day of April 2008 I came across a photo of a pleasant chap who seemed to be intelligent and interesting from his profile so I made an effort and wrote to him in French, telling him I would visit Paris in 2010. The next day I received a short reply back from him, offering me a place to stay whenever I chose to spend some days in Paris. His name was

Nicolas; and so began a relationship which would have profound positive and deleterious effects on me. It would set in motion a new direction for my life and a strange series of events I couldn't have predicted.

As the days and emails passed we quickly became closer and closer despite the language barrier. Nicolas was a teacher of primary school children, and one of the subjects he taught was English. His English wasn't good, but it was better than my French, so we frequently used dual languages in our communications. Initially we traded emails, but quickly we wanted to see each other to be sure we could trust the other and for curiosity's sake. My daughter Laura, being aged seventeen at the time, knew all about MSN Messenger and webcams and taught me all I needed to know.

One day there he was, for real, in his home outside Paris, writing in chat to me and watching my reactions. I was enchanted to realize it was him and that I was actually seeing him in France in real time. It wasn't love at first sight, but it was strong interest and a willingness on both our sides to see what could happen next.

Nicolas had a second job. He was a competent car mechanic and ran a little business on the side which afforded a greater income than his teaching did. He was also a textbook author, selling 150,000 copies in the previous year. Nicolas was comfortable in his lifestyle and had recently built a new house in a suburb north of Paris, where he lived with his son. His daughter spent much of her time with the children's mother somewhere else.

Nicolas sent me photos of his house and children and a few of himself. He told me he had his pilot's license and sent me photos of himself and his hired plane. The more I learned of him, the more I liked him. He was industrious, quite handsome and six years younger than I. He was clearly intelligent and tidy with a sense of humor. We shared many of the same interests in movies, gardening, and both of us had a teaching background. Our favorite color was blue and we gave each other hero nicknames; he was Indiana (Jones) and I was Xena (Warrior Princess). His middle name was Francis. He loved cowboy movies and I loved action and heroes.

By the 27th of April we'd exchanged many emails and he was considering coming to NZ to meet me. He told me his house was finished, but just waiting for a woman to help him with the decoration. He thought of me all the time and was anxious to see if his heart would truly beat when he saw me, but that he thought it would. He quit Match.com and decided to wait for me. On the 30th of April Nicolas wrote that now he thought I was the woman he'd been waiting for and he had only to wait. He said he was in love with me.

After four weeks of sharing our ideas and hopes online I was a major part of his life.

This evening I'm going to dine at a restaurant with friends, then see Ironman at the cinema. I'm going to tell them about you, Frances Lawson; a very beautiful woman, beautiful voice, magnificent smile, and very sensual. At last I have found the woman I was always searching for ... even if she is very far away I'm going to look for her ... I hope that I will be the man you're looking for to erase the past, and me ... I need to find the woman I've been looking for such a long time. It's why I go to the ends of the earth.

I write to you while you sleep. I love to write to you, to know that you read what I write and to know that I am thinking of you. I think the day we meet will be amazing.

There are important turning points in life; for me, you are one of them. I feel so much for you and I try not to get carried away, but my heart doesn't obey. My feelings are there and they invade me. I have a lot of hope, too, in coming to NZ. Even when it rains you are my ray of sunshine.

And his signoff *bisous* had now changed to *baisers tendres*, indicating a new, deeper level of intimacy.

I was moved by this tender, intelligent, and hard-working man who displayed so much courage and determination. I lived for his letters and our meetings on webcam most evenings. We didn't often speak to one another because my oral French was so weak, but we chatted away in writing on Messenger in both languages and somehow the connection was there, beautifully shared.

I was constantly thinking of him. I bought a couple of books for him. One was on New Zealand and contained short articles which had shaped moments in our history, including the infamous Rainbow Warrior debacle. It was bilingual, an absolute rarity in New Zealand. The other was a book on NZ itself. I bought a card, wrote a message, and drenched it in my perfume so that he would have a preview of me. Later he told me he went to bed with my perfume every night and had two sorts of dreams. One was Category One, as he called it; gentle and warm and wonderful. The other sort which became more dominant as time went by was Category Two; strongly sexual. We both had a wee smile at that. He was always charming.

Despite the wintry weather in Auckland I spent a lot of time in my garden. I wrote some poetic prose for him, in French.

In my garden is a camellia. Its white flowers are enormous and in the center of each is an explosion of golden stamens. I think of you and me. We are this flower, a great feeling one for the other, without any stains on our relationship, pure and honest. Simply a thing of golden beauty for all the world to see.

I look at the autumn leaves that fall from the tree outside my bedroom. I know that inside the tree new life is being made and the tree will become bigger and better. There is a promise of good things to come. You and I are at the beginning of spring at this moment.

The sky above my garden is blue with grey and white clouds that float across the world. We are both under the very same sky.

Sometimes he couldn't sleep and wrote to me. I was constantly in his thoughts. We had both experienced tough times as children and tough challenges in our adult lives. He felt moved to explain to me that in 2004 he'd had a serious motorcycle accident on a highway to Lyon.

Barreling along on his big BMW, he was struck by a low-flying bird with a wingspan of 1.2m, sending him flying through the air and his left leg clipped a metal power cabinet. His leg was left in pieces which he stuffed into a plastic bag inside his cycle jacket. I don't know how he stayed conscious long enough to do that. The surgeons told him they would normally amputate, but that since he was young and strong they would like to have a go at rebuilding his leg by harvesting from parts of his body.

It took eighteen operations and many long stays in hospital. His description of what he had to go through was chilling and so were the photos he would eventually show me on his mobile. Bone, muscle, and an artery were missing, so those were harvested from both sides of his lower back, above the hips. He was quick to assure me that soon he'd be able to run as before and that only the doctors and any woman he had in his life would be able to see the scars. This ordeal had left him wanting to make the most of life and not waste time. He said once he made a decision he just went for it, and that's exactly what happened with his interest in me.

His letters began now with *Ma Chère Frances* rather than *Bonjour Frances,*

> *I already miss you so much ... I say to myself that afterwards, I'm going to miss this woman to death. I need to talk to you every day because you are from now on my life, it's an absolute certainty. My heart understands it clearly. What more can I say? Wait a few weeks, I'm coming. I ask myself who will make the first step, who will be first to kiss the other, who will be the first to hug strongly and show that they are in love? I am already in love with you, so I don't look at any other women; I don't need to. The woman I love is the only one who counts.*

His flight tickets and new passport were all arranged. He purchased an international driver license and exchanged Euros for NZ Dollars. I had everything organized at my end. Things were set. His letters now opened with *Ma petite Frances adorée.*

I told Nicolas I wanted to write a book one day and what it would be called, but I warned him it would include a story about us. I offered to let him read it and suggest amendments if he wished.

"No no," he replied, "you're the author, you must write the book how you wish, just don't put in too many intimate details."

He told me he'd introduce me to his publisher and see if there were possibilities there for me. I thought that was an amazing idea. Everything seemed to be fitting together so well.

Then I broke my foot. My old Le Bop dance partner Kevin invited me to partner him to the annual ball. I thought that was a great idea. I didn't get out much or have opportunities to dress-up. I went decked out in my old wedding gear as I didn't have any other gown or fancy shoes. When I was married to Stephen we'd dress up in our wedding finery to celebrate our wedding anniversary. It was the first time I had worn the ensemble for a man other than my ex-husband. The weather was frigid, so wearing a sleeveless ball gown wasn't all that comfortable and I had to meet Kevin in the parking lot so he could finish lacing me into it. I didn't know anyone, but I was happy to tag along. Kevin took photos and we swirled around the dance floor.

"No helicopters," I breathlessly told him (this is a dance move where the man spins the woman just above the floor; it's stomach churning stuff).

He was careful with our moves as he knew I suffered motion sickness, and I enjoyed his expertise. I'm light on my feet, and I pick things up quickly. It was lovely having a partner instead of having to do everything solo. What fun!

After the buffet dinner we twirled and jived and strutted and chacha'd, and on one set of brisk turns my taffeta ball gown slid under my high platform shoes. I slid and, to save myself from falling, I stamped down the ball of my right foot quite hard to slow down. It worked; close call. We were a little more careful after that but, as the night wore on the burning in my feet intensified. Burning feet weren't new to me. High heels did this to me at any time because I had literally worn off nature's padding, which is never replaced. I walk on flesh and bone. The intensity got so bad I had to say something to Kevin, who gallantly took me outside to a seat, took my shoe off and massaged my foot.

Other women walked past. Rather enviously, some asked if they could have a foot massage, too. It helped a little, but I had to leave earlier than I would have liked because the pain was too great. The next day it had diminished, but as days passed it became unbearable. An X-ray revealed that my two sesamoid bones under the big toe were in six pieces scattered about. An orthopedic specialist said not to worry, it would be healed in six weeks, but that I'd need to wear an orthotic boot instead of a shoe, so no dancing, no bellydance performing for me. The pain carried on for months. I had an MRI, but it seemed the bones would never migrate back. The tendon still occasionally slips without its two guides to keep it in place. So there I was with a damaged foot. Nicolas and I had something else in common.

My daughter Laura decided she wanted to go down to Christchurch for three weeks holiday. This coincided with Nicolas's visit to me. It meant that he and I would have three weeks alone to explore our relationship and share intimacy, then Laura would return and join us for the final three weeks of his stay. It was all arranged and I was so excited. My colleagues at work shared my happiness and excitement, and I promised to take Nicolas to visit them.

Nicolas was keen to meet Laura and show her he was a normal guy and that there was nothing bad about him, that he could be trusted. This is important when using the Internet for dating. He appreciated her help when we had Internet connection difficulties. Laura, in her turn, was happy that I was happy with someone in my life, but was understandably nervous that I might get hurt badly yet again by trusting a man who might prove faithless, as had happened so often before. I told myself that surely, a man who recognized my value and spent time and money and effort to come to the end of the world for me must be a good person?

> *The first thing that you must never forget, is I adore you and I weigh my words when I say to you that you are a woman such as I never expected or who I no longer hoped for in my life. In one of your emails you describe a special man whom you would like to meet and how he should behave. I believe that I am what you are looking for. It's astonishing; you describe, too, how you would behave toward this man and what you offer him. It's exactly what I am searching for in a woman ... and what I have never found. This meeting is strange. Sometimes I tell myself it's too beautiful to be true. But I see you every day and I know it's true. It's not often that I think of you now, it's always, without stopping.*

I felt so warm and content inside when I read his loving words.

The difference in time zones had always been a challenge for us. Nicolas had to be online at 7.30am to speak with me before he went to school. Sometimes he was late to arrive and we were left with ten minutes only in which to communicate. At other times, if we had a public holiday, we could spend an hour or more just talking about anything. We really could talk about anything together and this was a source of gentle happiness for each of us.

A month out from his trip I decided I must tell him something personal, very intimate about me so that there were no misunderstandings when he arrived and if he wanted to pull out of the relationship at this stage and get his tickets reimbursed he could. I was rather tearful as I explained to him on webcam that since menopause I found intercourse painful, damaging, and often impossible, and that my sexual response had diminished to almost zero; a great source of disappointment and sadness to me, and this had had a negative effect on my last marriage. I was afraid how this would affect this new relationship. If he wanted to cancel his trip I would try to understand. His response surprised me greatly.

He told me he appreciated my effort to tell him something difficult like that and not to worry and not to cry. He didn't want to see me sad and that he was certain that when we were together we would find ways around the problem and all would be well.

"This changes nothing," he said. "I'm coming to see you because I think you're the woman for me. If we become intimate, and I think we will, I feel all will be well and we'll work something out. We'll take things carefully, don't worry."

This impressed me, and I loved him all the more.

Laura was moved to say, "Well, that's an encouraging sign. He must really be interested in you."

Here's a gentle and considerate man who really wants me, I thought.

Two weeks out from his arrival I received a short heart-stopping message from Nicolas to say he had received some bad news from his surgeon. During one of his checkups his surgeon had noticed that part of the underside of his left toe was necrosed. This didn't worry Nicolas because he'd lost feeling in that toe since his accident, but the surgeon said it had to be removed. My lovely man explained to the doctor that he absolutely had to be in NZ in two weeks' time. Incredibly, the surgeon, who was one of France's best, told him to report to hospital the next day and be operated on the following day. He would then spend a week in hospital. The doctor assured him he'd be able to get on the plane to visit me. This was nail-biting stuff and it unsettled Nicolas. He sent me a message that for the first time he was afraid; not of the operation but of not seeing me. Whatever happened, he said, he'd find a way to come to me.

With no Internet in hospital we could only communicate intermittently by SMS. He texted me, *Je t'aime*, and told me that he needed to hear from me 'for courage,' and I tried to be reassuring to boost his confidence. I wrote him an email every day, giving him news and telling him how I felt about him each day he was in the hospital. I knew he couldn't receive them but I thought it would be good for him to read once he got back home. The hospital stay was more than a physical setback for him. He was snowed under with car repair work and preparations to be out of the country for six weeks. Poor darling, I wished I could help.

In the end the surgeon amputated the first section of his big toe. This would mean walking with crutches for the whole of his trip to New Zealand and daily bandage changes. He wouldn't be able to take showers, but would have to have baths dangling his leg out of the water. We didn't care. We just wanted to be together. The next few days flew by.

His son drove him to the airport, then he was in the air, having texted me before takeoff and again when he reached Singapore. Now there could be no more communication until I saw him at Auckland Airport. It was so hard to concentrate at work, knowing that something momentous was happening for me, wondering what would happen when we met, and hoping we wouldn't have our dreams dashed.

CHAPTER TWO

Sharing our adventure

On Sunday 06 July 2008 what a frisson of sensations sparked inside me as I busied myself to tidy the house, prepare dinner in advance, and make sure I looked my absolute best for my date with destiny; hope, fear, anxiety, excitement, happiness all took turns to swirl inside me.

I arrived in plenty of time and wouldn't you know it the plane took hours to discharge its precious cargo. I sat in the arrivals lounge trying to focus on my newspaper but I couldn't. My eyes kept wandering to the display board showing Landed, Processing, hoping I looked good enough in my jeans and boots. Unable to bear it any longer, I positioned myself at the end of the entranceway so anyone coming through arrivals could see me clearly at the end. Where was he? It seemed as though every man but Nicolas was there. It took a moment to realize that the tall man halfway along the passage was indeed him. He wasn't as big as I had imagined; above average height and a nice build.

I grinned and waved to attract his attention. He caught my eye, but he didn't smile. He was leaning on a crutch while pushing his luggage trolley. I raced over to give him a hug and welcome him to Auckland. There were his sparkling blue eyes- such a clear and vibrant blue. It would be interesting to get to know him. He gave me three *bises* (the wee kisses of welcome that French people make).

"You'll need to do that," he explained, "if you want to be French."

My heart asked me where was the hug? Where was the smile and the excitement?

We made our way to the parking machine, then my car, loading his luggage into the boot and installing his crutch in the back seat. It all felt a bit awkward so I smiled warmly at him, trying to make eye contact. I put my hand lightly on his leg and told him it was wonderful to see him and I'd get him settled first, then if he needed a rest he could do so. No, he replied, he didn't need a rest; he'd fit in with whatever I suggested. His leg was like concrete to the touch and his face never moved. I put it down to being extremely tired from the long-haul flight and being out of his comfort zone. It was probably all rather over-whelming for him.

I took him to One Tree Hill to see the view. Alas, a storm was raging and we could see almost nothing up there between the large splashes of rain and the mist. I felt disappointed for us both. Things weren't going as I'd imagined. We drove around for a bit, then returned to my home in the suburb of Pakuranga.

I showed him Laura's bedroom which had been set up for him with every comfort I could think of, including maps of Auckland. The atmosphere between us was still rather stiff and awkward; not at all as I had expected after months of an online relationship. What to do? I decided that I'd better make the first effort at breaking down the walls so I asked if he would like a hug. I needed to explain what it was but I lacked the vocabulary so I had to demonstrate it instead. He seemed ill at ease but tried to go along with things. It was a little difficult to know what to say because we hadn't had a face-to-face relationship despite the fact we knew each other quite well. It was like starting all over.

It seemed we were both busily assessing things. It was forward of me to take the step, but I felt someone had to make things more relaxed. After a bit more chatting I asked if he would like a cuddle and explained it was a little more than a hug. It was nice and he kissed me, though tentatively I thought. He probably didn't want to make any mistakes. Eventually he fell asleep on the couch, truly exhausted. I felt tender toward him. He looked so vulnerable and sweet as I covered him with a rug and tried not to disturb him. He'd been though a lot recently. He slept more than an hour so I finished preparing dinner for us. I was quite nervous about cooking for him; after all, he's French and the French are famous for gastronomy.

We tried to watch a DVD of *Love Actually* but he was more interested in chatting and too tired to concentrate I think. He slept in Laura's room. It was strange, but special to say good night to him.

I knocked on his door the next day to say good morning, made him some breakfast, and sat on the bed chatting. It was lovely. Later in the morning we went to Botany Town Centre as he wanted to look for a jacket to combat the wintry weather. We looked, but couldn't find the right size and style. Nicolas decided to buy us lunch at the *crêperie* there. After we'd ordered and sat down, he had a startling and unexpected turn. He was dizzy and sweating, feeling sick. He apologized and had to put his head down on the table, suffering greatly. I didn't want to embarrass him and make a big fuss so I just held his hand

and talked to him. It looked suspiciously like a panic attack to me, but I also realized it could be a reaction to all the anesthetic from his operation on top of a long-haul flight and jetlag. I took him home and settled him on the sofa with a rug, stroking his hair until he fell asleep. He did a lot of sleeping on the sofa while I got the tea ready again. Later in the evening we had some hugs and kisses.

The next day I took him for a drive around the local area: Bucklands Beach, Musick Point, Dannemora, and Point view. I told him he could sleep in my bed if he wished, but intercourse was off the menu for now. I hoped my body would be able to try that on Saturday. In the meantime we found ways to explore and learn about each other and to be happily intimate. I was surprised I'd let things move so fast but felt quite comfortable about it other than his snoring which seemed to be as a result of a blocked nose from travelling.

It was awful having to get out of bed at 5.30am each morning to go to work, leaving Nicolas behind, but it was wonderful to come home and have him waiting there for me. It was a little stilted between us at first, but he put in a lot of effort to practice his English and I'd throw in a bit of French. We shopped at the supermarket together. He was always interested in what was available, but never impressed with the choices and prices; the situation he considered superior in France. He was also disappointed to discover that I didn't supply bread and cheese with every meal. That would be too fattening for me, I explained. He made an apple tart one day, onion tart another, *Tartiflette* yet another and a quiche. Each time I watched and helped him find the right tools and ingredients. We enjoyed cooking together in my little kitchen, and sometimes he'd reach around and put his arms around me.

I had decided to create a special romantic evening for our first Saturday together but it got off to a late start. It was difficult to get out of bed with such an attentive lover. I did manage to cook the lamb and vegies and prepare the Pavlova for my traditional Kiwi meal experience for him. The evening went well and we finally made love completely; a little uncomfortable for me, but at least successfully. I was so relieved.

After that it seemed there was no stopping us. The guy had stamina, and making love many times a day became the norm. I was incredulous that I was able to be with him like that, after years of tearful sexual difficulties as a consequence of menopause. I suppose we were physically well-matched.

One night he said to me, "This isn't normal, I can't understand how we can keep making love like this."

"I don't understand it either," I said. "I'd never have imagined it possible for me. With you I can do the impossible, it seems."

We had a chemistry where the best part of each day was being intimate as long as we could. Other than the constant urinary tract infections, my body was handling love marathons well even though it was mostly an emotional experience for me.

One late afternoon as we lay there relaxing he said, "If I had met you ten years ago I would have married you."

My heart and breathing should have stopped at that moment. That comment was so unexpected because he normally didn't tell his women that he loved them, though he did say it once to me during his stay. He had never married any of the women in his life (two major relationships) yet he was saying that to me. He said he preferred to *show* women that he loves them. I didn't know how to react so I said nothing. On reflection it was a bit odd--why only ten years ago? Why not in the future, too? I was too afraid to spoil the moment with discussion, but I regret that now.

As the days passed there was no real improvement in Nicolas's toe. It continued to bleed a little and didn't close. He kept off it as much as possible during his stay with me and I guess, in terms of recuperation, being with me was a good thing as I could run around doing things for him. He didn't have to drive and work; he could just get better. It became normal for me to see his crutch leaning against my piano stool or accompanying us in the car on our excursions.

One of these outings was to visit my best friends the Hilalis. I'd known them, for many years, since their arrival in New Zealand from war-torn Iraq. I'd befriended them when they moved into the house next door and even when they moved away years later they remained my best friends. They treated me like one of the family even though I didn't see them often as they were busy making their new life. Muhab had 'given me away' at my last wedding, and Yasmin had been my matron of honor. They were curious to meet and assess Nicolas because they didn't want me to be with a man who was going to hurt me, and they were concerned about the safety of Internet dating.

Yasmin and Muhab took an instant like to him and tried to greet him in French. Nicolas did his best to speak in English, and everyone was mesmerized by his life in France, the tale of his accident, and how he'd come 18,000 kilometers to see me. Dinner was delicious and the whole evening was a great success. We took photos of us all together. Nicolas and I popped in to visit them a second time just before he went back to France. A Chinese friend, called in one day and also met him. She thought he was handsome.

I'd made arrangements for us to spend Bastille Day (14 July) at a French event at Freeman's Bay. We arrived early in the pouring rain. The room was set up well, but the entertainment was uninspired. Nicolas recognized many of the French styles of music and particular songs. Who should turn up later but Kevin (my old dance companion with whom I had broken my foot) with his female consorts?

I introduced the two of them but had to decline Kevin's offer of a dance. Nicolas and I spent the evening watching Kevin's fancy footwork and everyone else dancing. We couldn't join in with our damaged feet. We just sat there gloomily and Nicolas didn't seem to be enjoying himself at all, despite the French music and entertainment. There was no affection between us either. Even when I'd occasionally touch his hand or shoulder there was no response. I felt sad and uneasy.

I took a week off work so that Nicolas and I could spend quality time together and for him to see a bit more of this part of New Zealand. We started off with a visit to the Waitakere City Council where I worked as a public relations advisor specializing in the environment, to show him parts of the 'green' building and to introduce him to my colleagues. I wanted to share my world with him.

Nicolas's voice was so smooth, round, masculine and melodious, like warmed butter and honey. My colleagues fell immediately under his spell. They were so excited to meet him and their eyes gleamed as they sought for things to talk about with him, in English. He understood them and they were captivated by his charm. Later they told me they were struck by the strong chemistry between the two of us and how right we looked together. They also saw the irony of how we were both wearing orthotic boots with mirror foot injuries; he with his left, me with my right. Twins.

Leaving Waitakere we headed out to Piha Beach and Karekare. I'd packed a picnic lunch and included some other snacks in between, but the weather continued to be disappointing. The sun came out quite a bit but the wind was strong and cold. Lunch had to be taken sitting in the car at Piha. We braved the cold for a quick view of the famous beach and Nicolas agreed that in summer it must be delightful. We shared some intimate moments in the car before heading to Karekare. I wanted to show him the beach where the movie *The Piano* had been filmed. It's a wild and lonely area when in the middle of a Kiwi winter. We were alone and it was good to have his undivided attention. As we walked along the track to the beach we discussed the future.

I suggested I visit him in April the next year, eight long months away, but at least the weather wouldn't be icy by then, and he agreed. I asked if he thought I'd be able to find work in France. He said he was optimistic of that because multinationals would always need native English-speaking staff. He told me he would sponsor me into the country, but I would need to leave my NZ culture behind and embrace French culture. He advised me not to sell my house immediately, to be sure I was happy living with him. He'd look into the visa situation when he got back. Maybe I could teach some English, he said. We planned my new life. He also offered to fly me over Paris in a plane so I could see everything from the air. He seemed genuine, and I had no reason to doubt him.

On the beach the visibility was poor, but I wanted to capture the atmospheric mood of the place so that Nicolas could go back to Paris and show his friends he'd been there. He looked so small and shy standing there in the wind, on the sand, in his special boot. It was difficult for him to walk in sand with his sore foot but he always put up with the pain, leaning on me when it got most difficult and never complaining. It was a good day. We'd both enjoyed getting out and about together. It was also an opportunity for him to appreciate the sights and scents of NZ. Tired and hungry, we made our way home.

The next day, after dropping my cat Disney off at the cattery, we headed off for two nights on the Coromandel Peninsula west of Auckland, me driving because Nicolas's foot couldn't cope with that. I'd already booked and paid for a room and dinner for us. I was so looking forward to having his undivided attention; no work, no domestic chores, and no Internet. Whenever I was within a close physical distance to him I just wanted to hold him, smell his delicate scent, feel his warmth and strong softness, and look into his beautiful blue eyes. He was in good shape for his age, and the scars on his body from the numerous operations he'd had didn't matter.

On arrival at the hotel we discovered we had a bonus. The hotel was half empty, being the low season, so they upgraded us to a bush chalet. There we were in a lovely big room with a super-sized bed surrounded by NZ native bush and privacy. Nicolas was impressed and took photos of me there. I wanted to photograph him. He was uncomfortable with this and told me he doesn't photograph well, but I cajoled and asked his advice on how to change the settings on his camera. In the end I took one of the nicest photos of him ever taken; he's smiling, which he normally never does in photographs. At best, at other times, he gives his 'man smile' as he calls it--sort of a minor wry lift to one side of his mouth. The weather was cold and wet so we couldn't sit outside on the balcony and listen to the native birds, but our three course dinner was delicious and it gave my French man an opportunity to try NZ wine; palatable, he declared, but not as good as French wine.

Our first full day there started later than we had planned. We drove along the coast to Whitianga to have a ride on the little train there, but when we arrived we discovered we were too late to book the railway excursion. I was disappointed with myself for lounging around in bed too long and missing the best part of our short stay- all we did was drive around that day- tiring but at least Nicolas got to see some of the countryside and take some photos.

We had expected to pick up Laura from the airport on Sunday night, but her plane was delayed so her boyfriend's grandmother dropped her home after we had gone to bed. Nicolas slept on the rollaway in the computer room as a courtesy to Laura so she wouldn't feel uncomfortable coming home to a man in her Mum's bed.

I had to go to work Monday 20 July without Nicolas and Laura being introduced so they had to take care of that themselves. After work Laura said it would be okay for Nicolas to sleep in my bed, so the new rollaway barely got christened. I appreciated her giving us the opportunity to spend the last weeks together at night. Laura and Nicolas didn't have a lot to do with each other, but one day she sat down with him, while I was at work, to discuss Europe. She was interested in Italy and travelling. She remarked to me later that she found it a bit disconcerting that Nicolas was so expressionless with his face. One could never tell what he was thinking. That was certainly true, though I experienced small changes in expression on his face when we were together and on the webcam. Some guys are like that, and I tried to accept that he wasn't demonstrative in that way and somewhat shy at times. The language barrier for him was also a factor.

During several of the Saturdays during his stay with me Nicolas would come with me to my bellydance classes with my teacher Monique. I'd been having private lessons for years and was a professional entertainer. I needed to keep my choreographies sharp. Nicolas would hobble into the studio on his crutch and take photos or try to video my practice sessions and in the evenings accompany me to the Kashmir Indian Restaurant where I would perform around 8.30pm.

The first time I got ready for my performance, Nicolas took a long look at me and said,

"You're not going out like that, are you?"

"Don't worry, I'll be covered up on the street".

"But men will look at you like that," he said.

"Yes, that's the idea; women and children, too. I'm an entertainer, it's normal. And it's work for me. I need the money," I explained. "Do you have a problem with my hobby?"

He was very uncomfortable but realized there was nothing he could do, so he took his camera with him each time and made the best of it. The restaurant owner had no problem with him doing that. I was always happy to have his company on what could be lonely and stressful evenings. Though I performed for only thirty minutes each time to restaurant patrons, the environment full of staff, tables and limited space always made it fraught with difficulty and, as a performer I did my best to minimize problems. They inevitably arose from time to time, such as table layouts in the way and malfunctioning sound equipment.

During his stay with me, Nicolas visited a farm owned by my publishing and scientific friend. I had realized early on that Warren and I would never be a good match but he was a kind and thoughtful person. He'd given me my first freelance writing opportunity to contribute a book review to New Zealand Geo-graphic magazine. We'd both found someone else but the four of us got together one day on his farm north of Auckland and shared a meal together, a good opportunity for Nicolas to see a bit of the countryside and a New Zealand farm. As always when meeting people, Nicolas handled it well and was popular with everyone he met.

We explored the view from the Sky Tower together in the heart of Auckland as well as the souvenir shops. He asked what I would choose from the Duty Free store. I told him but nothing happened when we visited it. I helped him choose presents for his children.

Another day I took him to the Auckland War Memorial Mu-seum to give him more of an appreciation for New Zealand's history and arranged for him to see a Maori Cultural Presenta-tion. He found it interesting but later when I sought some of the performers so he could have his photo taken with them he was visibly uncomfortable and tried to keep his distance. He clasped his hands, crossed his legs and looked like a startled opossum. Maori cultural displays can be quite intimidating, but I was sur-prised by his reaction.

I felt sad for him being stuck in the house for weeks while I was at work. He couldn't drive, so he couldn't get himself a rental car to explore Auckland and farther afield. His foot was-n't healing so after one painful attempt he gave up trying to walk down the road for some fresh air. He seemed to spend his days watching DVDs and surfing the Internet.

A few days before his departure my oven decided to die. We had noticed the bake function hadn't worked properly last time so Nicolas checked it out before preparing an onion tart. Just as well, both elements were dead. It was a disaster for me as I had no savings other than what I had started to scrape together to visit Nicolas in Paris. We had to rush out and buy an oven to be delivered next day. Nicolas discovered the old oven hadn't been wired well for access, which created big electrical rewiring problems for him. We scoured electrical supply outlets for what we might need, but Nicolas's experience was European. He put in a huge effort dismantling part of the kitchen and wiring the oven successfully. I was stressed but grateful. I'd never had a man who was so practical as well as intelligent.

Wednesday 20 August 2008 was a difficult day. It was hard to wake up and know we wouldn't be able to touch each other again for a long time. I loved him very much. I felt vulnerable to hurt now and afraid in case anything went wrong to spoil our plans for our future together. I was rather disappointed to find his idea of spending our last hours together was surfing the Internet for camera prices. I sat on his lap, trying to absorb his presence as long as I could. He said he didn't like unpleasant goodbyes at airports, so I tried to be calm but I was in for a shock on the way to Auckland International Airport.

Driving along the motorway I asked what he would say to his friends about us. To my astonishment he said he'd tell them that we had met at the airport.

"Well, it's true, we did," he said.

"But what about all the months we spent online with our relationship?" I retorted.

He looked uncomfortable and angry. I was hurt and angry too but there was no time to pull over and discuss anything. I was in a situation where the man I loved and wanted to be with whom I wouldn't see for eight months needed to catch his plane. I didn't want our last memory of each other to be a nasty scene. I told him I couldn't support a lie and that if anyone asked me in Paris how we had met I'd tell the truth.

"And what will you say you were doing here then?" I inquired.

"Flying planes. I'm here flying planes, freight, getting my flight hours back up."

It was much later that I realized this could never have been a credible excuse for him as with his foot the way it was he couldn't fly planes solo. His license had lapsed because he hadn't kept his flight hours up since his accident, and he had declined my offer to go up with an instructor during his stay. What a truly bizarre bald-faced lie; and how on earth did that just trip off his tongue like that?

"Am I a secret?"

"Of course not. My closest friends know all about you and it's no business of anyone else."

"Okay, but when I come and stay with you in Paris I'm not going to go around telling lies. I don't see why I'd need to. It's normal to meet the way we did, on the Internet."

I felt uneasy and hurt, but put it down to him possibly being embarrassed we had met online. Perhaps his man friends would have given him a hard time.

He collected his luggage from my car and we hugged and kissed a little with him looking unreadable and me trying not to cry. I bravely turned my back and walked toward my car. I looked back over my shoulder. He was still standing there watching me. It seemed he watched me a long time until I turned the ignition and drove off, and then he was gone. I could hardly see to drive through my tears and the pain in my heart. How on earth was I going to survive the eight long months until I saw him again, in Paris; my beloved in my most beloved country?

The Jardin de Luxembourg, Paris

CHAPTER THREE

The long wait

I felt bereft after I dropped him at the airport. For six weeks he'd been waiting at home for me and now there was no one. Suck it up, I told myself; you just have to be strong at times like this. I loved him, but several days after his departure I was becoming concerned about the desperate situation I would leave myself open to if I moved to France. I didn't know of a way to protect myself which didn't involve money I didn't have. I wanted to be with Nicolas, but if anything happened to him or us for whatever reason I could be destitute for the rest of my life. I wasn't sure I should take that chance. I decided I would have to be brave and see how my visit to Paris went and tell my concerns to Nicolas then. It was too soon to worry him with it, but hard for me to feel confident. Maybe if I was patient, I told myself, I could find a solution.

I started sorting through my things in preparation for leaving NZ. That was my way of coping with the separation, trying to move things forward, trying to make things happen. The stuff in the garage was first to be sorted, but without a fixed schedule or plan it was hard to decide what to throw away. Somehow taking action, even a little action like this, on faith, made me feel better and that perhaps I could move things forward with the universe. Unfortunately this didn't stop me feeling highly sensitive and vulnerable. I had the impression something wasn't right.

I sent him an email to welcome him back to Paris and to let him know I was thinking of him. He didn't reply directly to it. After he'd been gone some days he sent a short email to say he'd been overwhelmed with stuff to do since he'd got back and was hoping that the next week would quiet down. He made no reference to his time with me and there were no tones of love or missing me. I felt hurt and nervous, but tried not to worry as I knew he had a lot to deal with at the time.

Eventually we re-established our webcam meetings most evenings, but he often didn't turn up or he was late and, when he was there he didn't have much to say; it was usually me getting the conversation going, yet he continued to want contact and would get up to spend time with me on the webcam before he got on with his day or went to school (it was morning in France). Sometimes he'd take his laptop around the house with him to show me a snowfall that had occurred or how his garden was growing. I knew his home well, inside and out. Still, there was a big void of emotion, and his chat sentences were usually brief. When I asked why, he said he preferred to listen to me and I had more news than him anyway. How different things were before he'd arrived to visit me. It seemed such a lonely and rather empty shell of a relationship now but I wanted to keep my faith and my dream alive.

I spent many hours and a fair amount of money having selected photos from our time together printed, and I arranged them with maps and handwritten comments into a large album. I sent it with a card for his birthday. He received it in good time and in a short reply said that it brought back good memories, and if I'd been there, we'd have spent a special evening together and I wouldn't have gotten any sleep.

As the months passed I just couldn't stop thinking about my trip to Paris in the next year. It was so important to me and so exciting. I just knew I'd love France, so that wouldn't be an issue for me, just the logistics of moving. I said I'd have to sell my piano if we decided I'd definitely join him, but he said no, to bring it with me as he had plenty of room.

He didn't turn up for an expected assignation with me on the 10th of October, but it wasn't a new situation; I had to wait. Three days later he sent a short email to say that his foot had unexpectedly become painful and he'd been admitted to hospital overnight. They had trimmed his amputated toe and put him on antibiotics. He felt confident that now the toe would heal properly, but his lack of two arteries in his lower leg meant that there was always less oxygen available there for healing.

I asked if I should buy my tickets because there were some good deals this far out. I also wanted to check if he really still wanted me. He said yes, go ahead, so I did. It was the most money I had spent in many years and the first time in my life I had bought a plane ticket to another country for a holiday from just my own resources. It was a big deal. I felt like a normal adult, not just a solo Mum watching every cent. I'd have to save up and pay it back but for now it was paid, travel insurance, too. I sent him my itinerary.

Christmas was on the horizon so I asked what he'd like for a present. Oh, nothing; he had everything he needed. I told him I would send him something nice from New Zealand. Our trip to the Coromandel had been lovely, so I found a fine art print, by a popular artist, showing the area, and arranged to have it sent to him in plenty of time for Christmas. I kept asking, he kept saying it hadn't arrived. I contacted the print company who are experts in international posting to explain it had never arrived and what to do? They were surprised as they often posted to France, but sent a replacement off. This one never seemed to arrive either. Each week I would ask him to check his local post office in case it was too big to fit into his post box, though it probably wasn't. He didn't seem to be concerned. I asked if he was sending me anything. He said he was.

"Are you sure?" I enquired.

"Of course, it's certain, Miss Frances, I promise," he replied.

What fun; a pressie from France, my first from him.

I sent him a Christmas e-card with all the love I had. He sent me a beautiful Christmas animated Powerpoint presentation (made by someone else) with a romantic song and French captions which I managed to save onto my computer. I adored it and wept. He went away for a week with his sister to Strasbourg after the New Year, so again I had to be patient to see him, but it was hard, I missed him so much.

On his return in January I told him I had still not received my present. He laughed and said he had decided not to send it as there seemed to be postal problems between NZ and France. He'd give it to me when I came to see him. This disturbed me greatly as by this stage I was having doubts about his integrity but the problem for me was that, with the language barrier and the time differences and never being together, it was impossible to be certain of anything.

Often things didn't ring true, but there was never any proof they were not as he said. I kept wondering if I was putting my own interpretation on things through my own fear. Any time I asked a direct question or wrote a letter telling him of my unhappiness he either ignored it or said okay, we'd talk about it tomorrow, and if he didn't want to talk he always found a way to end the conversation by being late for something or interrupted by a neighbor or a nurse or just losing the Internet connection.

From time to time he would send me digital files of photos of France or an interesting link to do with environmental issues so I knew he was thinking about me, but the communication was sporadic and unsatisfying. His interest in me seemed to be mostly sexual. How could this be so different from what we had shared at the beginning?

He would often ask me to lean back in my chair and stroke my hair. He found me sensual and exciting. I refused to get naked for him until we were in the same room together in France. He was comfortable in taking off all his clothes so long as I told him exactly what to do. He joked I was the boss on the webcam but he'd be the boss in the bedroom. This type of sexual sharing was certainly more satisfying for him than me. It was a sad and lonely way to connect and share intimacy, but it was all we had. He told me he needed to feel close to me as we had been in Auckland.

April came; just two weeks to go and my suitcase was mostly packed. My work colleagues were happy and excited for me and kept asking for details. I'd arranged for Laura to stay with her father while I was away for five weeks. I knew Nicolas wouldn't be able to fly me over Paris because his license was still lapsed but he had suggested picnics and walks and restaurants and spending time with nature together. All that would be better with me, he'd told me.

He was still having Internet connectivity problems and would spend a lot of time trying to get it to work so we could see and chat with each other. On this particular morning I asked if he had news about when his foot might get sorted out.

"Yes, I was on the telephone all day on Tuesday. The surgeon must operate on the joint and shorten it a bit to try to close the wound. It will happen soon and it's not me who can decide the dates unfortunately. He's going to try to do it quickly like the last time before I came to NZ."

"So he doesn't know the date?" I asked.

"Not yet. Afterwards there would be two weeks in hospital, but that's not the worst. I telephoned the teaching academy and yesterday they called me back to say I have to have a medical exam next Monday. They want me to go to a medical center for three months in order for me to start working part time. It's a catastrophe! Otherwise they will no longer pay me sick leave and I can no longer teach. New law, thanks to Sarkozy. They're eliminating all the part-time positions. I can have one but I must go to the center after the operation under surveillance and a panel of doctors will decide when I can go back to work. I have no dates about that and it's a catastrophe for my car business, worrying for my children and worrying for your visit here. I think it will be me who goes to NZ when I get out of this center."

"But I can't change my trip- it's arranged with my work," I said in panic.

"I know that too," he replied. "Can't you get your ticket reimbursed?" he asked.

"If I cancel I'll lose $1200. It's taken an enormous sacrifice to save for this trip. Laura and I don't eat well. There have been no restaurant meals, no cinema for me, no house repairs, no expenditure on anything for eight months, in case I move to France. Can nothing be done to wait until after my trip?" I pleaded.

"I think the problem is not the surgeon, I wasn't worried about that. The academy is the problem. They'll let me know. I think they want me to go to Menucourt. This foot has been a problem for a long time. I'm waiting for the administrators' decision. Two women phoned me yesterday and told me I have no choice, it's the law, and they're doing their job. I spent the day phoning to find a solution but every service told me the same. Of course I can resign; at the moment they want people to do that but I can't. My children still need to study and it's very expensive. I need to stay a teacher for a few years still. I think you must postpone your trip. I know it's difficult for you … so I say I'll come. It's easier for me if my foot is better."

"But the whole point was for me to see France, to see if I liked it and to be there with you, to see how you live," I retorted.

"Of course. I'm sorry about that. I need to save my foot if I can and not lose my job. What would you do with a man without a foot? I don't want them to cut off this foot. I need it to walk and be whole."

"Yes, of course," I replied. "I understand. Your health is important and so is your job. But I would still want you even without your foot."

He said, "Okay, we need to wait longer than expected. That's difficult. We mustn't be too sorry … we must wait and see. I'll find a solution and will know more in a few days."

I was beside myself with despair. I walked down the hallway to Laura's room and burst into tears and told her I wasn't going to France. She looked a bit stricken herself. She didn't say much; there wasn't much to say.

It took longer than I'd expected for him to go to hospital. Waiting for appointments and decisions always seemed to drag on, and when he was in the hospital for two weeks I only received two short text messages to say the operation was finished and he was okay. He never answered any of my voice messages or text messages. He later explained his mobile phone battery had died and his message box was overloaded.

My annual leave had been arranged but I changed it to spend just the first two weeks of what would have been my trip at Easter, at home. I needed time out to process my sadness and disappointment. My heart and soul hurt so much. At work my colleagues looked at me helplessly, wanting to be of help with the disaster, but knowing there was nothing they could do.

Those weeks were truly difficult. I was alone. Laura went to her father's home as arranged, but for only two weeks. So much had been riding on my visit to Nicolas. I loved him passionately even though he didn't treat me as well as I'd have liked since our separation, and I didn't completely trust him.

This tragedy began to affect my health. My bowel stopped working most of the time. I tried all the medications obtained from my doctor, specialist, and over-the-counter supplements too. Pain and bloating were daily trials. I felt pregnant all the time, and my colleagues watched my bulging abdomen with disquiet. There was no obstruction, but it got so bad my doctor prescribed the powder that's used if someone is having a complete cleanout before a colonoscopy. Enemas only helped the rectum, and the problem seemed to be higher up.

In the end I had to pay for a private colonoscopy. These are no fun, but a good idea when one is over fifty years of age. The specialist found some polyps which they removed. They weren't cancerous but there was no point in taking a risk. They also found diverticulitis. Unfortunately there's no cure for that and it's often a source of pain. None of this explained paralysis of the bowel, and that situation continued for so many months. Nicolas was relieved that I didn't have cancer or anything else life-threatening.

In the meantime he had gone to the medical center for a couple of months. Contact from him was rare. Those rare emails contained perhaps two sentences and never any loving thoughts as they had more than a year before. I'd kept reminding him to send me documentation of his hospital operations for the past two times. He forgot or he was too busy or his computer broke down, but I impressed on him that I needed them to try to claim travel insurance. Eventually he sent them to me along with a letter I had asked him to write stating why he was unable to have me as a visitor.

My travel insurance claim was rejected because at this stage he had had twenty operations on his foot and I had purchased my plane tickets after one of his hospital stays. I'd had no right to have done that, they said. He was high risk so they refused to pay out. My money was lost.

I saw the hospital note for the previous October and a letter saying he had to have an interview in May, but there was nothing concrete concerning his last operation or the requirement for a stay at the medical center. Dark thoughts would pop into my mind but I had to trust him. To do otherwise would have created more shit for me, and I couldn't walk away from him and my dream. I was still officially on the Match dating site, but no one approaching the likeability of Nicolas had ever made an appearance.

Once he was back from the medical center we settled into

our on/off webcam sessions with him having connectivity problems and not letting me know, and me waiting for him in my fresh makeup and nice clothes, in vain quite often. He got a nasty case of the flu and I was very worried about him, but the dear man still tried to get out of bed to see me in the morning. There he was in his blue dressing gown, unable to sit up, lacking strength so much so that he had to lie down, trying to type on his laptop which was propped on his stomach. He was genuinely ill. If I'd been there I could have made him much more comfortable.

There was never any word as to when I could come over or when he could come to me. He was always waiting on the French education administration or the French health system. Our webcam sessions often seemed to focus mainly on having a slightly sexual connection and this became rather boring for me. He wanted me, he told me, and I believed it was true but was it now only sexual? I once asked if I was just a bit of Internet pornography for him. He seemed surprised and denied it. He reminded me he made an effort in the mornings to see me and that showed I was important.

I tried and tried to uncover the truth of our situation but to no avail. If Nicolas didn't want to say something, he didn't. A man wouldn't have gotten away with this 'live', but with time, distance, and language obstacles it stayed like this. I had no choice other than to quit. I didn't quit. I wanted to believe that this incredible meeting had significance, that the wonderful man I had fallen in love with would come back. Nicolas explained that his former persona was busy with all sorts of worries and that the distance made things bad. He excused himself by saying that since the accident he'd forgotten how to be romantic. Well, he'd remembered enough in the first months of our relationship.

My colleagues became concerned and Laura became annoyed.

"Can't you just go over there? Turn up on his doorstep?" my colleagues asked.

I didn't think it was an option spending all that money and flying so far to find him not at home and I had a feeling that wasn't the right thing to do even though I really wanted to do it. Laura was annoyed that he treated me so shabbily now with no love and effort.

I was admitted to hospital because my bowel had ceased to function for seventeen days. The treatment wasn't pleasant. I ended up on antidepressants after an overnight admission to the emergency department due to a major panic attack and the return of my general anxiety. I fully understood the horror of anxiety, panic and depression, having been susceptible to that since the death of my first daughter back in 1989.

One day I tried to explain that he didn't seem to want to discuss emotions and only thought about sex.

"What's so funny, Nicolas?"

"What you say."

"Not to me. I'm serious. Emotional intelligence is important in a relationship."

"Yes, I know that."

"You never seem to have time to discuss it."

"I prefer to keep it for later."

"Keep what for later?"

"All that I have in me."

But I've been waiting thirteen months. I deserve better."

"Yes, of course."

"Many times I've thought about ending things. Not because

of your foot or the distance but because you don't contribute feelings or romance.

"I see a woman who's thinking like a woman," he said.

"I'm still waiting for a man who disappeared a long time ago. I never saw that man again. He seems a shadow, that man I fell in love with."

"Lots to read this morning ... I'll think about all that. It's 8am and I have to go to school. I kiss you and I'll see you to-morrow."

"I miss the man I fell in love with. The man who wrote beautiful letters to me."

"Okay, I kiss you .... Friday."

Another Christmas came and I still had the third copy of Nicolas's original Christmas present. I had expected to hand it to him back last April, but perhaps it would be another April before we'd be together. He told me there would be workmen in his street for a bit, replacing Internet cables and we'd not have much connection. He seemed to have an extraordinary amount of Internet problems. The connection would cut out, then return. Often the webcam was blurry due to lack of speed. I waited and waited for him. For three weeks I waited with only a couple of short text messages from him. I sent an email, but he did not reply. I sent an e-card for Christmas and he sent one back with a short message ... *Merry Christmas Frances*. That's all. I felt so hurt.

Still I waited. On New Year's Day 2010 I wrote to him desperately and sadly, feeling afraid and knowing there was nothing left to lose by saying what was in my heart.

My Dearest

This situation is causing me a lot of concern, understandably. Each day I wait for you on MSN and make myself pretty for you. Each day I wait for news that's important for my life, but nothing happens. Never an email of hope or love, neither feelings nor sharing. You make almost no effort to keep me. I'm wondering if perhaps you don't want me but lack the courage to tell me. I'm only guessing, but is it true?

It's been three months since we've had a good conversation. I don't know what's happening with your foot or your job. You say nothing about coming to NZ to see me and you don't allow me to come and see you in Paris.

Since you left Auckland you have been so completely different, so cold to me and careless and not as attentive as a man in love would be. You have not clearly explained this though I have asked you many times. You make excuses and blame your foot, but I'm not convinced that's the complete answer. After all these long months of waiting I deserve better. I deserve the truth. I love you with my body, heart, and soul. Do you feel the same? Please tell me yes or no. Please help me understand.

What have I been waiting for so loyally? Was this all a game or a lie? If so, why would you be on webcam all these days? It doesn't make sense. You say you want me sexually but you do nothing to create a real relationship, to be with me.

This year will be difficult for me with so many changes at work and at Auckland, but I'm waiting to find out what will happen with you and me because you are so important in my life. I have to know if I will see you this year. I don't know what will happen, but I must make decisions and preparations, so I need you to answer this letter.

If you don't want me, tell me and I will try to accept it. If you don't want me then perhaps I will go one day to Paris but always it will be with a great sadness because I will know that just a few kilometers away is a man I will always think of, but whom I will never see again. So my dear, where do we go from here?

He didn't reply to this email, just as he hadn't replied to any of my previous letters to him, over all those months, seeking clarification. I received a short email simply saying,

> *Good evening Frances ... I'm at a friend's house ... my MSN isn't working and the new one won't install ... I'm doing all I can to fix it. I kiss you.*

Something didn't feel right. I had a chat with Laura and asked her if there was some way of finding out if he was really online but deliberately hiding from me on Messenger. We created a fake account. I became Fabienne Mazet. I found a photo of a Fabienne (young and fresh looking with long hair the way he likes it) on the Internet. I went online at a time I knew he would be available. Messenger indicated he was not online and not available, but I sent him an online chat message anyway.

I said, "*Salut*" and he replied.

"*Salut*. How do I know you?"

My jaw hit the floor. I couldn't move. I was so shocked. Why was he online talking to others, but never contacting me? I sat there staring at the screen and his conversation as he typed it, Laura beside me.

He said, "I have to go now, but I'll be back around 2.30pm so we can talk then. You can leave a message if you like and tell me how we know each other."

I knew I couldn't come online at 2.30 because that would be 2.30am my time and I had to be on a film set early in the morning. Of all days to have a job as a film extra; it wasn't even a good movie, Yogi Bear 3D. My heart was twisting in knots, my soul was screaming at me. What to do?

I added to Fabienne's chat conversation to him:

What, forgotten me already my dear? I'm crying tears over you. I see you have the connection. I've been waiting such a long time and I'm feeling very sad that you are not contacting me. Please for the love of God at least say something, be kind, and send me a message. This is a terrible situation for me.

I had to work on the movie, wondering all day if there would be a message waiting for me. There wasn't. What had happened? What was going on? What was it all for? Had I been a stupid woman to love a man? Why had he changed? All these questions had no answer. I had no closure. And that was the damaging part of all this. I needed to make some closure for myself so I wrote an email to Nicolas telling him how I had felt about him, hoping he would be okay in life and of my great sadness because I had never received a goodbye from him.

I never heard from him again. I so needed closure to heal and move on, to know the truth, but it never came. I could have accepted an honest rejection, but this was downright cruel and cowardly. I felt betrayed and lied-to. If only there was a little black box of our relationship that could record all thoughts, feelings and motivations, so that I could know the truth about us and deal with it. I wanted to play back the black box record so other people could see what had happened.

How much had been real? I struggled for a long time to accept the situation; back to square one. My mental state wasn't good. With my dream in tatters, missing what we had had, depression, despair and anguish had kicked in. I'd wasted almost two years of my life for brief snippets of happiness and hope.

France and love were just as out of reach as they had ever been.

The biggest coward is a man who awakens the love of a woman without the intention of loving her. Bob Marley

What did I learn from this episode in my life? France was important to me; in fact, it was clearly essential to my happiness, yet I couldn't explain why. It was simply resident in every cell of my being and resonated whenever I saw a picture in a book or a television program or movie that featured that country. It moved me to tears. In the end France was bigger than any man.

I knew I couldn't pick up my life and just carry on as I was before I met Nicolas. Fate made that impossible, even if I had wanted to choose the previous status quo. The politicians decided that Waitakere City and my job must disappear and become atoms in a 'supercity' concept. I was now losing my job.

I'd always found it difficult to get employment, even though I have decades of good experience and good qualifications. There was no guarantee that there would be a job for me in the new Auckland Council. It was looking increasingly unlikely as I saw the tactics of politicians and businessmen. It seemed to me they had little commitment to helping residents use water more sustainably. I had specific expertize that wasn't wanted in the new order.

I was honest enough to accept that I hadn't been happy for some time in my little house and garden. My house needed money spent on it, but it could never be truly comfortable because it was simply too old and modest and needed an expensive upgrade. I could no longer imagine myself staying there for the rest of my life. I'd been in a holding pattern with my garden for years, having done as much as I could with it and just maintaining it with little excitement.

What's more, Laura, the center of my universe, and I were starting to get on each other's nerves. It was a sign we both needed to become independent. She needed to have to make her way without me always paving the way for her. I loved her to bits and I loved that we were close and could talk about anything, but her problems were always my problems too, and I had so many of my own to deal with. The truth was I was tired, tired from struggling and trying and fighting and hurting in life. How could things be different? I needed to find a way to live my own life, discovering what that looks like without living each moment for other people.

I needed love, real love, genuine love, lasting love. I needed quality human connections where I mattered on a long-term basis. I wanted a relationship that merited the love and attention I would put into it. I'd proved I could survive; now I needed to find a way to thrive.

Joan of Arc, Mont Saint-Michel, Normandy

CHAPTER FOUR

Picking up the pieces

It's often said that if you keep doing the same things you get the same results. If you want your life to change you have to change yourself, but it takes courage and commitment. I needed gobs of both.

It was clear to me that my life in New Zealand was going nowhere, and that had been the case for years. I'd always found it a struggle to get work despite increasing experience in diverse sectors, and qualifications. My age was now against me, and I knew I was losing my job at Waitakere City Council. The fact was, we all were.

The national government had decided they wanted to amalgamate seven councils into one enormous 'supercity' run out of Auckland Central, despite the fact that each city council was servicing different types of communities across a large region. I worked for New Zealand's first and only true Eco-City. It had been founded on the principles of Agenda 21 at the summit in Rio de Janeiro in 1992. Mayor Bob Harvey and his team had courageously decided they would manage a city in the west of Auckland based on principles of sustainability, being green; an idea a little ahead of its time.

I'd fought my own environmental campaign against ecosystem destruction by my own city council Manukau City back in 2006. I won a battle but lost the war. A developer's money was just too lucrative for that council to care about buffer zones between industrial and domestic zones, beautiful established trees, and residents' wishes. I gained the respect of residents, some local politicians and local media, but it took a lot out of me, fighting the fight virtually alone. However, I discovered I really did care about our planet and the injustice that was going on around me where there was, politically, no honest commitment to living more sustainably.

Waitakere City, on the other hand, had a record of putting their efforts where their mouths were, and after three attempts I succeeded in getting a position there as a generalist communications advisor. Eventually, as a result of some effective efforts and campaigns, I succeeded in gaining a more strategic environmental position. I felt at home there; a good match for my values, and I felt valued.

Much of my time became spent in helping the water division of the council, EcoWater, to promote its messages concerning drinking water, wastewater, and stormwater. With my teaching background and experience in marketing, I came up with new ways to get the sustainability messages across to the public as Public Affairs Advisor-Environment. I enjoyed this work. I felt that at last I was making a positive difference in people's lives, especially after I established the Water Ambassadors Kids Club. This was based online with information and interaction on environmental matters pertaining to water use.

I formed a group of young public speakers, some as young as six, who would go out into the community, schools and speak at events to spread the message in the community. Retired folk got involved and I was encouraged and supported by teachers, club members' parents and my bosses. It was satisfying hard work, and it was getting positive outcomes.

EcoWater became the regional, if not national, leader in this type of work, and from time to time I was asked for advice on water management campaigns, by other councils or to peer review government research papers. I was also called in to advise and help implement other Waitakere City environmental programs. The pay was poor, and after a few years I started to get a bit restless, but on the whole it was a good position, and I worked with lovely people who cared for each other and the planet. I won an internal award for innovation and received a couple of little bonuses in recognition of my efforts.

Unfortunately, this special city in the west of the Auckland region was all unraveled by politicians and businessmen who had much to gain financially and politically by setting up organizations that would spend a lot of money, give high salaries to a few and destroy careers and jobs for many. It would obliterate many local community connections and initiatives and cause untold stress. Now there would be just one all-supreme council answering to the government, saying it had the ratepayers' interests at heart, even though the ratepayers had never wanted this.

Auckland had been bureaucratically dysfunctional for years but that's the nature of the place. Restructuring in this way could never change the problems and culture of Auckland. Better ways were proposed, but the decision-makers ignored them, so it was in this climate of dissolution and uncertainty and the loss of Nicolas that I found myself suffering gobs of stress and physical symptoms of headaches, anxiety, bowel dysfunction, and minor health issues.

It became clear to me, despite the positive expectations of my bosses, that the company that supplied water to the region would never hire me as a public affairs/environmental education advisor as they seemed to have no intention of encouraging people to use less water in the future. They publicly admitted they were there for the bottom line, and it didn't seem to be the triple bottom line. Their management also stated publicly that they were "not in the business of consulting with anyone." The guy heading that company was also the guy in charge of the dismantling of all the city councils and the creation of the 'super' city. My bosses became more and more despondent about the situation for staff and environmental sustainability messages. My colleagues were becoming stressed.

I searched for an alternative job, and a new way to see my beloved France. In January 2010 I enrolled in a residential course based at Plélauff, Brittany to study for a TESOL qualification. This is an internationally recognized certificate demonstrating that the holder had the skills to teach English to speakers of other languages. It was my hope that I could find a way to teach English to the French and at the same time have a mini holiday. The course would last four weeks and I'd then take a holiday consisting of less than two weeks, a total of just under six weeks in France. Many hours were spent researching language schools in France and preparing a cut-down CV in French and English. I started taking French conversation classes in Auckland as preparation.

Financing this trip was a major problem but I had to do it because the clock was certainly ticking. I discussed my hopes and plans with Laura. She was understandably anxious because we'd spent her entire life together, very close, even when there had been her father and my last husband on the scene. She'd been the center of my universe and I hers.

That relationship would change, inevitably, one day. I decided that at fifty-five years of age I needed to be the one to leave home, rather than my daughter. She understood, but she wasn't comfortable about it. She'd watched my struggles and knew how important this was to me. Laura was undoubtedly scared of what success from my trip could mean for her, and we talked about it whenever we could, to acclimatize us both a little to the possibility of me leaving.

The folks at work used to ask me for updates on my planned trip and nudged and encouraged when I started to worry about the craziness of tearing off to the other side of the world for a qualification and a hope. One day Judy, who worked in the Cleaner Production unit of the council, passed by my desk one day.

"Frances, there's a sustainability conference being held in Auckland at the end of the year. It's something that might interest you."

"Sure thing; tell me about it. Is there a website I can check out?"

I checked out the information online. It certainly looked interesting, and I read the profiles of the key speakers. As I scrolled down the conference information I came across a professor interested in ecological economics and sustainability. How interesting! Perhaps he might know of an opening for someone like me? I searched for him on the Internet and eventually found an email address for him. I wrote and told him I would be in visiting his area on a certain date and could I come and talk to him about some sustainability projects I was involved in? He replied yes, and said to keep in touch, but at this stage he was available on those dates. This was an encouraging development for me.

Creating opportunities for oneself can take time, so I thought that attending the conference might be good for networking and that why not become one of the presenters myself? After all, I had some special experience and expertise. I offered to write a paper and present it, and this was accepted by the organizers. I started to write the manuscript so that all I'd needed to do on my return from my trip would be to finish it off.

In the meantime I was busy organizing my trip, finding somewhere for Laura to live while I was away and completing all my work commitments. The garden needed lots of effort to tidy it to a high standard ready for my absence, and I discussed my plans with friends. I had created my Facebook page earlier so this could be used for regular communication and I created a Hotmail account so that I could access email while overseas. It was clear I'd need to buy a laptop for the course work while in France; an additional expense, but a worthwhile one. So much to do but all rather exciting.

My ex-husband suggested I use my interest in writing to start a blog about my trip. I had no idea how to do it, but a few days later I'd taught myself and on the 23rd of April I wrote my first blogpost.

I couldn't see how some folks could make sudden decisions to up and go overseas; blink and they'd be gone. Not me. Long-haul seemed to require army precision and a major packing campaign even though I could take only essential small items in my suitcase, plus the required course materials.

My trip had taken so much planning, dreaming, hoping, and effort; those myriad tasks that demanded attention before I could relax into the idea that I was almost on my way: finding a safe board for Laura, getting on top of my work at Waitakere City Council, obtaining a Warrant Of Fitness for the car and paying the registration. I discovered my driver's license would expire while I was away. I asked myself what bills would come in while I was in France. Would my luggage be overweight?

I learned about all the crazy regulations in place at airports for security. Mascara had to be in a plastic bag. Mascara for heaven's sake? In reality there's never enough of the liquid in those dinky little tubes to last long. What was I going to do with a mascara wand, threaten a gay pilot?

The most direct long-haul flight takes at least 24 hours. I'd have to shove spare knickers in my laptop bag if I wanted to arrive 'fresh'. Well, I hoped the nice man at customs wouldn't get the idea I was trying to bribe my way into France if I accidentally deposited my G-string on the conveyor belt along with my passport; then again, being French, maybe he'd understand perfectly and wave me through with a twinkle in his eye.

I had a rather odd mix of items in my suitcase: bellydance practice gear, hair dye to cover my grey for several weeks, copies of key documents, CV and cover letters, language course binders and materials, enough pharmaceuticals to look pretty dodgy. Madam, please explain all these enemas you're carrying--I could just hear it.

There was no room for a raincoat or umbrella and I'd only packed three pairs of shoes. Three! How on earth could I look presentable in the fashion capital of the world? My mind reflected back on a previous period of packing my bag for a trip to France. Here I was, two weeks out again, but this time I was making every detailed arrangement myself. This time I was going alone into the unknown. There'd be no one to meet me at the airport and share my trip with me. I felt sad, but determined. This time it was going to happen; then a little-known volcano in Iceland decided to erupt and European air traffic ground to a halt due to ash.

French planes were grounded; the backlog of passengers became enormous. People had meetings, family events such as funerals and wedding arrangements ruined. Each day I scanned all the information sites for any news that might show my trip was still possible.

With only four days to go now until I left New Zealand for the biggest and most important adventure of my life (other than becoming a mother) I was unsettled. The previous week I had been happy and excited, but over the last two days those positive feelings had been smothered by anxiety; smothered by the cinders threatening French airspace, smothered by molten rock from the center of the earth.

I absolutely had to be in Paris on the Friday or I would lose the opportunity to get my new qualification, I would miss my job interviews and the hope of the new life I had always dreamed and worked for. It couldn't be rescheduled. So much detailed planning had gone into creating this window of opportunity; so many encouraging moments from friends and colleagues, the little synchronicities that had occurred lately.

I busied myself in setting up my new laptop and it was great to have my ex-husband's help to do that, to receive Laura's best wishes for Mother's Day. There had been so many contributions to this milestone in my life. I felt as if I was taking many well-wishers along with me on this journey.

"Please make it happen for all of us," I pleaded with the universe.

In the nick of time the dust clouds thinned a bit and airlines became bolder in sending planes into the skies. I settled Laura with a lady I had known when I was studying for my degree in Applied Communication. She had teenagers and I thought that could be a safe place for Laura to experience not having me around for a while. Bag closed, just, I was driven to the airport by my best friends. What a civilized way it was to start my first journey to Europe; my friends hugging me and wishing me well, taking me to the airport and lingering long enough to see me settled with a hot chocolate.

On my own and strolling through the international departures it all felt so natural; no great excitement, no anxiety, just at peace with everything. This was rather unusual for me because I'm quite a worrier, a bit intense and always full of feeling. Instead, I'd been living in the now all day.

As the plane launched itself into the blue, I felt no emotional connection with Auckland at all. I wasn't leaving home; I was leaving a place where I lived, simply a fact, just an observation and mild surprise at this discovery. I'd never taken this flight path before so it was a pleasant surprise to look down at a couple of Waitakere dams showing signs of emptying from the drought, then we skimmed over Piha and out to sea.

It was a long flight, first flying for eleven hours to Singapore, a five hour wait at the airport there, then on to Paris for thirteen hours. It wasn't pleasant squashed upright in an economy class seat even though I'd taken a few sleeping tablets along the way. I'd had enough of watching Leonardo Di Caprio in *Shutter Island* or gazing at The Tasman Sea, watching Denzel Washington in *The Book of Eli* or checking out the Northern Territory of Australia. Outside my window the Northern Territory was looking bleak with a color palette limited to muddy tan and blackish green. The straight lines that dissected the landscape were the only sign of man's attempts to tame nature. This country didn't seem to want or need people in it.

I couldn't see much out the window as we were coming in to land at Roissy Charles de Gaulle Airport, so I tried to curb my impatience and just wait until all the processing was complete before working out how I felt about being on French soil. As the plane taxied on the runway at CDG, heading for the terminal, I was a bit surprised to see numerous rabbits bounding about as we cruised past. Surely their burrows would be a menace for the planes?

What an odd feeling to see all the signs in French and to have to be completely reliant on myself every minute. I was glad I had planned thoroughly, but there was a nail-biting moment when the disembodied voice on the Air France Bus to Gare Paris Montparnasse announced we would arrive at 9.58 am. My train to Rennes was to leave at 10am. A Singaporean man and I looked at each other in horror. Two hours to bus from the airport to Paris? I sat there for a moment feeling helpless and silly, but then thought I'd better see what I could do to get back on track. I spoke to the bus driver in my pitiful French and explained my situation. He said there'd be no problem, I would arrive on time. I had to trust him.

Paris traffic can be challenging but on this occasion the motorways were flowing freely. The Singaporean made his stop at Gare de Lyon and I made mine in time too and in the meantime I'd had my first glimpse, briefly, of Notre Dame Cathedral as we'd crossed the river Seine on our way to the train station. A little tingle went up my spine, then it was gone.

Despite years of trying to get there, dreams in flames and unexpected obstacles, I was really in France. Was I jumping up and down in excitement? Strangely, no! I remained relaxed.

Everything was new but everything was so normal. I realized, quite profoundly, that I had been living in a foreign country all my life and now I was home.

Les Invalides, Paris

CHAPTER FIVE

A Breton introduction

The TGV high speed train is a wonderful creation. It usually leaves on time. It was almost imperceptible that we had taken off. I saw the station moving, but there was no sensation that it was really me inside the train which was moving. It was so smooth and quiet. I could even plug in my laptop to the free power socket. There was no Internet connection available, but it was great to replenish my battery. That just left me to be replenished, in Rennes. Meeting me at the station would be Alain.

What a beautiful countryside. The trees were wearing their newest clothes; everything was so ordered, tidy, beautiful. I suppose that when a country has been established for 2000 years even the grass and trees know how to present themselves at their best. Even the wind turbines seemed to be at peace alongside the pretty little farms and villages, and coming up, the next stage of getting to know France would be to meet and get to know Alain, whom I had never met, but who had so kindly offered to be an ambassador for France and look after me for two days.

Alain and I had met on the dating site. We hadn't exactly agreed to have a 'relationship', but he had suggested that he be an 'ambassador' and provide hospitality when I arrived in Brittany. He had renovated a bedroom, working extra hours to get it ready in time for my arrival. So here I was meeting a man I knew a little, but had never met before, at the train station in the capital of Brittany. I knew he was of a similar age to Nicolas, that he had little English, that he was a dental technician with two children. His son shared time living with his mother as well as with Alain. I'd bought a little stuffed Kiwi which made the cry of the Kiwi bird when he pressed it, as a gift for his son.

I wondered if I'd recognize Alain in the hordes of people bustling on each level of the station and I felt just a little vulnerable. What if he and I never connected? I'd have nowhere to go, but there he was, not tall, a kind looking man with a twinkle in his blue eyes. We studied each other to check if we did indeed have the right person, and off we went to his village about fifteen kilometers from Rennes. I was soon settled into my room which had a view over Alain's unkempt garden.

The next day I woke up at 8am feeling reasonably well after my jetlag, but no one else was up so I decided to take some photos, and then go back to bed for a while. Suddenly it was 10am and time for breakfast with Alain, his son, and his daughter who was accompanied by a girlfriend. We drove to another village. The countryside was just gorgeous and the villages with their stone houses picture-postcard. I loved the French architecture -- medieval but beautiful, strong, and functional but always in harmony with the scenery.

Alain and I visited Rennes, the largest city in Brittany. Once again, I fell in love with the older buildings, the shops, and municipal buildings. There was a civil marriage at the town hall and many markets and buskers. We visited some jeweler friends of Alain where I explained my father had been a manufacturing jeweler. It was great to be back in such a workshop. It reminded me of the times I visited my father's workshop because I could recognize a lot of the equipment. Some things don't change much.

After a coffee we walked through Rennes for a bit before collecting Alain's son from the birthday party he was attending. He seemed to greatly enjoy the toy Kiwi I gave him. It went everywhere with him and seemed to inspire a great deal of imaginative play.

That night Alain created a BBQ for some friends. It would be interesting to see if I could manage enough French to cope with a French social event. I knew it would be difficult in a room full of native French speakers, especially with my reduced hearing. Each day I spent in France I felt I was living in the present because everything was fresh and genial. There was no baggage, only new experiences and good people.

I enjoyed the BBQ. What a challenge for my French language. In the end I had to concentrate on one conversation at a time, and even then it was extremely difficult, but I joined in when I could and Alain and his friends were great company. Alain was a great cook. His chocolate dessert was amazing and so was lunch. I drank French champagne (no, not Dom Perignon) and something alcoholic made from apples (no not cider or calvados). The weekend ended and it was time to head to Plélauff and the language teaching training center in the heart of Brittany, more than two hours' drive away. Alain so generously drove me all the way there, wished me luck, and had to drive all the way back to his home near Rennes. What a lovely guy.

I bought a few groceries to get me started for the week as

Plélauff was isolated with no public transport, no supermarket, not much of anything. For some reason my Outlook email wouldn't send mails. Thank goodness I had organized a Hotmail account; so much more practical when travelling. My jetlag was starting to catch up with me. Well, I hadn't rested much since I'd arrived in France so I took myself off to bed for an early night.

I didn't sleep well with the sound of other students' voices, the cold, then feeling too hot, nightmares (which are uncommon for me), then the rooster crowing at 6am. I got only three hours sleep which was not that unusual, but not good on top of jetlag and feeling unwell. The sore throat I developed before my trip hadn't improved and my chest was feeling more and more painful. There was no access to a doctor in a nearby village for at least two days so I had to box on somehow, but it made sleeping, studying and enjoying myself more difficult.

The facilities at the Centre were primitive; an old 'cot', begging for a blanket which had holes, stuffing toilet paper on rolls under my postage stamp pillow just to raise my head a little, and my diet was 'student-like', but I learned how to work around the limitations. We visited a supermarket in Rostrenen to stock up on provisions, and I ended up spending more than I had anticipated. That's because I discovered I needed non-food items like toilet paper, clingwrap, stuff for hand-washing my clothes, shampoo and conditioner and, horrors, a hairdryer. Twenty euros went just on that, but with my long hair and not feeling well, I decided not to risk getting a chill from wet hair in the cold weather. We were hoping the temperatures would increase because it was certainly not summer-like as I'd have expected in May.

The TESOL course was interesting and certainly covered a

completely new approach to language learning. I had the opportunity to participate in a French lesson at intermediate level with two other students there who'd had a lot more exposure to French than I had. Happily I found I could hold my own at that level, which was all in French with no English. The thing now was for me to learn how to do that for students of English.

My French got a workout at the supermarket. Having never done shopping in French before and not knowing product types, the different culture, and with my limited vocabulary it took longer than usual to find what I needed. I had to check labels carefully. I discovered I had no idea what hair conditioner was in French so I asked a friendly-looking lady shopper for her advice. She seemed a bit surprised and bemused to have me ask her in French but kindly helped without giving me too much assistance. This gave me self-confidence, but included the challenge of being resourceful for myself. The Plélauff locals there were used to English speakers arriving in the village to study.

Activities and assignments came thick and fast right from the beginning. I had to deliver part of a lesson as well as finish another assignment. It was full-on so I made sure I got some exercise during the afternoon in the dance studio. It was a large new building which had a great dance floor and a sound system I managed to operate.

Originally I had arranged with the center director, who was also a dance teacher, that I would put on a paying show and she would handle the payments. I'd created all the promotional posters in New Zealand, but at the last minute I cancelled as I realized there was no way my suitcase could hold even one costume set. My bellydance costumes were made of glass and weighed a lot. I could only take twenty kilos. It was a shame. How cool it would have been to have put on a one-woman ninety minute bellydance show in France.

In the end I only practiced three times over the four weeks. I was just too busy and too tired from all the homework. There was also the fact that doing anything normal was difficult due to the primitive facilities we were paying for. I discovered that I definitely didn't pack too many clothes and that every three days I needed to do a little laundry. The problem was, there weren't any laundry facilities.

I took my life in my hands and asked the formidable director of the center if there was somewhere to wash my clothes. She pointed me to a couple of old sinks outside and an old string washing line. Cool, I thought. Cool indeed. It turned out the cold water was so icy I couldn't get my hands, in it let alone wash my undies. Back at the accommodation I thought perhaps the basin in the 'bathroom could be used? Nope, no plug could be inserted as the old arrangement was permanently jammed open. It was a little unorthodox, but I had no choice but to do my washing in the communal kitchen sink, then rinse it in the outside sink. Brrrrrr! I then hung it on the outdoor line with little confidence in it drying before nightfall. Not much different from washing in a river and no chance of it turning out whiter than white, but at least it was clean.

My special task the next day was to teach a 'warmup' language session which went okay but needed some adjusting to enable more communication between the students. During the afternoon and evening we watched a demonstration lesson by our trainer with a class of beginner students, mostly middle-aged ladies from the village. This was followed by a demonstration intermediate-level lesson.

This 'communicative' method of teaching English is a far,

far cry to what most of us had experienced if we had learned another language in our youth; I know it was for me. It requires a lot more effort from the teacher, but the students eventually learn the second language without needing to have any instructions in their native tongue. It was quite exciting to see.

My days totally revolved around study and how to eat as cheaply as possible. My bread had to last a week and was usually at the toasting-only stage. Dessert was an over-ripe banana on bread which followed a packet of minestrone soup, half of which had to be saved for lunch the next day. I reckoned I could give a pensioner a run for their money in the efficiency stakes. Lunch was usually a miniscule pot of yoghurt and a piece of fruit but was occasionally supplemented by some vinegar crisps for added carbohydrate.

It was amazing how I could manage on a lot less than what I had back home. Certainly things were rather simple and required less technology there; no oven, no washing machine, no TV or DVDs, just keeping in touch with friends via the Internet and lots and lots of homework. This was my second time as a 'serious' student, and it was no easier this time around.

I loved the quiet there, no traffic noise, nor noise from neighbors or lawn mowers, no planes overhead; only the sound of the nearby animals at the center, only the enveloping calm and quiet of country Brittany. I was enjoying La Bretagne.

With Alain's generosity and assistance, the next weekend I visited the Cote Sauvage, Carnac, Quiberon, and Saint-Goustan. Friday night we settled in at Carnac with a late night pizza, different to those in NZ. The base was thin, but not hard, and was covered with various types of thin sausage, cheese, and sauces, washed down with a nice red wine of a beautifully dense color. We walked for a bit in the village and headed back to our room for urgently needed rest. I was surprised to see there was only one double bed in the room. Alain had asked what I preferred and the big bed hadn't been my answer. Cunning Alain, but I didn't mind the little hug goodnight. I enjoyed spending time with him. He was intelligent, funny, and attractive.

On Saturday we went kayaking off the coast with one of Alain's friends who ran a kayaking business. The location was Saint Joseph de l'Océan à Portivy. We had fabulous weather, and Eric our teacher spoke a bit of English, as did his wife, so I had a productive lesson on what to do and not do in a kayak. Most of my efforts had to be with my feet and legs, not my arms. Somehow I made it to a little island in the Gulf of Morbihan with a sandy beach where we could rest before the row back to the mainland. There we discovered that the sun-cream we'd been using wasn't actually sun cream. It was simply a light moisturizer. Oh oh! After a few hours in bright sun Alain was looking like a bottle of Rose, and I was only slightly better.

I was disappointed that Alain left me, his friend and guest, to my own devices all day on the water, He wasn't much company at all, but I had a challenging and interesting time. Along the way to and from the island I saw enormous orange jellyfish swimming near my kayak. Fabulous! The temperature was an amazing 29 degrees Celsius. I saw topless bathing too.

Was I tired and relieved to be back at the beach? You bet. As I sloshed through the slippery seaweed at the water's edge I found some cute crabs. The male was on top of the female, protecting her from me. The male was much bigger than the female. Neither was at all aggressive, simply trying to sashay sideways out of my hands.

After a quick clean up and change of clothes we headed to our kayaking instructor's house for a BBQ with his family. Invariably, the French people I met were extremely hospitable, generous, kind and jolly. Alain has a large group of close friends. The men seemed sensitive and extremely supportive of each other. Friends and family are the center of French life. It's not really the case so much in NZ. The differences between NZ and France were becoming more obvious to me even though I was still in the 'honeymoon' stage of my French experience.

The strawberries I'd eaten in France were smaller and had the most wonderful flavor. It was also easy to buy strawberry juice for drinking, the juice of Clementine oranges and other tasty delights.

Another delight was the shops at Carnac. I was so impressed. The presentation was exquisite; the staff was so friendly, helpful, and professional that just the experience of going into a shop (and not even to buy) was enjoyable.

We visited an amazing wine shop. 'Fine' is how I'd categorize it. The choice of French wine was purposeful and high class for any budget. The proprietor really knew every wine intimately and provided a professional advice. Also in the shop were other fares to match a dining occasion such as beautiful chocolates, specialized ciders, and unusual jams. If anyone found themselves unexpectedly invited to dinner there would be no excuse to arrive empty-handed. The bottle of red that Alain bought was automatically wrapped as a gift with a beautiful and classy sticker on it to acknowledge the shop it was bought from. Everything was done with care and extra attention.

One Sunday we went farther afield to Quiberon at the end

of a peninsular and very scenic, then on to see a field of mega-
liths. Carnac is famous for its megalithic alignments- dolmens
(with a stone across the top) and *menhirs* which are placed sin-
gly, but often in arrangements. No one is certain what they
mean, but they were established 4,000 years ago. The area is
much bigger than Stonehenge, but is of a different style. The
stones are now protected by a fence so I couldn't give them a
hug.

I'd struggled with my health for the past ten days and finally
had an opportunity to see a doctor, a French doctor who spoke
no English. It wasn't easy to give a quick summary of recent
treatments, my date of birth, explain the intensity and duration
of the malady, in a second language. If I didn't understand
something I asked him to repeat it. If he didn't understand me I
found new ways to say something. He checked my throat--very
red. He checked my ears--slight temperature. He tested for bac-
teria -none. Of course it was viral and giving me a nasty cough
now too. I had to make an appointment for a blood test to determine the virus. The laboratory (in Rennes) would send a
report to the doctor, then the doctor would contact me for treatment options. In the meantime I had to suffer, not even a
painkiller, (luckily I had a few with me). It was clear there'd be
no possibility of treatment until the next week; understandable
but miserable for me.

As I sat on the train on my way from Saint Brieuc to Rennes,
watching the green, green fields and their civilized wildness,
quaint villages with town church spires reaching to the heavens,
I wondered about all those French people who were related to
me. What were they like two hundred years ago? Were they
happy, struggling, fighting, and gardening? Would they have

welcomed me back if I could have stepped through a time portal to their time? Did any of them look like me?

The answer came, "They are you. It's the reason you feel so settled here."

I'd lived in Christchurch, Wellington, and Auckland. Each city was a different experience. I had travelled most of New Zealand, especially the South Island and its rugged beauty. It had been interesting, beautiful, and it was all I'd known apart from the odd trip overseas. Sometimes places had the wow factor but none of them had the *is* factor. To simply be there was enough, in harmony with myself and I scarcely noticed that I was a separate entity from it. It's not a romantic notion, it's not a theme-park ride. It's all about being at peace somehow, and I'd found that place.

I'd come from one of the last countries on earth to be established, to one of the first. France had a different language that I wasn't skilled in, a culture very different, a different hemisphere, different food, yet it was a place of belonging. I hadn't expected it to be quite like this for me. I thought it would be fun and exciting and full of adventures. That's not the way it had been so far. For those friends who had been a little concerned I might have expectations of France that couldn't be realized, it wasn't the case, it was much more dangerous than that.

Yes, I had achieved my dream to visit France and yes I was having a lovely experience but it would never be enough. If anything, it had made things worse. My key dream was to live and work there, and the more time I spent in France, the more desperate I was to make that happen. To be denied that was becoming insupportable and I wasn't sure how to deal with it as it truly was something connecting with my soul. I still had a few weeks left for a miracle, and that's exactly what I need because effort is not enough. If only I could secure some employment there. I was becoming quite anxious about that. I'd sent out more and more enquiries to language schools, but still only had the one interview. My nationality was a huge barrier, otherwise I think I'd have had a Teaching Business English job by then.

I stood outside, leaning on the old stone fence by the gate. The morning was fresh, but comfortable, and everything was peaceful. Chirrups from the sparrows, the occasional 'caw' by a crow flapping in a tree and the lacy patterns of the trees against the sky were so different from life back home. I was waiting for the French phlebotomist to arrive to determine why I was feeling so unwell.

Corrine drove through the driveway and walked over with her highly organized 'blood collecting' kit. She made an effort to speak some English words, but we ended up speaking in French. Corrine was good; one of the best I'd say. Usually phlebotomists have a dickens of a job finding my fine veins, and then getting any blood out of them. I was about to point this out to her in advance when I realized I didn't know how to say it. While I searched for the words, she had the task finished.

There was the paperwork to do and me handing over yet more euros for medical expenses. I was now informed it would cost me quite a bit of money to pay for the lab tests. That was the easy part of the day over with.

Each day we had a brief feedback session with our trainer to make sure we were on track with assignments and to discuss anything relevant. I was in for a nasty surprise. I was told my performance in the classroom the previous day wasn't acceptable. I would have to repeat it and be certain to get it just right or I would have to come back for the following month's course (impossible and he knew it). Well, I knew I had made a few mistakes in the process but the outcome was that the students had thoroughly enjoyed it, learned what they needed to know, and I had discovered I enjoyed doing it.

My good feelings about being in the classroom evaporated instantly and were replaced by extreme anxiety. Here was I, a successful teacher of more than ten years' experience, being told the main portion of my lesson was a 'mess' and that my charisma, personality, rapport, and interesting exercises meant nothing. A lack of mastery of a robotic but complex maneuvering of flash cards had let me down.

There's no intelligence required with the process, but it's extremely easy to get the sequencing out of whack. None of us had been aware in advance that passing the course depended on robot-like precision. We did now. I was shocked. My colleagues were shocked. I hadn't seen any of my other colleagues do it perfectly yet, but so far I was the only one who could fail this course and if that happened I felt my life and dreams would be down the toilet.

"Perhaps you should reassess how you spend your time on the weekends. Some students stay here and work to make sure they're on top of their work. You'd be advised to do the same, since you're clearly having problems," my trainer informed me.

"I don't see anyone else here staying in these cramped conditions all weekend. I work my butt off for hours every night, usually past midnight, then I have to start sending out letters and CVs to language schools. Frankly, I need some time out to unwind a bit and see a tiny bit of France; otherwise I'm not going to be fresh for the next week's lessons," I replied

Giving up my weekends to stay at this cold and primitive

spot wouldn't have done my sanity, health, or performance any good. I'd have ended up going back to NZ having never experienced Brittany at all. Still, I had to pass, and there were many assignments still to come.

I spoke to fellow student Caroline, who agreed to let me practice on her early the next week. I sent a message to Alain to request an opportunity to practice on his son or even himself. In the meantime I had to start over and plan a different lesson as I wasn't allowed to repeat the previous one. I got the feeling my trainer was being disproportionately hard on me for some unknown reason.

The next week was massive in terms of workload. I needed to complete all the materials preparation; finish writing out my lesson plans as well as prepare for doing language-use diagnosis on one of the village women. That has to happen on Monday. I also had to plan and prepare for the ninety minute grammar lesson.

I sent off nine more CVs to language schools in or near Paris. I changed the beginning of the email to be a bit more daring and try to catch the reader's attention. I was starting to run out of contacts as the 'yellow pages' didn't list the email addresses or Internet sites (if they had them) of all language schools. I was running out of ideas and time; time to catch the interest of a language school, time to make and conduct an appointment, negotiate and arrange a contract. I would be in Paris only five days and two of those were the weekend with another set aside to go with a fellow couch-surfer Veronique to visit Monet's garden at Giverny. I reminded myself to keep focused and enjoy the time I had.

I practiced my intermediate lesson with Alain and my beginners' lesson with his son. I still had some process issues to fix with the beginner process, but hopefully it would be easier at Plélauff because the students were used to the process.

Alain was cutting things fine when we left his home to take me to the train station. Cars and lights were against us; there was no parking to be found. The two of us dashed across the pavement to the Gare de Rennes. On the departure board my train was no longer to be found. Disaster. No more trains that could connect with the bus from Saint Brieuc to Rostrenen. *"Merde! merde! Merde!"* was buzzing in the air. Poor Alain had to drive me all the way to Plélauff in the center of Brittany after dropping his son off at his mother's, two and a half hours each way. It doesn't pay to treat the French transport system casually because it doesn't wait one second for tardy passengers.

Back in my little room at the Camina Centre, I checked out the times for travel to Rennes for the next weekend, the last time I would see and spend time with Alain and his son. I felt rather sad about that. They were wonderful people who had opened up their home and friends to me. I felt I was beginning to know them and I was fond of them, especially Alain. There was a connection there. I hoped they would remember me kindly.

After spending hours making materials for my next lesson, my trainer (who had already known I was making a Snakes and Ladders game) then told me he didn't think my game was suitable because there wasn't enough speaking involved for the students. Of course I could still go ahead if I insisted on using it.

Well, what would have been the point of that? I go ahead and not pass? I wasn't falling for that so I said I'd think of something else before I had to teach in less than two hours. This was a big disappointment and huge pressure. I never knew what was really wanted; it seemed the goal posts moved depending on the mood of the trainer and sometimes I felt he had it in for me. Somehow all my efforts ended up having to be re-done because the requirements weren't what I thought they were. If effort and student enjoyment had been the criteria I would have had no problem, but particular processes were required. I felt disillusioned because I would never have treated students the way I was being treated by this trainer.

This was all foreign to my way of thinking, caring and operating from ten years of successful teaching but I had to pass this course. I was not enjoying it. I felt like a loser compared to the others who had no training nor experience. Only one other person was more confused than I.

No one else on the course had set their future on this qualification as much as I had. Some had parents helping with money and education, some had jobs to go back to, some had husbands who financially and emotionally supported them. I was feeling squeezed by events. I'm pretty resilient and I don't quit easily but when students didn't know exactly what was required to succeed it was a bit demoralizing. We had all had to sign a disclaimer about the stress causing problems for students there. I thought it was a bit over-the-top at the time, but now I could see why people packed their bags and walked out, as some had done in the past.

I passed my intermediate class lesson. Apparently my rapport with my students was great; they loved my lesson, it was well planned, and the last-minute substitute activity worked well. So that bit was in the bag, but there was the dreaded grammar lesson to demonstrate. In the end I passed my grammar assessment with flying colors. Apparently I displayed excellent knowledge and was helpful to my colleagues. I put in eight hours work for a ninety minute presentation, but I really needed to nail it. It was crammed with technical stuff and plenty of worksheets. I'd never given such a presentation before, and I had to teach myself the grammar before I could plan the lesson. Although I had a teaching background, I had never taught formal grammar to adults.

After more than forty emails to various language schools, I still only had the one interview. I treasured it, but was still trying to find other work opportunities in France. I was excited about seeing Paris, my job interview, and my short trip to Provence which lay ahead. In a week I hoped I'd have my TESOL certificate. It was vital to what happened in Paris, what would happen after I got back to New Zealand, what would happen for the rest of my life; a simple and modest little piece of paper within arm's reach, but a treasure I hadn't yet earned.

Friday started very at 5am to catch the bus from Rostrenen at 6.30am. As we drove through the Breton countryside the effect was magical with complete calm, except for the crows and ravens. An eerie fog and mist had formed in layers over the land. It seemed as if the rings of Saturn had come to Earth. We didn't see the wild deer which are often to be seen at that time of the morning. Apparently there were many 'bambis' at this time of the year. I did see some laid back cows, literally, as they lolled about on the dewy grass. The fields of crops were immaculate. Every seedling gave the impression of having been planted with care, though undoubtedly they were planted mechanically. Crop farms in New Zealand seemed more industrialized and lacking in charm, in my opinion, or perhaps the magic of France had me under its spell.

Brittany is beautiful any time of day but first thing in the morning before the sun has lifted above the horizon is particularly memorable. If Napoleon were to drop in I'm certain he would recognize the countryside instantly, despite the passing of almost two centuries. He had the canal from Brest to Nantes constructed to facilitate the movement of his army through Brittany. The canal passes near Plélauff.

On the TGV travelling from Saint Brieuc to Rennes I reflected on a day spent with Anna, a fellow couchsurfer who had agreed to host me for the day. She had collected me from the station and had taken me home for breakfast; tea, baguette, butter, and a delicious jam. We drove around the Baie de Saint Brieuc. I was dismayed to see the environmental degradation occurring in this wild and beautiful part of France. I was informed it's mostly due to pig farming. The effluent and run-off adds too much nitrogen and other unhelpful nutrients to the sea and causes nasty build-ups of stinking green algae.

I could smell the sea before I could see it and not in the way I was used to. This stinky, algae-riddled water chokes, and is dangerous for bathers, pets, and children. It was disappointing that at every turn we could see the effects of greed for money destroying the only planet we have.

We went as far as Val Andre. I was delighted we visited this town because I saw a photo once (a rather dated photo) and thought it looked quaint and picturesque. Yes and no; it's a beautiful beach and town, but time has created a much more modern and bustling little mini-metropolis. It still has much charm but it's vibrant and extremely popular for tourists. There seemed to be a bit of an influx of English tourists that day.

It was still hot at almost 7pm. I imagine the temperatures probably made thirty degrees. When I arrived in Rennes where

Alain collected me I had to pour myself off the train. It was great to see him again. The weather being so hot, we dined on the terrace with a lovely wine and I tried some rather unusual sausages (*boudin*) which I definitely didn't like. I found myself trying (sometimes accidently) all sorts of things, some I liked and didn't like, over the weekend.

After a leisurely lunch on the terrace, under the umbrella, we set off for Dinan. This medieval town is a must-see in my opinion. Its buildings are hundreds of years old, it oozes charm, and it's truly beautiful. I took a lot of photos of the interesting and ancient architecture. The shops were beautifully presented, and the whole place felt less touristy than other towns or cities such as Saint Malo. We entered a patisserie and Alain bought us each a special Breton cake, *Kouign Amann*. It's chocka with butter, more butter, and sugar. It was heavenly. I washed it down with cider while Alain drank a beer.

To polish off the day and also my last weekend in Brittany, Alain took me to a restaurant and bar owned by his friend Bruno. We debated the issue of my insistence on having my meat well-done because it's just not done in France. The customer isn't right and doesn't get what he wants, how he wants it, necessarily. This is a cultural difference between France and NZ, when it comes to food. It was with some trepidation that I awaited my beef; would it be bleeding all over the plate? How many times would I need to send it back?

It arrived reasonably well done with a hint of pink so I could cope with that. Bruno had made a concession for me and I appreciated it. However, there was something odd about the 'thing' on the top of my meat. I thought perhaps it was some sort of potato cake, but it was actually melting somewhat from the heat of the steak. I asked Alain what it was. He wouldn't tell me, simply saying it was a vegetable. I wasn't convinced, but he wouldn't tell me more.

I took a bite. It tasted and felt like one hundred percent blubber, pretty disgusting really. Alain still refused to tell me what it was, but he was prepared to finish it for me. In the end I had to ask Bruno what it was and he explained it was raw duck liver. Well, no wonder I didn't like it. It wasn't all in my head.

Earlier in the weekend Alain had cooked some rather suspect sausages. He wouldn't explain what was in them. I never did find out, but I didn't like them either. I think a fair amount of blood was involved in their production.

Alain stayed late to converse with his friend Bruno and his staff. Bruno supplied a bottle of champagne, and somehow I ended up entertaining everyone with a rendition of one of the Maori hakas (war dances) I used to teach kids so many years ago. It went down well, even if it's frowned on culturally for a woman to perform it.

I was looking forward to a real bedroom and a real bathroom. In my opinion, the training center could have been a lot more customer service focused. I was tired of sleeping on toilet rolls because I didn't have a proper pillow. In the last week I was sleeping on my bag of dirty laundry but after I'd washed all that I had to resort to my leftover toilet rolls to support my head. The thin, lumpy postage stamp that masqueraded as a pillow was utterly useless. The spit-thru blanket I had to ask for was full of holes, and if I'd wanted a change of linen it would have cost me extra, so I slept in a bed I'd had for a month. This course was definitely not for the faint-hearted, physically or emotionally.

I met wonderful people such as Caroline and Patrick, and found myself being completely myself ... fun, silly, outrageous, helpful, encouraging, dynamic, and understanding. My sense of fun came out in the shared living experience despite the fact I was old enough to be the mother of the other students. The student life was novel for me. I never had that when I was a teenager because I either lived at home or behaved like a wife to my future first husband. I felt completely free to be open to enjoyable experiences as well as stressful ones. There were moments of despair, moments of loneliness. This was one of those times, a bit like childbirth where, over time, a woman can forget the pain and just focus on the positive outcome, and that positive outcome was that I graduated and received my international certificate.

I had another 'bite' from a language school in Paris. Unfortunately, as soon as they found I didn't have working papers, they lost interest. I'd sent out seventy CVs in total and I'd run out of time. My destiny was already decided, but I was giving Paris my best shot. I slept more fitfully than expected. Too many thoughts were buzzing around in my mind like demented bees. My experiences of the past month, logistics ahead, job interview challenges; all demanded attention.

Pastries, Le Marais, Paris

CHAPTER SIX

Despair and hope

The TGV from Saint Brieuc to Paris took three hours and along the way somewhere La Bretagne changed to Ile de France. After I'd settled into Veronique's apartment in the 13th Arrondissement I let myself loose. I took my camera and just walked. This way I got to see the real Paris, not the touristy bits. I found my way to the Jardin des Plants in south Paris, not that far from the Sorbonne. It's a beautiful facility for Parisians. I enjoyed the leafy corridors, so cool and relaxing despite the crowds and noisy children. The men playing petanque thought I was delightful.

Paris wasn't covered in doggy-doo (I only saw one example of that) and there was no such thing as rich meals with creamy sauces. Apparently that died out many years ago. Meals seemed to be simple, uncluttered, and healthy. I was getting used to olive oil and goat cheese and was definitely not putting on weight after the Spartan living at Plélauff.

My first night in Paris, Veronique and I checked out the neighborhoods of Paris by car, munched on some takeaway food from a Feminist-Lesbian rally, and enjoyed a drink at a bar. We also attended a free theatre/music performance given by a writer friend of hers. I couldn't understand any of it as it was delivered at speed in French using a style that's not conversational. A few words here and there, that's all I could get, damn. I did enjoy being out at night and wandering around as if I was a local.

We drove part of the way along the Avenue des Champs Élysées, but the traffic was awful. I had to risk life and limb leaning out of the car to get a shot. I don't know how Parisians survive traffic. Pedestrians risk life and limb, cars whiz in all directions. They park so closely it's a wonder they get in and out without an airlift. Small cars are essential for maneuvering narrow streets. I wanted to see the Tour Eiffel sparkle, but the timing wasn't right. It happens on the hour, several times each night but I needed the opportunity to be there for the important five minutes worth. Veronique decided she didn't want to go to Giverny after all, so I decided to explore Paris.

Up and showered early, I headed off to the Tour Eiffel before the crowds got too thick. It is, of course, lovely but it's at its best at night. It positively glows with light when it's dark, and it has a searchlight revolving at the top.

I got fed up with being hassled by 'Bosnian' women who would come up to me and say "do you speak English?" They would thrust a piece of hand-written paper in plastic at me. It usually said the same thing. They couldn't speak French, and they were in Paris and there was a sick relative and they needed help, and then, I learned to wait for it, the theatrical performance of looking so sad and destitute would occur.

So I would say, "Why are you living in Paris if you can't speak French?"

They had no idea what I was talking about and it ended the conversation, mercifully, but I was accosted four times around the Tour Eiffel.

I also got fed up with the black hawkers who were not amused when I didn't want to buy their Tour Eiffel trinkets no matter how cheap and nasty they were. Even speaking French to them didn't help a lot.

I zig-zagged across the Seine from one side to the other via various bridges to get interesting shots. I asked an old lady how to get to Les Invalides; she was completely wrong but charming. Foreign tourists would stop and ask me how to find places. I was asked by French people how to find places. A Spanish woman screamed something at me about the Tour Eiffel, and when I tried to show her on the map she shouted and stormed off; weird.

I eventually found Les Invalides, built by Louis XIV for the army. It's impressive, but I couldn't afford entry fees to anything so I skipped seeing Napoleon's tomb and museum. I was lucky to whip off a shot inside the church before a gendarme came up and explained that mass was about to start. I beat a hasty exit. I asked another gendarme to please take a photo of me, but he refused. Maybe they have a rule not to be helpful to tourists who look like me and are wearing a camera.

The Jardin de Luxembourg is another treasure for Parisians. It's large, well designed, and beautiful, varied, and caters extremely well for all ages and interests. I was rather surprised to find a pond lined by folks, mainly women, sitting on chairs, working on their laptops. Couldn't they stop and admire the beauty all around them? I popped in to look at a free art exhibition featuring Russian artists being held in the Orangerie. Bronzes of French painters and other characters caught my attention, but the rest didn't.

Sunday is a good market day in Paris. I wandered over to

the bio fresh food market. Wow! It would be fun to do this on Sundays if I lived in this city. The food looks great, it's fresh, and there's so much to choose from; interesting tomatoes and asparagus that you'd never see in NZ were there. Prices were high and I couldn't drag shopping bags around with me all day so I had to make do with photos. Flowers, vegetables, fruit, cheese, meat, wine and cider, pasta and preserves, soap and essential oils (and the ubiquitous jewelry), and then there was the vegetable paella.

After getting up early so I wouldn't be late for my appointment I put extra effort into looking the part. Oddly enough I hadn't seen any 'fashionable' Parisiennes and no Parisiens in swanky suits. Everyone looked ordinary and rather *decontracté*. Really, I wouldn't have known it was the world's fashion capital, or I wasn't moving in the right circles.

I followed a common practice in Paris and took my dress shoes with me in a bag. So there I was, throughout the day, pulling off or on my socks and sneakers and changing to my high heels, depending on the circumstances. I arrived in plenty of time, negotiated the door entrance which inside was covered in huge mirrors, and experienced the smallest lift in all my life. It was only just possible for me to turn around in it to press the buttons.

I waited in the reception area for a bit, then was courteously greeted and we settled down for a chat. Rosmarie was friendly and encouraging.

"Well, Frances, you have an interesting background, especially your extensive business experience. Business English is popular with our corporate accounts and you seem to have a solid grasp of several different industries. We could be interested in you. You'll find that few teachers here have set numbers of hours a week. You'd be paid an hourly rate. It can vary on demand though many of our teachers can get twenty hours a week. And what's your work status?"

The earth dropped beneath me.

She said, "We no longer sponsor, and practically no language schools do so now. It's just so much easier to hire EU citizens, despite your CV."

She wouldn't hire me without my having a working visa, but I couldn't get one of those without a job. She simply shrugged and suggested I consider becoming self-employed but for that I'd need money behind me and it could take a long time still to be accepted into the country. She'd never asked that obvious question before she granted me the interview, but she must have known to ask it if it really mattered. The whole experience was set up for despair. I also felt the advice I'd received from my trainer and TEFL International hadn't been realistic. They'd suggested it might be difficult, not that it was impossible. My expensive qualification was, in fact, useless in Europe because I was a New Zealander.

Well, I thought, that's that. It was a devastated Frances who made her way to the train station to head for my meeting with The Professor. Things seemed miserable as I had literally spent hundreds of hours, before the trip and during, to find work. In NZ I couldn't get employment; I couldn't even get an interview, yet in France a number of language schools were interested in hiring me so long as I was legal. How ironic, but just as impossible.

The Professor was head of a research center in one of the universities. When I arrived I was shown to him and went to put my bag on the table.

He looked up and snapped, "Don't put that there. It's hard

enough finding anything; you'll mess it all up!"

I was taken aback at the lack of courtesy, not even a hello, but he seemed to be very busy and his papers certainly didn't look very organized, so I waited a long while in another room for him to get back to me. We went to lunch in one of his favorite haunts and I explained why I was in France and what I did in NZ. This was of interest to him as I had the background and experience to contribute to a future project, but there was currently no job.

"What I really need is a visa," I said.

"Well, I can get you one of those," he replied.

I'm sure the earth stood still for a moment right then. The appointment continued.

There was a glimmer of hope. He would discuss the situation with his colleagues and get back to me. To use my talents in France would be fantastic, I thought. I could gain valuable experience and contribute something worthwhile to sustainability projects while I improved my French, thus making myself more employable and visible.

"You don't know what it's like to work with me," he said.

It seemed a rather odd question from this tall, overweight, disheveled and somewhat eccentric-seeming person.

"Okay, yes, so what is it like?" I politely enquired.

"I have a tendency to take on too much, get too stressed and pass that stress onto everyone else."

It was the greatest understatement anyone had told me in my life, but I didn't realize it at the time, nor could I have imagined that it was a red flag, nor what could have been behind his statement. This meeting was a thread of hope which really could make my dream come true. There was nothing concrete at this stage, no offer, but I left him my degree transcript and CV and

DVDs I'd produced on sustainability.

I dithered about what to do next with my afternoon because I was feeling a bit churned up by the day's events. I took a train to Versailles as I had never been there but often admired it in photos. There was plenty of walking, queuing for train tickets, waiting for trains, queuing for entry tickets, cold and windy weather. By 4pm I was in Versailles; not enough time or sun to explore at leisure but a start. A charming young man from Texas, of Indian birth, asked me to take his photo because he was on his own and was never in shot. I was happy to oblige because I had the same problem. We ended up touring around the palace together, taking shots for each other and chatting non-stop. This made the whole experience more fun.

As I walked to the Metro I felt rather 'full' as it hit me that today's experience may well become commonplace later that year. I also thought about Laura. What would she think? How would she feel about me living in France? We'd talked about it many times, but now that it might really happen did that change things at all? I knew she'd never want to come with me and I had no resources to support anyone else. I received an email from The Professor the next morning asking me to get in contact with the French Embassy in Wellington to get the process underway to obtain a work visa. There was no contract at this stage, but there was a proposal underway.

I travelled from Paris to Marseilles on the TGV to meet the sister of my French conversation teacher. She had kindly offered to put me up in her village for a couple of days and to show me around Aix en Provence. Valerie was fun and generous and a great cook. She gave up her bed so I'd have somewhere comfy to sleep, which I thought was incredibly hospitable.

The sun rose hot, intense, and very Mediterranean, very Provencal. The difference between Provence and my experience in other parts of France was startling. It was less wild and a lot warmer. After my usual breakfast, Valerie and I headed out to one of her favorite haunts, a bar and restaurant just outside Aix en Provence. I had a tea, she had a coffee. It was lovely under the leafy shade, and I marveled at my life right now.

Aix was pretty much as I expected. I had a photo of a part of Aix as wallpaper on my desktop computer at home. Incredibly I found myself staring at the same building for real, so too a small shop that I had a photo of at home. The experience was weird, seeing them for real. Aix is beautiful, completely different from Brittany, Paris, or even Marseille. The people are dressed more elegantly, there's a lot of attention to detail, the shops present their wares exquisitely, and there are fountains, tidy though old buildings, quality and a great lifestyle.

Lunch, a salad, of course, was delicious. It was amazing what a few large raisins, dried apricots, warm deep-fried goat's cheese, basil, and olive oil with balsamic vinegar can do to a green salad with tomatoes. I was impressed with the matching olive oil and vinegar spray dispensers. What a great way to deliver just the right amount of flavor.

I woke to the moaning of the wind around the building. Ah the Mistral. It wasn't unpleasant, but it was a forecast for a windy day. We all hopped into the car and went to Valerie's parents' house just outside of Gardanne. What delightful people, and their guests too. What friendly, generous and welcoming people they all were.

Oh là là, the food. Valerie was a wonderful cook, and so was her Mum, who whipped up extraordinary delights. I even ate a snail. The pastry and garlic were nice, but the snail wasn't very exciting; as rubbery as I remembered from eating them in Form 2. The battered and fried courgette flowers were a bit of a surprise, but quite edible. Veal in pastry, dessert, cheese, coffee, and that was after the aperitifs. Her father makes wine out of oranges and it was good to drink. He also has a talent as a painter.

The train from Marseilles to Cannes had been pleasant. I wished I'd been less tired. I struggled not to close my eyes because I wanted to see the countryside. It was lovely with the vineyards that stretched in endless kilometers punctuated by olive groves and houses (with orange roof tiles) set in the middle of fields. The French seem to value trees. They add great amenity to the country.

Occasionally I would catch a glimpse of the Mediterranean. It was choppy out there and the sky was mostly an ominous dark grey. They'd had some nasty, fatal winds and floods here. On my way into Cannes on the bus it was sad to see the olive groves all on the ground, the vineyards under silt and the wheat fields destroyed. There were a number of farmers out surveying the damage as we passed by.

After I caught a bus from Cannes I found myself waiting for the weather to stop raining so I could start walking to the center of Grasse, perfume capital of the world. I'd already seen the billboards for Molinard and Fragonard. Time was short there. It was lunchtime and I had to leave tomorrow morning. My room at the Mercure Grasse had recently been renovated so I was pretty happy with it.

This was my third to last night in Provence so I needed to find a way to maximize my time. It was hard to believe this was the end of June in Provence. It should have been fine and scorching. Instead it was cold and wet, a bit of an understatement really. Wandering the narrow streets of Grasse on a Sunday is, I discovered, not the best day for a wander with most of the shops closed.

After leaving the hotel on foot, determined to manage several kilometers to the center of town, it dawned on me fairly quickly that since Grasse is a somewhat perched town, it was all going to be uphill. There was no choice. The bus timetable told me I'd have to wait two hours for a bus; not an option. After a while I got to thinking that at least I wasn't wet from rain, but soon I was running rivulets of sweat as the clouds parted. Just as I got to the center of town someone turned the sun off and I got cold as the sweat evaporated.

Thinking it might be a good time to go indoors, I visited the Fragonard perfume factory. They had a free tour so I joined it. It was interesting. The person who mixes all the essential oils together is called The Nose. These specialists have spent at least three years studying and seven years gaining experience so that they can identify 3000 ingredients used in perfumery, where the ingredients come from, and the exact quantities in each perfume. Of course, the perfumes don't have 3000 ingredients, usually up to fifty, but the fifty noses around the world (Paris, Grasse and New York) are very special individuals.

They can only work two hours a day because their noses get saturated. They're not allowed to drink, smoke, eat spicy foods, or get colds. The Nose uses a perfume 'organ' to concoct a unique scent from base notes, heart notes and top notes. Five hundred oils are arranged in three levels like an organ.

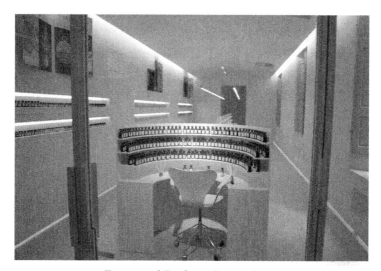

Fragonard Perfume Organ, Grasse

I discovered a small, boutique perfume house down an alley and spoke to the owner who turned out to be the The Nose for Parfumerie Artisanale Guy Bouchara. Indeed it was Guy himself. He proudly showed me his old copy of the novel Perfume, with the signature of the author Patrick Susskind, and a handwritten note from the production company of the film Perfume which came out a few years ago. What I learned about perfume manufacture, in the film, is absolutely correct. The crew visited Guy's perfumery for ideas on dressing the set. He was proud he had a hand in the film, and he was a charming man who was pleased to speak French with someone from NZ even though he had some English. That was a nice little adventure to stumble across.

The weather took a nasty turn for the worst; thunder and torrential rain. Of course, being a tourist, I had no access to an umbrella and nowhere to buy one. The bus timetable didn't work for me, and taxis seemed to be only in one's imagination in Grasse. Back toward the hotel I went, but I soon became lost in the myriad of narrow, look-alike streets running torrents of rain. I could hear rivers of water gushing through the storm-water courses down the water-stairs inside walls. Interesting engineering. Nothing for it but to hoof it and shelter under dripping trees or lurk in doorways.

Things became unpleasant. My shoes had earlier alerted me to the fact that all my walking in France was just too much for my aging Reeboks. The sole of one shoe announced its impending detachment by making desperate squeaky, sucky noises. That now turned to squelchy noises as my shoes filled with water, my hair and jacket clung to me, and my best trousers slapped my ankles as I walked in any direction that said Cannes. This went on and seemed to take forever, but suddenly the hotel came into view and I soothed myself with the thought of a nice warm shower. No, not yet.

My room decided to be uncooperative. I tried to get the electricity to work by inserting my room key. Nothing. Drip drip. Again? Nothing, drip drip. Eventually a housemaid arrived and announced I must move to another room. Hairdryer working overtime, I set about drying off my sopping leather handbag and camera case.

The bus to the center of Grasse the next day cost only 1€, and the driver told me to hang onto the ticket and present it to the bus driver at Grasse Gare Routiere which I did. Wow! When I presented my ticket I didn't have to pay any more money, so I went from the hotel to Grasse central to Nice on 1€. It had only cost me 2€ the day before to go from Cannes to Grasse. No wonder the buses were well patronized. Not only that, but the services were integrated and easy to switch from one to the other.

The trip between Grasse and Nice was lovely; the houses and leafy sections climbing up and down the hillsides, glimpses of the Mediterranean. The properties are larger and have a great lifestyle, I think. The French who are not in apartments seemed to like to grow things like vegetables, flowers, trees, and fruit more-so than New Zealanders. They seemed to appreciate the quality of life that brings them. Everywhere there were trees, yet in NZ we seemed hell-bent on destroying them in our urban areas. The bus rumbled through many leafy tunnels which I appreciated in the growing heat.

Ah, Nice. It was big and beautiful and not as brash as I expected. In fact, as I wandered around the city I found I liked it more and more. Where were the playboys with the bling, the open shirts and sunglasses perched on their heads? Not a one to be found. I wasted one and a half hours trying to get to my hotel. I called two separate taxis at two locations but none ever arrived. I had heavy luggage but there was nothing for it but to hoof it again. At the Hotel Ascot the doorman gave me a map of Nice and away I went.

My reservation at my hotel was in order. My room wasn't quite as nice as I had hoped. There was nothing for making a cup of tea; I had to drink water from the bathroom. The shower was old and held together with tape. The stairs had a nasty habit of not having any light. If I started off with some, I was then plunged into darkness. It was dangerous in my opinion. There were no hotel instructions of any use in the room, but the TV worked.

I wandered around Old Nice which was lovely and quite crowded. Nice had so much choice for all budgets. I spoke briefly to a gold pirate who was more interested in watching le foot than in being a street statue. I continued on my way and experienced one of those rather weird adventure moments.

There was a small group of French police on segways hanging around the market. I wondered what could be interesting about other people's cast-offs, and there he was ... surrounded by Secret Service men. Just another day at the markets with President Bill Clinton. French stallholders were surprised but chuffed to see him. I became a stalking member of the Paparazzi. I got close. He moved on. I walked ahead, then, near his official car, he stopped to say hello to some Americans and receive a hug. One said thanks for being our President.

Why not? I thought. I stepped forward, put my sunglasses on my head, and waited for him to notice me in front of him, and he did. He hesitated, and it seemed he wanted to shake my hand. I offered mine and said, "Here's to American-New Zealand relations, Sir"

"You're from NZ?"

"Yes, sir."

"Where exactly?"

"Auckland."

"Ah yes, I know it. It's a great little country. I've always enjoyed my time there," he added.

Then he walked off to his car. He did shake my hand (his was soft and warm), our eyes met, and we had a 'moment'. I was so disappointed I had no one to take a picture for me on my camera. Somewhere on quite a few cameras there are photos of me and Bill, but not on mine, Bugger!

The next day started out a scorcher. Breakfast was on the waterfront of Nice and consisted of *pain au chocolat*, a strawberry juice, and a hot chocolate to set me up for a lot more walking. I caught a bus to Eze from the Gare Routiere. The bus rumbled along the Cote d'Azur and the view was spectacular. It was what I imagined, but I was doing it as a bus passenger instead of driving a red Ferrari, as I'd imagined eleven years ago. Oh well, I was doing it, and I felt a million euros just breathing the air, feeling the breeze and the sun, seeing the hedges of bougainvillea and the towns clinging to the mountains.

Eze required a climb again, but it was worth it. This town is spectacularly beautiful and just reeks quality in everything. Yes, some things are expensive, but they're unique and the design is astounding, but budget-minded visitors are catered for, too. I hoped I could come back and explore more at leisure one day and maybe buy myself something. The weather was rather warm, but I persisted and found the Chateau de la Chevre d'Or. It's part of the Chateau et Relais chain so I knew it would be first rate.

I sought it out because I had been told it was the restaurant featured in the movie The Bucket List starring Jack Nicholson and Morgan Freeman. Perhaps it isn't really, though the film crew visited the establishment and took ideas. The staff had no idea where it was actually filmed and thought it was a pastiche of ideas with a lot of set dressing, but the dinner restaurant, which wasn't open for business, certainly looked remarkably like the location and the magnificent view was identical. Never mind, the location was on my bucket list.

Thanks to my last ex-husband's generosity I was able to actually have lunch there. How incredible to sit there on the terrace like a wealthy woman, enjoying the hospitality, the colors of the Mediterranean, and relax. For the first time in France, I had the opportunity to really sit and be waited on in such a fabulous place. It was totally cool. I had an apricot juice and they brought out some tiny dried fruit and other things as munchies until the restaurant opened. I had to wait forty-five minutes and I thought perhaps my skin had had enough sun so the waiter pulled over a parasol for me.

I didn't need a full meal; it was just lunch and the impression of being a member of the rich and famous that I was looking for. I ordered a glass of rose champagne to celebrate my stay in France and the possibility of moving there later that year. It cost an incredible fifty euros.

Nice

The train tracks often skirted the Mediterranean when they weren't going backstage in Provence. The countryside was civilized, beautiful, red volcanic rocks erupting through the shrubby trees; so different to the colors of Marseille. I wasn't sitting on the Mediterranean side of the carriage or I would have taken more photos, but how much sun, sand, and trees can a person take, really? For me the Cote was eye candy at any time, and now the rocks changed to white and I knew we were skirting the back of Marseille and on past Aix en Provence.

I bought a couple of *pain au raisins* before I boarded the train, just to keep me going on the almost six hours to Paris, a cheap and agreeable way to keep one's blood sugar up. There was a woman in my carriage marking papers, another breastfeeding a young baby, a mother and teenage son scoffing sandwiches and Coke. Someone with a broken leg, on crutches, had just negotiated the aisle and two passengers had to move to another carriage because they are sitting in someone else's seat. One guy was reading *L'Equipe* with the headline La fin d'un monde. It must have been referring to the French Le Foot World Cup disaster.

On to the airport, stopping over again in Singapore, then the last leg back to New Zealand were taking it out of me, but I consoled myself I'd had an unforgettable experience and that more may be in store.

Returning home wasn't smooth sailing. After I emerged from Auckland immigration I headed toward biosecurity where I received a steely look and was told I would be searched. This rather concerned me. Could I have accidently left an apple in my bag? If so, instant fine of $400. I asked what the problem was; they wouldn't tell me.

I felt the guilt of the truly innocent swamp me. Eventually, after making me sweat a bit, they decided to get a special search guy to come and go through my suitcase. They found what they were interested in but I explained it was a gift and not what they might think. No mercy, rip, rip at the gift wrapping, what a mess. I was not impressed and they weren't apologetic about it either, just sheepish. I realized, of course, they were just doing their job but after being awake more than thirty hours I wasn't in the mood for unnecessary stresses and destruction of the gift wrapping. Too bad because there was more to come.

I couldn't find my friends at the airport. It wasn't like them not to be there. I was unnerved, what to do? After fifteen minutes of searching through all faces in the terminal I decided to catch a taxi as I had no NZ phone nor cash to buy a phone card. The taxi driver had great difficulty in finding the address even when we were on the correct road. We were both becoming frustrated. At last we saw the letterbox and a light was on.

My friends were understandably surprised to see me as they had expected to meet me the following day. I'd made a mistake with the time zone differences. I asked for my car keys. Unfortunately my car battery had given out. My friend dropped me home before returning to watch a World Cup game of football.

Safely inside my home, having turned on the water and the hot water cylinder, I realized I had left my passport and travel documents in the back of the taxi, in the dark. Phone call to a taxi company, phone call to the police. Was it time for bed yet? I crashed.

I arranged an appointment at the French Embassy in Wellington for 30 July. Now I was waiting for the official contract from the university outside Paris. Everything seemed to be a goer but I wasn't 'safe' until I had that and the visa. These were nail-biting times. In the meantime I tried to plan and organize logistics for the move. I would have to sell my home contents to fund the transportation of my personal effects and to pay for the flight and to survive until I received my first pay, five weeks after I arrived. There was so much to do and I'd a lot on my mind, but it all felt right.

Royal bedchamber, Fontainebleau

Roman amphithéâtre, Saintes, Charente Maritime

CHAPTER SEVEN

The great unravelling

Each new day I was looking for evidence of moving myself forward to the life I wanted and needed. Though I had not yet received the official contract, I now knew what my salary would be; modest, but better than if I was teaching English in France. It seemed the university was happy to have me and find me useful. The Director of Human Resources and The Professor employing me there were writing the required documentation.

I allowed a little more excitement to make itself felt each day. Looking around my home in NZ, I gently tried letting go of my attachment to my belongings. That also meant my garden. I felt it was unlikely I would ever tend to it again, after I left in September. Normally that month would be a time for new things in my garden and for me. Already the jonquils were flowering, offering their sunny faces to me in greeting.

I promised myself that one day I would make a lovely garden somewhere in France. In France there are more opportunities to plant the plants I enjoyed in my childhood and early adulthood because the climate is a little more like that of the South Island of New Zealand. Auckland is warmer, quite humid most of the year, but there are many English plants that don't do well there, a bit like me, I guess.

I was making a list, checking it twice, in the immortal words of that song. Divesting myself of my belongings had begun. I'd already made a list of key items to sell online via the online auction site, Trade Me, and another, longer list for a garage sale, earlier rather than later. I'm not a big hoarder after so many relocations in NZ during my lifetime and so many situation changes, but after fifty-five years I'd kept things which sparked off memories of experiences. Memory alone is fickle. I've forgotten much of my life, much of the detail. My 'things' help me remember. What would happen to me when I no longer had my 'things'? When I no longer had the people I had now, in my daily life, to remind me of shared experiences? That's an awful lot to lose.

I'd kept receipts of things I'd bought nearly forty years ago, special things like houses, first motor bike, and previous cars, first table and chairs on hire-purchase. One afternoon I spent time throwing out a lot of such household documentation. When one has to consider how to pay for getting stuff to the other end of the earth, and then find a place for it over there in a bedsit, the rubbish bin becomes a lot easier to use.

It would be as if I was eighteen years old again, just starting out with little in the way of possessions. But this time I'd have added experience, wrinkles, and arthritis and lost youth, less energy, and a lot less future years to rebuild, and I'd be doing it completely alone in a foreign country with a foreign language and culture. Hmmm, where did I hang my 'balls'? I needed to find them. Somehow, being materialistic was no longer appropriate in my life. Having attachments to things and places

wasn't part of my immediate future. I was born with the sur-
name Free. Now I thought I was about to find out exactly what
that meant.

It happened! It finally happened. I received a *lettre d'en-
gagement,* a letter of appointment, from the head of the
university in France. My dream was coming true; I had been
appointed to communications/teaching resources for a research
center and its associated projects; a worthy sort of work, important work, I thought.

It was hard to price my belongings. I knew they have to be
a bargain, but what was the market value for second-hand? It's
what people were willing to pay, of course, but how to determine that in advance? Research on Trade Me?

I made a list and guessed pricing for both Trade Me and a
garage sale. What if no one came to my sale? Oh, horrible
thought. I wondered what the best way to advertise it would be.
I'd never done this before. This process seemed much worse
than getting in a moving company and having the cost paid by
an employer. For my move I had to find new homes for things,
empty the house and shift personal effects at my own expense.
One quote was for only one cubic meter. How on earth was I
supposed to manage with only that? Sheesh! I asked for a quote
for four cubic meters for my clothes, books, DVDs and documents, guitar and violin.

It was about this time that the enormity of what I was about
to do started sinking in. I searched Google Earth to see what
my new address looked like in in the village of Caféolait.
Would I have one window or two? My space would be only
about thirty square meters. I was used to 100 square meters and
a garden. I would be living more than 16,000 kilometers from

all I'd ever known, and it wouldn't be just for a couple of months, and it wasn't a holiday. I was not having second thoughts in any way but I was thinking about the scope of the changes I needed to deal with all at once. The biggest one would be language.

English is like breathing to me. I write well and sometimes it's effortless. Certainly it's easy for me to express myself and be understood. I enjoy listening to others' ideas. All that would be gone, at least for a while. I could barely survive with my current knowledge of French, but if I needed to live and thrive, well, that was another story. Sure, eventually I would improve but ... in the meantime?

I was thinking about the positives, and there were a great many. I accepted that it was essential in the great scheme of things that I make this move; in fact, I couldn't imagine a life without this opportunity. But I was thinking ... crikey! What's the process going to be like? Would I manage this emotionally, all alone? Okay, yes I would, but this was the angst stage, and there would be another one after I got to Caféolait. Good things take time; great things require courage, I reminded myself.

I was very happy that Laura would soon have a full-time job at a local supermarket. She would be able to make her own way in the world. I imagined she was having similar thoughts about coping with major change as I was but it seemed a positive change for us both, even if it wasn't comfortable. This time I would be doing something for me. Like many women and mothers, I'd sacrificed job opportunities and hobby opportunities; having to put men and children first; now I needed to shape my life around me before it was too late.

Such a lot was spinning around in my mind and I was experiencing some unpleasant headaches as a consequence. They say that moving house is up there on the list of the most stressful things to do. Well, I asked for this; it was a wonderful opportunity and I'd tackle it head-on. I find the best way to deal with uncertainty and anxiety is to get stuck in and move things forward. It's tempting to procrastinate but there comes a point, fairly quickly, when I just know I'll feel better when I've achieved some forward movement instead of worrying about the current situation, and forward movement was happening.

I engaged a property manager to look after my home in my absence and an accountant to make sure I wasn't wasting money and was meeting my legal requirements such as taxes. I'd also signed my new employment contract. That was all go, but still the documentation had be finished by the university and sent to the government in France, who would consider my case and (I hoped) would direct the French embassy in Wellington to issue the work permit after my visit there the next week. Time was short for a government department to make a decision before I arrived at the embassy.

I was still looking at options for my belongings. The small stuff had to go, but I was a wee bit nervous about getting rid of my large stuff, my furniture. My contract was officially for only one year and although The Professor had told me there was a good chance that it could be rolled over indefinitely, that wasn't on offer right now.

What if I came back to Auckland to no chair, no bed, nothing. I'd never be able to replace it so at the moment I was investigating minimal storage. It was expensive, but less expensive than having to replace furniture. I figured if things worked out indefinitely for me in France, I'd come back to NZ and wind up my affairs.

It was going to be odd for me not to have a garden for some

time. Gardening had been an important interest for me and had supplied great organic produce. My time would, in the future, be directed onto other things. What would they be? Would I be able to continue my bellydancing? What about Toastmasters? There were no clubs near my new home or workplace in France. More changes in the wind, it seemed. I wondered what would replace these interests, so I decided to take some dance costumes over to France, just in case.

I'd had a number of people say to me recently that they felt more at home elsewhere in the world than in NZ. Generally they felt most comfortable in a country from which their ancestors had come.

It was the same for me. I felt far more calm, comfortable, and at home in France than I ever had anywhere in NZ or any other country I had visited. My ancestry includes Irish, English and Norwegian immigrants, but a large percentage on my mother's side is of French descent. The Libeau family were original settlers of Akaroa, Banks Peninsula, South Island of New Zealand, in 1840. They were enterprising, gardeners and many other things. My grandmother was proud of her ancestry. Even my grandfather was equally related to the same family (with several generations in between I must add), all on my mother's side.

New Zealand certainly has much going for it; its beautiful scenery of mountains, plains, volcanos, forests and lakes and rivers. There's relative safety, and a relaxed lifestyle, but you can't live on pretty scenery and I'd had a whiff of an alternative. For me France had so much more depth, nuance and richness than what we had developed over two hundred years in NZ. Plus, I felt I needed different experiences to grow more into the person I wanted to discover in myself. If I wanted something different to happen in my life, I'd have to change what I was doing.

My daughter told me, once I was back from my trip to France, "Mum you were dying before you went. You were miserable and getting sick and starting to look old. Once you were in France you looked so happy and ... younger".

When I look at my photos from that trip, I do look remarkably comfortable and even radiant. Maybe we're so busy rushing around we don't notice what really works and what doesn't. What opportunities have we missed by being so run-into-the-ground? The supercity had made many of us re-evaluate what life meant to us.

The day came when I watched as people decided whether my belongings were worth a small amount or nothing at all. People arrived much earlier for my garage sale than advertised, catching me off guard, and I must admit the whole thing flustered me. I made a major mistake in not putting the price on each thing. This seemed to be an invitation to visitors to insist on what I should be selling it for, not what I wanted and in my 'need' to get rid of things I did let some go at silly prices, just to feel I was making some forward progress. When my friends arrived they pointed out I had been a 'silly billy' to let things go so easily. I was careless in selling my stepladder and clothes dryer so soon too; ouch!

Their advice was to put the worthwhile stuff on Trade Me, even if I was rather busy. I was hoping Laura could help me with that as my head was spinning with all the myriad things I had to deal with at once. At least my beloved piano was going to a good home; my best friends. Some things about this move made me sad. Some important things were irreplaceable and had been part of my everyday experience for decades. Some things I had chosen to buy because I really enjoyed them, and now they were gone. I knew I would have regrets about giving up things I still wanted to keep, but I discovered I didn't have the financial resources to store them in NZ or transport them to France.

My bank was going to charge me for the privilege of topping up my mortgage. Hey, they should be paying me, it was all of benefit to them. Yet more sneaky new charges appeared. I knew my future property manager from our forays into dating each other from the Internet. I had to trust that he and future tenants would go kindly on the home Laura and I lived in for fourteen years.

My home was starting to empty and I tried not to notice that too much. There was a big blank space where my piano, stool, and art print used to be. Drawers were also emptying, pictures left the walls. My colleague Liz bought a rug and bookshelves from me, as well as my garden worm farm. Saturday next weekend the packers would arrive to pack and send away the few belongings I needed to take with me to Caféolait.

It was the first day in a great many years that I had no pets to feed or say 'hi' to. The last of my lovely goldfish were now living with neighbors. There was still a lot of stuff that had to go. That was the tiresome part. A few bits and bobs were put away for Laura; online auction site Trade Me and garage sales would need to take care of the rest. Anything left had to go in the wheelie bin.

I was burning my bridges behind me because I couldn't afford storage and I didn't intend to return to NZ to live. I wanted a different life containing more people, friends, fresh experiences and the hope of some comfort later in life, to live life more on my terms, to live with an open heart; to be where there were more opportunities, professionally and personally.

Despite having some good times in NZ and meeting some wonderful people, I could honestly say most of it had been rather dark, painful, lonely, and always a struggle--lots of hurt, tragedies, and feeling that my efforts and determination amounted to nothing. Going to France changed that for me. When I was there earlier in the year I had celebrated in my mind that I'd actually achieved an important goal; just being there. Now my medium term goal could be realized and I'd be working hard on my long-term ones.

My future was hanging by a thread. My financial situation was precarious and it was quite the day from hell. It began when I looked out the window that morning and saw fog. Oh shit, what about my flight to Wellington for my visa interview? That was rather unsettling but I hoped things would be alright. It seemed they would be as I logged onto Air NZ and checked the departures; so far so good. Having parked at Auckland domestic airport I went to check in; waiting, waiting, waiting. The staff person asked if I would like to transfer to an earlier flight as she suspected my flight would be cancelled. Oh-oh, yes, please. Just as she handed me my boarding passes they announced my original flight was cancelled, then they announced my new flight was delayed and a decision would be made later. All around me flights were being cancelled, it wasn't looking good.

I went through the gate and hoped and hoped. More cancellations were announced. I was now quite unnerved and I couldn't rebook. I had to get to Wellington in time for my interview at the French Embassy for my work visa. I had all my documents and more to prove I had been offered a job in France, and documents had been sent to the French government. Alas, when I finally arrived at the embassy with not a moment to spare, Madame took all my documents and passport, then went through everything. She stared at me.

"I can't process this, it hasn't got any stamps from the French government," she said.

"Well no, I'm still waiting for that."

"You'll have to go away and start over another time if the government approves the visa."

"This visit is all organized, the payment is here. I can't afford the flight money nor the time to come back again because I'm on a tight time frame for this job. The university told me to get onto this right away, so I rang this office and was given this appointment."

"I don't know who gave you this appointment but you shouldn't have been given one. It's not how things are done."

She got angry and raised her voice saying it was nothing to do with her, over and over. I became more desperate. Madame kept reminding me the website said appointments were made after approval. I explained the university was closed for the summer holidays, the government was on go-slow for the same reason, and The Professor was unreachable, on leave. She admitted the situation was stressful and unfair, but ... I burst into tears. I couldn't help it. This was my only chance to make my dream come true and to survive financially.

I'd been selling my belongings to fund my flights and living expenses until I got my first monthly pay in France. In a few days the moving company would arrive to take my personal effects to France. It would take months to get there, so it had to be done now. I needed to resign from my job at the council in a couple of weeks; I needed to refinance my mortgage now. If I didn't get the visa in time to take my flight to Paris I would end up with no job, no means of support, no belongings, no ability to stay in my home and what few books and key papers I had would be sitting in a warehouse in France, costing me money.

I couldn't suspend the leaving process or I wouldn't meet the deadline to leave NZ if my visa came through. I showed Madame the papers from the university with the official stamp on them.

"Oh, you could have forged those," she retorted.

She then pointed out the pile of folders in her in-tray and stated she didn't want any more work sitting there. This could take months, even years, she informed me. Eventually she softened. Was it the tears rolling down my face? Was it the fact they had given me the interview appointment anyway? Eventually my biometric data was taken; ten fingerprints, face scanned. All I could do was wait and hope they would not take a month or more to approve my application. There was nothing more I could do and I wasn't permitted to contact the embassy to enquire as to progress. They kept my passport; I couldn't go anywhere right now.

My friend Helen, whom I'd known since the late 1970s, texted me and suggested we meet up for a coffee. What a godsend. It was so good to see her, but especially so when I was so stressed from my appointment. So the two of us munched our savory scones and had a hot drink in a cafe in Cuba Street and discussed my situation and her recent trip to England. It was helpful to have a friend to talk to and to hear about her adventures overseas. I wondered if I'd ever see old friends in Christchurch, Wellington, and Auckland ever again.

She drove me to Wellington Airport, which was kind of her. After she left, the airport announced my flight was quite delayed but eventually I made it home, collected Laura from work and settled in with a takeaway, put the fire on, and determined to assume that things would work out. It would be too cruel and a waste of effort if the universe didn't see this thing through, fairly. I had no good choice other than to proceed to dismantle my life, but I did feel as if I was heading into a void. Was it reckless to follow my dream like this, at my age? The consequences could be magnificent or a disaster. I wanted the French government to welcome one of its daughters home but would they grant my visa?

Okay, enough already. Last week it was hassles with the French embassy. Now it was hassles, major hassles, from my bank. They wanted to translate my work contract in France from French into English. Well, they had better not charge me for such lunacy. Apparently rental income for one's property wasn't enough to keep them happy, they had to delve into the rest of my business as well. I wasn't impressed, and it was taking days and days. Moving on my small scale was a nightmare. There was no employer paying a company to uplift all my belongings in one go and pay for the move. Independence is expensive. Sorting through everything into three piles seemed to be my life right now.

1. Pile one (the biggest) was everything I couldn't keep in my life.
2. Pile two consisted of personal effects to move to France. Stuff I needed, a few things I really wanted.
3. Pile three was what would fit into my suitcase and weighed only twenty kilograms.

Changing my life to this extent was the hardest thing I'd ever had to do. It wasn't all falling into place, but I couldn't go back. I wanted the life I'd worked for, in France.

I looked around my home and the reality certainly was setting in. In particular, what was left I couldn't keep, no matter how much attachment I might have to it. I felt sad. I couldn't keep my *Starlog* magazines from the 1980s, nor my record collection and there were some great albums in it, like *Thriller*. I didn't want to sell them but they were heavy. What could I do? I asked my ex-husband to look after them until I could arrange to have them sent over one day.

I'd kept a few of my bellydance costumes, some DVDs and CDs, some clothes and collectables, a dinner set and some china, my guitar and my violin. My second oldest possession was my violin. I acquired it when I was almost eleven years old, and played it regularly, sitting exams, until I left high school aged seventeen. I'd pottered around on it only a handful of times since but I'd always intended to take it up again, so I could play in a chamber group or orchestra; and my oldest possession? My teddy with the tummy button that still played *Twinkle Twinkle Little Star*, after fifty-five years.

I hadn't been at work all that long before I received a phone call on my mobile. It was a 04 number, Wellington. Could it be? At the end of that call I was punching the air. Yyeeesssss! The embassy had rung and confirmed approval for my work visa. I would receive it in my passport in ten working days.

So it was certain now. I would be living and working in France for the next year. The Professor had also said there was the possibility of rolling my contract over indefinitely. I would make new friends, work my way further toward bilingualism, discover the intricacies of a different culture, stretch my intellect, discover new places, and maybe even explore new countries.

How awesome! I'd deal with the sadness of leaving things behind and somehow I'd deal with the separation from daily life with Laura. I'd deal with my fragile financial situation and those moments of loneliness in France. I'd stay open to what I can be and do and feel. I hoped I could be of service to people and our planet and fill my life with love.

I had no idea what my little bedsit in Caféolait would be like. Would there be room for my few personal effects when they arrived? It might be touch and go. Never mind; I was keen to get on with it, but it was still important for me to let go of my NZ life gently.

Laura was still nervous about not having a secure full-time job so she could move out of home. That was understandable. I wished the supermarket would give her some real certainty not just verbal comments. There were people who would look out for her, but I knew she wanted to manage things herself. That's admirable, but sometimes one has to seek assistance for a short time.

I remember that when I left home I couldn't support myself financially on my tiny income as a teachers college student, so my boyfriend and first husband, paid the rent for a furnished flat in central Christchurch. I was poor but with a little help I managed and I've survived since; not often easily but, hey, look at me now. I was like an eighteen year-old again.

On Thursday I resigned from my job at Waitakere City. On Friday my second ex-husband and I got officially divorced. On Saturday I threw out lots of stuff that had been important to me. On Sunday I held another garage sale, and Laura let go of things that used to be important to her.

Ironically, I went to the movies that day and saw Toy Story 3 which is all about folks leaving home to start a new life, and giving away their stuff that used to matter to them. Boy, did that strike a chord. I seemed to be freeing myself from all sorts of attachments; some precious ones like my few friends and especially my lovely daughter Laura, material things such as my belongings, my job, my garden, home, and country and language and culture.

My security had to come from within me more than ever. I had no idea what would happen but stagnation was far more damaging to me than the challenge of change. Maybe that's why my life had been one of constant change even though I'd yearned for the sort of stability and comfort other people seemed to experience so easily.

My time with the council had been a major and influential milestone in my life. In fact it had felt like home. Waitakere taught me how to be more aware of my values and my daily behaviors, and to be aware if they were sustainable or not. It also taught me that one person can make a difference when she is supported by the many.

Waitakere had been so different to the toxic environments I had worked in. Staff didn't go around resenting other people's successes. Instead they encouraged celebration of those successes. There was no tall poppy syndrome here; colleagues and managers were delighted whenever we did something well. How refreshing.

I'd been given a priceless gift during my time here. I'd been allowed to use my imagination and passion to create new things that hadn't been done quite that way anywhere else. My ideas to promote democracy via encouraging voting, to promote sustainable living to the community, were valued, and even budget put aside to implement them. That was a truly liberating behavior from the council. Be innovative, work together, be bold, speak positively, and do what you say you will; these liberating behaviors were truly displayed every day by my colleagues and managers. That was priceless and certainly made me feel comfortable at work.

Of course, there comes a time when the fledgling has to leave the nest. I was leaving 'home', but I could see where my battle against one council and my development and support within another had provided stepping stones to a much bigger opportunity. I was proud, privileged, and just plain delighted to be able to take my passion for the environment and sustainability, along with my experience of working for our eco city, to France.

I'd found a country and an employer who seemed to care about sustainability and our planet. I thought I could take those eco-city principles and let them loose where they were appreciated. That was liberating too, a good home for me. Unfortunately, I was to be proved wrong, that didn't happen. The new working environment would be considerably less positive than what I was leaving, and those eco-city work principles would become a distant dream. Even the concept of sustainability at my new employment would prove to be a 'greenwash'.

Normally I'd be sorting out my dance bag for my bellydance lesson on Saturday morning, but for the first time in six years there was no class, no Monique to talk to, no exercise, and no creative physical outlet. She was overseas on holiday and by the time she got back I'd be in France. Instead, I had my last garage sale to manage. I'd rather have been dancing and I wondered if I'd bellydance regularly again in the future. I hoped so, but it would be in France, and I'd need to find a new teacher.

Monique and I had had a great time developing me into the dancer I was now. We'd shared many personal stories and danced together, laughed and cried. There weren't many people in this world I could say had been influential on me but she was one. I'd enjoyed interacting with other dancers, but my natural place was as a soloist. I could focus on what I was doing rather than be distracted by others.

I'd enjoyed the harem evenings at Monique's studio, and learning how to conduct seduction dance workshops for women, learning how to use many dance props such as finger cymbals, veils, cane, wings, and feather fans. Pretty costumes I'd designed myself had been a terrific, creative exercise, and fun, too.

I popped into Elm Park School on my way home from work, hoping they would like my donation. I dropped off a large carton of unit boxes full of lesson plans and resources, an encyclopedia of NZ history, and a big carton of children's books for the library plus a big crate of craft materials, courtesy of my time as a teacher in NZ.

It was satisfying to help out others, and all it took was for me to let go of my stuff. The same for many of my belongings over the past couple of days; lots of people were enjoying my things, not just me. I thought that was rather cool. My shell collection was with a bright little boy who was also excited to have bought a kite and some model kit sets from me. My Halloween costumes for girls were with someone's Grandma. Garden plant food and other bits and bobs were with a Chinese man who seemed to want a lot for almost nothing. A friend was enjoying my container plants, and an old man was enjoying an eclectic mix of furniture and other belongings. My books and DVDS were all over the suburb. Some of my smaller musical instruments would be entertaining young and old for years to come.

The garage had never been tidier nor emptier. Shelves and cupboards in the house were voids. It shouldn't be too difficult to clean things before I left. It seemed my property manager had found a family as my first tenants, so the boxes were being ticked. I invited the Salvation Army in to collect the leftover linen, furniture, toys and books. I was enjoying being able to give and share, but I was now running out of stuff.

The public affairs team went out to lunch together at La Cigale Cafe to say goodbye to me. I ordered a scrummy rich beef stew. We shared wine, water, and bread and chatted. One of my bosses was disappointed he had to leave half an hour later to conduct job interviews for the supercity.

I'd truly miss my colleagues in public affairs. Most of us weren't 'young', and we knew how to share our personalities, hopes, tragedies and successes. We listened, debated, and supported each other. We were friends. We had spontaneous hugs and cups of coffee. I admonished the smokers in the group and they happily agreed, then ignored me. We'd seen our children grow up and seen politicians come and go. Crises had been managed, awards celebrated. We'd experienced the birth of an eco-city and now were watching it die. These people with whom I had worked had been like a family to me for four years. We'd each earned the right to be part of our group. Some of my colleagues would find work in the new Auckland Council. Some wouldn't and had their lives changed forever, like me.

I attended my last Toastmasters meeting. Eco city Toastmasters Club would continue on, despite the dissolution of Waitakere City Council but its membership would be somewhat different. I delivered my final speech, 'Know What You Want', which seemed well received. I enjoyed connecting with my fellow members. We knew each other well, and the club had added a new dimension to my life. I had more confidence in public speaking and often enjoyed training the less experienced. Being able to think on one's feet is a really useful skill to develop.

I didn't know if I would take up Toastmasters in France. There were several clubs in central Paris, but nothing anywhere near where I would live or work. I didn't know what would happen to any of the interests and hobbies I developed in NZ. So, for now, I'd be content with my Competent Communicator and Advanced Leader awards from Toastmasters International.

It was now my last night in Auckland, NZ. The past few days had been loaded up with dealing with cleaning my house, banking, and minutiae. Last night Laura and I had gone to dinner to enjoy some quality time together. It would be such a long time until we saw each other again. We went to our favorite Italian restaurant, La Padella, in Highland Park, and then Laura shouted me a drink at the Cock 'n Bull at Botany. Incredibly we had never been to the pub together before, and I learned what her favorite drink was.

My house was empty, and there was a void in my heart that had been constantly filled by Laura and my responsibilities as a custodial parent for nineteen years. We'd been Mum and daughter, confidants, friends, sharing ups but mostly downs. Now she would be living with her father, a new experience for her. I reminded myself life equals change for all of us and sometimes it's good.

I had no idea what would be ahead from one day to the next. I didn't yet know where I should go when I arrived at CDG Paris. I hoped the university would send me the info overnight. Trimming my suitcase down to twenty kilos was a job before sleep, and I needed to fill out my general election voting papers, too, my last democratic task as a New Zealander. I spent the last couple of nights in New Zealand staying in my ex-husband's spare bedroom.

My last few hours in Auckland were decidedly unpleasant. First there was the last minute tossing of things from my life that would not make the twenty kilo baggage limit. Space in my suitcase was taken up by essential documents and my computer keyboard. It was quite peculiar wearing clothes one day, and then throwing them out, only to start over with another set the next day. This had gone on for five days.

All the while I suffered a very strong headache brought on by tension, no doubt. I called in to see my best friend Yasmin to say goodbye and drop off my car. She and Muhab had kindly offered to sell my car on my behalf. That was immensely helpful, a burden removed from my already over-stimulated brain. Saying goodbye was even sadder than I expected. I had never seen Yasmin cry before but as I sat in the car while it backed down her driveway we both lost our struggle.

"I miss you," I choked out, then we were both inconsolable as the distance widened.

How ironic; they came to NZ from Iraq for a new life and now I was leaving for France for the same reason. We hadn't seen each other often, but each time it was always as if no time had gone by at all.

Ahh, the airport. It should have been simple enough. I checked in. My booking was in the system. Not enough, passengers must present the very same credit card with which they made their flight booking. This was impossible for me as I had been the victim of a phishing attack weeks earlier, and had needed to contact my bank and get a new card.

Two days earlier I had gone to the bank and explained that the info I had downloaded from the bank's Internet system did not give me much information on my flight purchase. The bank tried, too. They couldn't generate a bank statement for the old card. Information was in the system, but not all would integrate into one document. Eventually they wrote a personal letter to qualify my credit card use, regarding the flight, on letterhead, no less.

Check-in staff were sympathetic but the flight booking system was uncooperative and wouldn't complete my boarding arrangements. Time marched on toward my boarding call. Finally a supervisor worked some magic, but wait, there was to be more anxiety ahead. Check-in then informed me I could not be cleared for boarding as I had no return ticket. What? I was incredulous!

"What's the problem with me?" I asked.

They smiled nervously, "You're somewhat unique."

"How so? People leave NZ all the time."

"Well, the system is saying you have to be cleared by the French Embassy in Wellington. They have to be contacted and must approve your departure before you can receive your boarding pass."

"But I have a visa from them! They already know all about me!"

"Sorry, it's the rules."

Time marched further.

I was then told the embassy would ring the airport back, after a decision had been made about me. I lost it, I must admit. After all the crappy experience of obtaining a visa, to then be possibly turned away just before boarding, was just too much. I was in tears. In the meantime, my ex-husband was wondering what on earth was going wrong at check-in. We spoke via mobile phones at Departures. I continued to stand with my extremely heavy laptop bag and camera bag and even heavier heart. The clock was ticking loudly now. I thought a calm check-in and buying ex-hubbie a hot chocolate before departure would be good for our nerves and a nice way to say goodbye. It wasn't happening.

Finally the supervisor came back saying the woman at the embassy didn't know me, but if I could prove I could support myself in France it should be alright. What? The check-in supervisor waited for proof.

Totally exasperated, I said, "The embassy has a copy of my work contract, documents from the university detailing my salary; this is how I got my visa in the first place. There's nothing more I can do."

The supervisor looked embarrassed and said "Okay, here's your boarding pass."

My ex-husband and I bolted down a hot chocolate and an afghan biscuit to calm our nerves, then it was goodbye. It wasn't the sort of farewell New Zealand experience I'd wish on anyone.

CHAPTER EIGHT

The Kiwi has landed

I don't like long-haul flights, especially back to back, but I had no interest in staying in Singapore when I could be at my real destination of France, so; eleven hours plus hours at Singapore plus thirteen hours, and travel from CDG to my hotel (in stages). Auggh! No matter how good the service on the plane, there is no compensation for the torture of sitting upright in a seat for more than ten hours at a time. Get up and stretch, you say? Not much of an option these days as the planes are all full and the aisles clogged with people waiting for the toilets. There was no space to bend, so I was reduced to making tiny movements with my calves and ankles during the flights. The woman sitting next to me farted odiferously at regular intervals. I wanted to throw up. The frequent turbulence (even at 37,000feet) did not help.

No one wanted to talk to me on either flight. They sat beside me with 'cones of silence' switched on. After watching five movies I couldn't bear watching another, so I listened to my MP3 player instead. Sleep was impossible on the flight to Singapore, so I shouted myself a massage and shower at Changi. It's a good service, but very expensive. I needed it because I was facing another thirteen hours of sporadic, moderate turbulence. The Internet service was also good, so I dropped a line onto my Facebook page to update everyone.

On arrival at CDG, as on my first visit, there was no sign of customs checks, not even an arrivals card to fill in, just long waiting queues. Outside the terminal I tried to work out how to get to my hotel. There was nothing direct, so I needed to catch a bus to a major train station in Paris, but which one? I asked a bus ticket seller but he had no idea. Probably both Gare de Lyon and Gare Paris Montparnasse, he suggested. Oh, both? The bus driver wasn't helpful either, he thought maybe both? No matter, he was going to each station but I'd need to make a decision.

I had plenty of time to do that. The traffic in and out of Paris was so appalling that it took nearly three hours to get to Montparnasse (luckily I guessed the right *gare*). I then couldn't find anywhere to buy a simple one-way ticket to the location of my hotel. I asked and was told where to go. I stood in line for forty more minutes of heavy luggage wielding. There were hardly any tellers on duty. The lines of waiting customers were enormous. Eventually, as I asked for a ticket I was told no, not here, this is only for other tickets. I must go somewhere else. I found somewhere else and purchased a ticket, train leaving in four minutes; great, I thought.

As I put my ticket into the machine and pushed my way through the metal barrier pincers the machine stopped me halfway and refused to budge. My legs were trapped in the middle, my suitcase was trapped ahead of me, my laptop and camera bag fell off my shoulders behind me, and no one cared to help. I was pissed off, especially as the machine had swallowed my ticket. After painfully extricating myself and my belongings I marched over to the ticket seller and told him what had happened. He looked a little amused (I was definitely not) and eventually came out, having made me wait for him to dress up in a fancy official jacket and cap.

After identifying the offending machine he unlocked it and retrieved my ticket, but now I wasn't allowed to go through the machines. I had to go through a door. I discovered this door only opened one way, so I had to wait until a passenger wanted to come through to my side. Needless to say, I had missed my train with all this.

Next task, identify the correct platform, time of next train to the destination required and it's a good idea to check the names of the stations I'd pass through too, as a double check. Done; I'd now arrived at my destination. I was so exhausted, my back and hips completely done in from struggling with luggage for so many hours. I thought, stuff it, time for a taxi to the hotel.

My room was number eleven, and just to polish me off, I had to haul all my luggage up an old spiral staircase until the proprietor took pity on me and hauled it the rest of the way. I gave a shuddering sigh as I closed my room door behind me.

For the past couple of days I'd tried to get out of my room and explore, but the weather was horridly bitter, windy and occasionally wet. It was hard to believe it was barely autumn. How on earth would I stand it, namby-pamby little Aucklander that I was? Everyone was rugged up, but I didn't have an adequate coat.

I decided to travel back to Versailles. I explored a bit of the old city and then decided to explore parts of the Chateau that I hadn't had time for three months earlier (when it was cold and windy then too). This included Marie-Antoinette's estate Le

Petit Trianon, as well as Louis's Grand Trianon. I noticed again how worn everything was. They try to preserve things, but it's a far cry from what it must have been in its heyday. Even though things were tired and old the magnificence still shone out. This tourist attraction was one of my favorite places. If only the weather would be warmer so I could relax, instead of freezing and hunkering down in my thin little rain jacket.

I put on more comfortable shoes the next day, but the cobbled streets and footpaths of the town where I was staying were quite uncomfortable to walk on for any length of time. I stayed out all day and was physically paying the price, but staying in my tiny room wasn't an attractive idea. My toilet was like a tiny pantry. When I sat on it my knees touched the front wall. I had to keep the door open because I was no longer limber enough to twist around for the toilet paper in such an enclosed space.

Tomorrow another way of life would begin. I must catch a train to my new workplace to see what arrangements had been made for my studio in Caféolait. I needed to start creating a home base so I could settle.

I was doped up on painkillers. Was it any wonder with degenerating discs, two long-haul flights, dragging and slinging a total of thirty kilos of luggage around for days, walking screeds of kilometers on cobbled streets and then finding my click-clack bed in my studio had no idea how to spell 'decent mattress'. In fact, it had no mattress at all, just a thin slab of foam on top of all the metal and wires; utter agony, and it curved in the middle so all my weight when lying down concentrated on my lumbar region (my most unhealthy area). No sleep the first night; none at all.

The amount of space in the studio wasn't too bad for one

person. The studio had a good location on the ground floor and I was learning to cope without an oven (don't cook) but the lack of sunlight was a real problem for me. The windows could be lovely, but they were permanently covered by solid blinds which were not designed to go up and down. They were stapled to the window frames. It was like a dungeon, and the lighting was so dim I could barely see to read, so I went out and bought a table lamp the next day.

I spent quite a few euros getting some essential supplies; a hygienic toilet brush with a bit of life in it, ditto for a towel and bathmat, then a toothbrush and toothpaste, some tea towels that were recognizable, a mug (only a cracked one in the studio), a hot water bottle. I had to buy a fry pan and pot as what was here was so bashed and worn out I wasn't convinced it would be healthy to use. Teflon was flaking off. Now, with a few items of my own, I felt more settled.

Not having a car made any kind of shopping difficult. It was impossible to lug a week's worth of groceries from the super-market to my studio, and shopping every other day meant I spent more money, so I invested in one of those shopping trund-lers old ladies use. I discovered a market outside the *mairie* (town hall) every Wednesday and Saturday. It wasn't cheap but it was fun and the produce was fresh. That night I sat down with fresh strawberries and raspberries to have with some exceed-ingly dark chocolate ice-cream. Ah chocolate ... I found a tin of drinking chocolate, pure cacao from Monbana Chocolatier. I imagined myself as Juliette Binoche's character in the film Chocolat. Really, the tin even had Inca imagery on it. Nice tin; shame the contents barely filled it halfway. Never mind; I added a sinful hot chocolate experience to my fruity indulgence that evening.

It had been a good couple of days; new pajamas with great style and fit and great (as in big) price, so I now had two pairs of pajamas, a new haircut too. I was reinventing myself because, quite frankly, I was embarrassed when I saw my appearance and my clothes and shoes from last century, yes.

Tomorrow I would try to find some affordable clothes that suited me (so far only the outrageously expensive ones seemed to appeal). Six hundred euros for a coat? Choke! Not for me. Thank goodness for my bank loan, I could have fun looking around tomorrow. Apparently boots suitable for snow didn't arrive in shops until the beginning of December but people got caught out the previous year, when the snow arrived in November.

What a way to start my day, visiting social security and the predictable red tape. A pregnant lady had an appointment which I watched through a window. It didn't seem to be going well. The lady was getting sadder and more depressed as the minutes ticked by; I thought she was going to cry. I don't know what was going wrong for her but her body language was so dejected when she left. The office person interviewing her was completely dispassionate and unsympathetic. Oh-oh, doesn't bode well, I thought. Darned right!

I walked in with the paper the university had told me to bring. It was obvious I wasn't French, but they made no concessions at all and I felt they deliberately made it difficult for me to understand. They wouldn't slow down. They must have both had Botox because there was no amiability there at all. I felt bullied and a non-person. They demanded my birth certificate be translated into French. I asked why they couldn't read a name and a date without it being translated into exactly the same anyway, but they didn't appreciate anyone questioning anything; this can be problem with administration in France.

They wrote down a list of demands and told me to go away and come back with someone who understood French. Charming, not! I was so annoyed because this put the university out as well. I had my passport and visa but that wasn't good enough. My birth certificate wasn't showing my current name because in New Zealand you have the same birth certificate all your life; the details never change. What to do? I was sizzling even though it was grey and rainy.

I set out with my camera to explore the Chateau de Caféolait and the park. It was lovely to have a chateau down the road. It's a tad like Versailles but much more intimate with some lovely detailing on the wall panels. I had to hand it to Napoleon, he did restore and protect a lot of important buildings and works of art. His bathroom was beautifully done. Francis 1; well he visited the chateau and I saw his bed. The influence of Louis XV and Louis XVI is also strong there.

I struggled to understand the commentaries given by guides for the chateau. They spoke at break-neck speed in French. I only picked up a tiny fraction which was such a shame because I knew they were knowledgeable. I did wish the guide for the park visit wouldn't keep brushing his arm against my breast all the time he was explaining things to me (the others had abandoned the tour early so it was just me), it was very off-putting, even though he was a very enthusiastic guide.

On my return from the park I wandered around the chateau gardens. I saw a guy with a strange gait coming toward me, and he made certain I couldn't walk past him. He decided he was going to show me some beautiful gardens around the corner and would like me to accompany him. Well, er okay. So we chatted away in French. It turned out he was a fashion photographer from the ritsy Parisian suburb of Saint Germain, named Guy. He then insisted we sit down on a park bench for a chat. There was no sign of us walking around the garden.

Guy proceeded to light a cigarette and ask me questions about myself. I made sure I didn't give him the name of my street though he wanted to know it. After a while I started getting a bit fed up with him and his smoking. I told him I wanted to see the garden.

He said, "After."

Next minute he was taking my hand and stroking it and asking why there were no rings.

I said, "I'm going to look at the garden."

He tried to kiss me and was mighty put out that I didn't allow him any *bises*. A solid no from me and he vanished like a genie. Good heavens, was this typical of French men?

During my work days I'd been in the deep end. Not only was almost all conversation in French but so were all the university documents I was supposed to read and make sense of. Then I was expected to do data-entry in French. All the computer programs were in French, email was usually in French. Of course, I was in France, but I'd thought it was for my English expertise I'd been employed. Thank goodness I'd had the foresight to bring my QWERTY keyboard. It was a steep learning curve but gradually I adjusted.

My clothes washing was done in the kitchen sink. It was not easy as a sink isn't very large. I had to wring each thing out and dump it into an old broken plastic crate to transport it into the bathroom, fill the bath with rinsing water, swish and wring and then hang it all out on a little airer to drip outside (hoping it wouldn't rain out there). It dripped but never dried out there because the sun only hit my door briefly in the early morning, then it was gone for the rest of the day. I felt as if I was going down to the river, in the old days, before washing machines and wringers came along. A gel product proved useful instead of washing powder as it took up less room to store and mixed better in a small space. Later on I discovered a Laundromat, which helped a little, especially with bed linen. I'd pop everything into my shopping trundler to transport it.

It was pleasant in the autumn sun, walking through the markets to the supermarket and pottering around there. The checkout operator was friendly and attentive. Some of the security staff were starting to recognize me. It was a nice 'local' but selections were limited so I thought I'd go home, unload the groceries and try to discover a bigger commercial center. I wanted to look for small items of furniture and a TV.

Crikey, the gadgets one could buy for a French kitchen were amazing, and rather specialized. The electric crepe pan looked really good, but I didn't have room for any gadgets and I had no one to cook for anyway. I was thinking of getting a wee TV but when I saw the prices I thought I'd probably be better off doubling my budget and getting something decent in high definition. I had no entertainment and social life so a TV might fill the void and a decently big one might be pleasant to have during the five months of winter. Unfortunately, the studio couldn't accommodate a TV as it was at present, with all The Professor's broken down old things he was storing there. Renting the furnished studio was where the first culture shock came in.

As a landlord in NZ I had to ensure everything worked in the house before the tenants moved in. Every light bulb and blind, appliance, key etc. It was different in France. Here you just rented the space. I had extremely poor lighting in the bathroom and one specialized bulb has never worked. I was told to replace it myself. That wasn't easy as it wasn't standard, and I had no idea where to find one. I bussed all over Caféolait hoping to find a shop that sold them, an expensive exercise, so I could wear some makeup and wash at night.

The window coverings were permanently down. They didn't lift or lower, so they permitted no light at all 24/7. I was told by The Professor (my landlord) that if I wanted something that worked, I must install my own fittings and curtains myself at my own expense.

That's the way it is in France. Unless the electricity supply is not connected or the plumbing doesn't work, well, anything else, the tenant is on their own. Most kitchens don't have an oven or microwave or fridge let alone a dishwasher, just a sink, often not even any bench top. No curtains are supplied. Every time a tenant moves they have to change things. Hells bells, what an expense, and great for the landlords if they are renting an investment. No wonder people don't move if they can help it. What with changing service suppliers and all, it's a major hassle and expense to move.

I asked The Professor to please remove some of his old run-down stuff to give me some room. When my personal effects eventually got here (God knew when) it was going to be rather cramped. Both events took much longer than I imagined.

The sun was watery that morning, the air fresh, when I set out for the *gare* to catch a train to Chartres. It proved to be expensive as it was a long way. The train rolled along and stopped at some nice little villages. In between I could see even cuter hamlets but what really made an impression on me was the greenness; everywhere trees, trees and forests, trees and houses, trees and horticulture. Dense little copses with streams running through their dark centers like ribbons of clear midnight. Gorgeous!

Leaving Caféolait behind, I was thrilled by the picture-postcard villages with their steepled churches taking the high ground. This was all new for me. I'd never been in this part of France and I hoped to see lots more when I had a car. I especially liked French forests because they seemed so bio-diverse, not like the boring kilometers of plantation Radiata pine in NZ. All shades of green and gold, all sizes and shapes were cohabiting so well together in the French forests; composing such a splendid panorama for me to admire.

My first view of the famed cathedral of Chartres was splendid but, to be inside it was magical. Notre Dame de Paris is celebrated, but Notre Dame de Chartres has a spiritual magic and is so exquisitely beautiful with its stone carvings. They are almost like filigree. The talent and skill demonstrated by ancient artisans was so humbling and sadly well and truly gone.

Strike Day dawned chill but clear. Negotiating the wheelie bins on the footpath on my way to the station I wondered how everyone was going to cope with the strike. I knew there were a few rare trains running during the strike so I made sure I was up to get the early one. I could tell it was anything but a normal day as soon as I arrived; people everywhere, I couldn't see the ground. All over multiple platforms, lots of nervous smokers huddled. How the train managed to arrive on time was beyond me because at each stop it took so long for the mass of people to get on and off. Settling back in my window seat as the doors closed, I felt sorry for all the people left behind. They stood, watching intensely and solemnly, as the train pulled away, and then, on masse, they reached for their cell-phones. This happened at every station we stopped at. The snack bars were running out of lunches by 8am. Onwards the seething masses poured toward the commercial center of town as I indulged in some appropriate rock music by Daughtry. It seemed to fit.

As expected, the welcome meeting/induction in the afternoon was way over my head. We got there in a rather circuitous route in Victoria's car, despite her GPS. The meeting consisted of two and a half hours of listening to French speaking in a big room. Only two Powerpoint presentations were made. They were dry with far too many words on each slide. Apparently there was really useful stuff but I had no idea what it was. There was no effort made for non-francophones in this supposedly multi-cultural institution but at least I came away with a mug and a little satchel. Those I could put to good use.

I felt helpless and vulnerable. At the nibbles afterwards no one talked to me. This sort of occasion was hopeless; I couldn't contribute and I couldn't assert myself because my language was too limited. I was frustrated at the isolation that imposed on me, and felt rather childlike, but there was no Mummy for me.

The day came when I had to go to the bank to make my first transaction. I needed to collect a check book and to deposit some euros so I could write a check out for someone at the NZ Embassy to officially translate my birth certificate. As I stood in the queue I felt the sweat literally trickling in rivulets down my back. It was a big deal. I was on my own; bank staff didn't speak English, I didn't understand the system or how to fill in the forms. I was told I couldn't even put money in the bank without handing over my passport. I didn't carry that with me every day because I couldn't afford to lose it. My driver's license was not official ID. My credit card from the bank was not ID but the teller decided to make an exception for me this time and used my license as ID.

All French people have an identity card to prove who they are which they carry at all times. I wasn't used to that idea. A French lady behind me overheard and pulled her card out to show me what it looked like, and to confirm the requirements for bank transactions. I succeeded in obtaining a deposit slip and tried to fill it out. It wasn't laid out like those in NZ and the jargon was confusing. Another lady, who was waiting, offered to act as interpreter and taught me how to fill out a deposit form correctly. Each time I thought I had finished, she checked and corrected. Awesome young woman; so kind.

When I got back to work I discovered that Claire had decided to organize a welcome dinner for me with some of the ladies at work who lived in or near Caféolait for next Tuesday. I was impressed; then Claire joined me in the train for the journey home and we chatted in French and English. I thought the office was changing since I arrived. I thought perhaps I'd become a catalyst for my colleagues to freshen up their English. They were enjoying it, and I was delighted to help.

I was surrounded by good people, all with different personalities but accepting of me, welcoming and generous. I couldn't understand why the French had a reputation for being snobby or arrogant. Yes, there were a few but most people I met were a delight. I was so relieved.

The rhythm of my life was settling. Saturdays consisted of breakfast, strolling through the markets, then on to the supermarket. The markets continued to be a real pleasure and entertainment. I never ceased to be surprised at the incredible choice available. It wasn't top quality but the items ranged from five to fifty euros mostly, except for the big stuff. It was so enjoyable to wander about but I usually didn't go near the food stalls, especially the fresh produce, because the queues were awful. To me that was the downside of shopping in France. It was lovely to visit the little shops and markets for each item but so much time was spent waiting to be served.

My life was lived at a different pace now and it seemed to be good for me. I could decide when I did things and how. I fitted in with no one's schedule but my own (except at work of course). The pace was simpler, slower, and allowed time to just appreciate the now. I suspected that would change a bit the more I became ensconced in France, with better social contacts and reviving some hobbies.

I spent a lot of time working on the studio. It needed it; getting rid of big cobwebs and insects, washing walls and window frames and even the windows themselves, trying to fix one of the blinds so it would go up and down. I'd had a temporary success but the curtain coverings were unusable. I'd been wracking my brains as to how to attach curtains. I needed sheers and I needed curtains but space was limited and the old fashioned windows needed to be taken into account.

Most people use curtain rods in France, but there wasn't enough room under the ceiling for that. Small curtains are hung with *tringles* (small diameter, short rods with fancy end pieces that fit inside the frame diameter). I had no tools to do it myself, but I did visit a DIY after work to teach myself what was out there, costs, and to buy a measuring tape. If it had been my own place I'd have got someone in to measure up and make the curtains and install, but that wasn't reasonable for my situation.

The solution, I decided, was to string a wire up under the ceiling, just above the door and window frames, and hold it up with old screws.

The building in which I lived was built in 1787 by an important employee of King Louis XVI. He was a busy and important man because the king kept building many grand residences. There's a delicate ironwork design on the street-facing balcony with his initials. The entrance was wide enough for horses to be ridden through into a small courtyard. The house now consists of three wings. I lived in a space on the bottom level inside the courtyard, so I could walk straight out onto the cobbles, which were uncomfortable to walk on. My two windows faced a small, unkempt garden, but I was happy to have some greenery to look out on and see the changing weather.

The change came suddenly. I was there when it happened. When I arrived at work my French colleagues all concurred; winter had definitely arrived. We were all feeling it, and the evidence was plain to see; men wearing two coats at the same time, women wearing fluffy boots and jackets. Practically every woman was bound up in a scarf. Gloves were starting to appear or men thrust their hands firmly into their pockets. The chill arrived on Sunday as I was stepping out my doorway to catch the train to Paris. I'd looked at the sky and decided the blue skies must mean a nice autumnal day ahead.

I left without my raincoat or scarf. What a mistake! Tears were running down the sides of my nose as I reached the train station, and my cheeks burned with the cold. It was a different cold from NZ, in particular that of the North Island. The wind seemed to be off the arctic, and it probably was. By the time I arrived at Paris Montparnasse station I had no idea how I could possibly cope for a day in such temperatures. Thankfully Veronique, whom I'd arranged to meet up with, picked me up from the station as I was running a bit late. The train I had planned to catch was cancelled when I got there, due to the strike, so I had to wait for another one which stopped at every station and took an hour to do so.

Veronique needed to buy flowers and oysters, so I tagged along. The weather was freezing. I borrowed a thin jacket from her as anything was better than nothing, and then caught a metro to Chatelet station. My hands were so cold I couldn't easily get the money into the slot to pay for the tickets at the ticket machine. I kept dropping them onto the ground. Eventually I was on my way. I still found the metro system intimidating, probably because I hadn't used it much and had always had to do it on my own, so I learned the hard way. There were so many tunnels to walk along I needed to do my homework in order to have any idea what the various signs meant, and what station names appeared along my route.

I heard rather pleasant music down one tunnel. I emerged to find a line of men playing instruments and singing. They seemed Russian or Polish and they performed well, but I was pressed for time to make my next appointment. Chatelet is a major line change station on the metro. It can be difficult to travel from one side of Paris to the other without changing trains. It's like a rabbit warren. I eventually found a train to Porte Maillot, on the outskirts of central Paris, near La Defense. I was to meet Jacques there, for a wine. We'd communicated via a dating site. We ended up going somewhere for a hot drink instead of a wine, and then pottered around a convenience store which happened to be open on a Sunday.

We looked for Floc de Gascogne wine (alas no luck with that) and jam and a mild sort of goat's cheese for me to try. Then he helpfully dropped me back at Gare Montparnasse to go back to Caféolait. I didn't see anything of Paris at all and froze whenever I had to emerge outside. Jacques decided he didn't want to see me again as I didn't eat chicken. Another pointless Internet-initiated meeting.

Life was like learning a dance right now. Clumsy, frustrating, backward and forward motions. I was enjoying my 107cm HDTV; what a luxury--so nice to have some background noise and access to French language in my home. So far I had watched programs on Saint Malo and its links with Jersey, a yacht race off the coast of Brittany following the old rum route, tried not to watch the absolute crap of celebrity chat/indulgence/reality shows.

The other major project I'd been working on was the curtains. Victoria took me to Leroy Merlin to look for ready-mades. We had a long and frustrating search to find anything suitable for my window measurements and situation but I came away with five gorgeous terracotta/gold sheen curtains I could put a wire through. I still had to work out the wire arrangement and install it.

I'd been spending my Sunday trying to cut a length of fake lace into curtains (sheers) with a pair of nail scissors. It wasn't easy, but they were the only scissors I had. I'd got a lot of painful bruises from trying to balance on a table which was not connected to its legs, and a chair I was standing on which was rocking around on top of my bed. I had no ladder and if I had there'd have been nowhere to store it. After more window and floor washing, curtain-hanging and appreciating my lovely TV,

I was feeling chipper.

Little by little the studio was turning into a home. I'd adjusted to living in one room. The lack of facilities was something I had to be patient about and inventive with and organized, but I was content. I'd be even more content when The Professor got around to uplifting his big stuff that was taking up so much room in my bedsit.

Every day I had random moments of pure joy when something went well, or something looked beautiful or I felt I was behaving just like a French person. I couldn't understand why I seemed to be the only one not feeling joyful about the superb sunrise last Friday. It filled half the sky as the train carried us all to work, lasted twenty minutes, and covered every color tone from purple through red, pink, orange, gold. I wanted to shout to the commuters to stop sleeping, reading or playing with technology and just soak up the beauty. Instead, the sleepers continued to nod in time to the movements of the carriage. Walking through the town where I worked, in the morning I looked up at the lightening sky, saw a half moon, and sighed with sheer happiness. I was here in the only place I needed to be, wanted to be, should be.

One day I noticed many people in the town of Caféolait were carrying up to six baguettes in their arms. Perhaps there would be no shops open tomorrow, I thought, so I joined the queue outside the baker's and came away with a baguette, (a festive), an oval *campagne* and a *pain au raisins*. I topped that off with a visit to the charcuterie for a couple of mini *quiche lorraines*. Imagine me carrying all that in my arms through the streets of Caféolait, right at home. Yes, such things made me happy these days.

CHAPTER NINE

Darker days ahead

I contacted the Department of Births, Deaths, and Marriages in Wellington, NZ. It appeared the NZ Embassy in Paris found my birth certificate unacceptable. It was the only one I'd ever had; it was original and the price of 2 shillings was clearly printed on it. This sort of nitpicking really annoys me but, unfortunately, it's what many people have to deal with in moving to another country. I needed to have my birth certificate translated into French. Apparently numbers in one language are not acceptable in another. This keeps someone employed I suppose. I needed my birth certificate translated so I could apply for social security, in particular my *carte vitale* for healthcare. At the moment I had no protection for anything; sickness, accident, unemployment, whatever, but I still had to pay taxes.

I sent my birth certificate and the inevitable fee, to the Embassy in Paris because they must do a certified translation for the use of the French Government. No, no I must have a long version, as if my mother's maiden name is of any relevance here at all. Naturally, to get a new birth certificate copy and courier it to France was going to cost me another bundle. Oh, the money-go-round, for no real result. I was already here. My old birth certificate has been perfectly fine all my life until now. What happened? It's not worth arguing with oneself, *c'est comme ça* (that's just the way it is). For a small additional fee from Births, Deaths and Marriages one can have one's new New Zealand birth certificate covered in glorious artwork from a choice of designs.

Recently I had discovered that such 'milestone moments' in our lives are not documented as we assume. When one is given a piece of paper to sign at one's wedding it's not a true marriage certificate, it's just a notification. It's important to know that money and queuing is required to get a copy of the real Mac-Coy; otherwise it's not a legal document. Gee, I'd never had a legal one, in that case, for more than 35 years. My first husband and I never knew we didn't have a legal document and we still managed to get divorced quite simply. When my second husband and I got divorced, we discovered the document we signed at the wedding wasn't a marriage certificate. Good grief, I thought ignorance was bliss but actually, it's a hassle if you don't know these things.

I was still waiting to hear from the immigration department of France when I had to have an interview and a medical examination, do 'Becoming French' seminars, and have my level of French checked. None of that happened as expected. Some of it didn't happen at all.

I was fortunate to have some help from the administrative assistant at the research center where I worked. Michelle's job included battling the famous French bureaucracy. I couldn't have opened a bank account or taken out car insurance without her help. Consequently, I was now managing to fit in a little better to French society, and was managing my own life, to a limited degree. I could do internet banking, use a *Carte Bleue* credit/debit card and I sorted out a savings account to put the dreaded tax money in to meet the yearly bill. Employees' salaries are not Pay As You Earn, in France.

I decided I needed to get a car, to have more choice and independence. The Professor had told me he would sell me his car for a good price and it would be so much easier for me to buy a car through him, because the systems in France would be too expensive and complicated for me. I wasn't sure it was really the sort of car I wanted but he insisted it would be easier for me. I could still have declined the offer, but he was my boss, I didn't want to make waves with someone who was starting to make me uneasy at work, and I thought he might know best.

Michelle, The Professor's administrative assistant, and I spent ages trying to obtain car insurance for me. We had an idea how much it might cost, but I felt I couldn't afford it, and Victoria said, no, you can get it cheaper. So Michelle and I did exactly that, thanks to her negotiation skills. The car was insured, even though I didn't have possession of it yet, and I had taken out some personal accident insurance in case of disaster. Otherwise, I would have had no protection, would be possibly unable to work, or support myself anywhere if an accident had occurred. Accidents aren't covered by the social security system in France. Imagine what could happen to a new immigrant if he or she didn't take out personal insurance. It was another expense, but essential. Once my belongings arrived I could insure them too.

I caught two trains to Paris to meet up with Bent. I'll call him that for the sake of safety and accuracy. We'd met on the internet and arranged to visit the Louvre together. I'd never been there and I felt it was a good place to meet someone for the first time. The weather was dreadful. My umbrella was damaged within one minute of stepping outside my door. Being a public holiday, the traffic in Paris was atrocious. We drove through the tunnel where Princess Diana died. It still felt dangerous. Battling the elements we finally made it to the doors of the Pyramid not long after lunch.

Queues on queues; the facilities could no longer keep up with the patronage. After the effort of getting to the Louvre we just managed to secure a table in the restaurant, and have a quick bite before heading off to the Egyptian exhibit which interested us both.

Bent was 64, French, mostly retired, and spent a lot of time in Morocco. He told me he spoke eight languages; including French, fluent Dutch, German, Arabic, English, Spanish (he'd been a nightclub dancer there in his youth), and had an extremely colorful history, not all of it savory. A reformed playboy, he was good looking, kept in shape and was interesting to talk to. I was enjoying myself. We talked so much (mostly English with a bit of French thrown in by each of us from time to time) that we frequently had to remind ourselves to look at the exhibits. They're awesome in the full sense of the word.

We spent five hours in the Egyptian exhibit and still didn't see everything there. The Louvre itself had an extension added a few years ago and it's beautiful inside. The famous modern pyramid is a triumph of integration between the ancient and modern, and to be inside it and looking up at the night sky outside is magical. As we (tried) to navigate the Champs Élysées I saw the 'sparkler' for the first time. I had briefly seen the Eiffel Tower at night back in June, but I had never seen the lightshow that occurs on the hour. What a shame we couldn't get closer;

it was gone almost immediately as we tried to make our way to Richefort for some spaghetti.

Bent generously paid for everything, but when it was time to say goodbye at the train station he grabbed me and firmly helped himself to kisses with no warning. I was taken by surprise and felt quite uncomfortable. He informed me that his behavior was entirely normal, just ask any French woman, and that I'd have to get used to it. I wasn't sure about that explanation, but who was I to know what was true and what wasn't; I was a stranger in a strange land.

The next day I made my way by trains to Versailles expecting to go cycling with Bent in the grounds of the palace. The weather was horrid again, but I took my sneakers as requested. Nothing went smoothly. My train was delayed almost an hour by climatic problems on the line. Good grief, problems already and it was still above zero degrees. Poor Bent had to wait for me. This wasn't a good day for that to happen. When we met up he told me he was in a bad mood, and he certainly was. No wonder.

Earlier that morning his sports car had been destroyed by a massive fire in the car parking building where he stored it during the winter months. A nice silver Mercedes sports car, it was totally burned along with 300 cars; a major financial and bureaucratic headache, not to mention the disappointment. We saw several cars still barely drivable but black, trying to drive away, and several cars even more blackened, parked in various parts of his town. His car was completely destroyed. It wasn't insured during winter, as he only used it during warmer months. Luckily he had another car which he could drive. I thought to myself, it was rather foolish not to insure a car all year, especially when he had the money to do so.

We didn't end up cycling. We visited Saint Germain-en-Laye instead, a pretty and affluent town. I met folks who knew him. He was well known and popular. His apartment was tastefully decorated with Moroccan furniture; lovely pieces and in my favorite colors. He liked to write poetry; what I read was quite clever but dark. Bent was wonderfully helpful when it came to finding me a warm winter coat, in a style that suited me.

"No, that's for an old woman ... no, what you want isn't on offer this season but take a look at this one ... here's one for a good price."

So now I had a warm coat for a reasonable price, thanks to advice from a man whose taste in women's clothes I felt I could trust.

A few days later I decided I'd go to Paris to do some Christmas shopping for a couple of special people in Auckland. I had to do it now, in November, because posting stuff to NZ takes time. It was ghastly weather, but I took my camera, bag, broken umbrella, and an extra bag to put purchases in. I had no real idea where to go for anything because buying to send to NZ is very difficult and I didn't know Paris for shopping. I decided to head toward Boulevard Haussmann and visit Galleries Lafayette, a famous and enormous Parisian department store. Oh dear, the people. The store had set up their Christmas window displays and anyone with kids (and without) was looking at them, clogging up the pavement. Dancing cancan bears, Mamma Mia Abba bears popping out of cakes to the sound of the musical tracks in French; I'd never seen anything like it.

The store was huge, interesting but tiring, and I spent four hours trying to find anything suitable to send by post. I ended up having to be rather predictable with books, CDs and DVDs but at least things were ready to post. I got lost a bit trying to see past my broken umbrella in the wind and rain and darkening skies, but a friendly Metro cashier advised me how to make numerous changes of train until I could get back to Gare Paris Montparnasse. Second to last stop was Porte d'Orleans where I purchased my ticket to Montparnasse where from there I would purchase another ticket home. I never saw my wallet again.

Somewhere between my crowded experiences on the train and negotiating the enormous complex that is Paris Montparnasse my wallet disappeared. I was horrified, when I discovered it was missing, when trying to purchase my ticket home. All my money, my French and NZ credit cards, my driver's license, and sundry other things were gone. I had prudently hung my handbag around my neck but it was still easy for someone to pick. I'd had my arms full and everything was crowded.

The police in Paris wouldn't help me because I couldn't prove my identity. I didn't have my passport on me so I was told to visit the police in Caféolait and lay a complaint. How to do that? I had no money to buy a train ticket. The police told me to get on a particular train without paying. Oh, great strategy, as long as I could get past the barriers at the station, and avoid the on-train controllers!

I sent a mayday to Victoria. Thank goodness she answered. Like a trooper she called my French bank for me, and found the number to call for me to contact ASB Bank Auckland. Shaking from all the stress, I finally got through to the ASB via my mobile phone but couldn't stay on the line long because international calls on my prepay phone chewed up the credits. I called them back when I got back to my studio. Camille called me, (alerted by Victoria) and called in to pick me up, to help out with the language barrier of making a statement in French, at the gendarmerie. Thank God for those two lovely ladies.

My bank cards were cancelled but the other stuff was a problem. I had no money and no access to money for some days. I had to sort out the issues of my driver's license. I was so glad I didn't usually carry my passport. I could use that to prove my identity to the police in Caféolait but I had to stay inside my uncomfy little studio until work on Monday. I couldn't even buy a loaf of bread. What an awful weekend. I resolved that in future I'd always keep a tiny amount of cash at home, in case of emergencies.

The day I got robbed in the metro in Paris I spent part of the evening with Camille giving a police statement in Caféolait. We were seated by a French woman police person. We had barely got started on the statement when I proactively handed over my passport, but was asked what NZ is. Camille was a bit taken aback and replied that it is a country. And what nationality was I, asked the policewoman? Camille shuffled in her seat and tried to explain I was a New Zealander. How do you spell that? How do you spell Auckland? Camille and I looked at each other incredulously. That policewoman must have been kept in a cellar all her life without any communications, to have been so ignorant.

Little by little I put my life back together after the robbery in the Metro. I now had a replacement *Carte Bleue* and a new NZ Visa credit card. The later cost a lot of money to send to France but full marks to the ASB for having a 24 hour emergency service manned by New Zealanders and responding very promptly to cancelling my stolen Visa and getting a new one to me. It took a little more rigmarole to replace the French one but, once again, with the help of Michelle, I now had access to funds; not much, but I did manage to buy some groceries so that was a relief.

Replacing my driver's license was another ball game. There are no such things as Justices of the Peace in France who could sign and validate a photocopy of a document. I needed that because NZ Land Transport told me to send various ones to them, not original documents. I needed to ask the NZ Embassy in Paris if they could do that for me. If yes, I would have to take a day off work to travel to Paris. I didn't realize, at that stage, that there were cheaper alternatives, such as the *mairie*.

The next Tuesday, a holiday, Bent kindly picked me up from work and came over to install my curtains. It was a job and a half. The drill couldn't penetrate the wall properly and the windows were at the end of the reach of a man of normal height standing on a rickety table. There was no room at the top to install a normal rod, so I had to use a metal cable instead. It sagged a bit but at least the curtains were up. It was wonderful to have such a splash of happy red-orange in my room, and privacy too. Bent had sweated and persisted with the difficulties of the installation and I appreciated his efforts. An ex-gangster with a kind spot in his heart was helping with my domestic problems; amazing.

The following Sunday I showed Bent around Caféolait. We did the tour inside the chateau. We discovered that in some ancient buildings, air-conditioning was achieved by embedding thigh bones of cattle into the walls to conduct the humidity outside, very clever builders in the eighteenth century. We headed to my studio where I prepared a meal and we chatted and shared intimacies about our lives. Despite our different backgrounds and life experiences we enjoyed each other's company. We were not what we expected to meet.

Bent said he never expected to meet an angel. I said I didn't expect to meet a gangster. He said he regretted that part of his life and explained why a certain part of his anatomy was always, well, bent. He said he'd been a bit too enthusiastic with masturbation in prison and burst a blood vessel. The medics told him they could repair it but that he might prefer to keep it the way it was. Like that, he was told, he had a better chance than most men of hitting a woman's G-spot. So it was always leaning over like a banana, even at its best. I just nodded interestedly and tried to seem worldly. In hindsight, this explanation couldn't possibly be true. It was more likely someone had committed a violent act on his member, while he was on one of his stints in a foreign prison.

The rest of his body was in magnificent shape; in fact I kept wondering if at any moment his so-tight skin was going to crack under the strain of his muscles. He spent three to four hours most days in the gym and was very proud of his age-defying form. Combined with his naturally tanned complexion, flashing white teeth, and silver hair I found him attractive and the ten-year age difference of no matter. But I needed a second opinion about whether it was wise to continue with this relationship.

I needed to consult with the ladies at work to see if I should be considering a relationship with a man with such a past, but French attitudes are less rigid than in those in NZ. Their advice was that if he treated me well now and didn't have the old behaviors like cocaine, women, alcohol, and gangstering then give it a go, and I thought he deserved a chance.

On Monday night after work I finally took possession of my car, after waiting a month for the boss to get around to it; all the time I'd been paying the insurance. I didn't want to do the pickup at night because I felt it was too risky driving for the first time in France in the dark, in a car unknown to me, a layout different to cars in NZ, manual, out in the countryside without any streetlights or GPS. Unfortunately I had no choice. The Professor wasn't known for being considerate of others so I had to wait for his convenience. I asked Michelle to come along with me so I didn't get lost and to supervise my driving. Thank God I did. Things took an unpleasant turn in the road.

I tried to keep to the right side of the road but the country roads were narrow and most were unlit. I had no idea where I was going and just followed instructions from Michelle. I didn't feel safe in this situation. In hindsight I should have asked Michelle to drive but I'd been driving since I was seventeen. The car was practically a station wagon. As I negotiated the country road my right tire clipped the kerb. These kerbs can be tall in France, so clipping one is a big deal. I kept control of the car, but only managed to drive a hundred meters before it was clear I had no functioning tire/wheel. In fact, there were problems with two of the wheels. Here we were in pitch dark, two women alone in the country. What to do?

The first thing was to erect a reflective triangle and set it up on the road, then don a reflective vest. This is a legal requirement for all motorists. We couldn't locate the spare wheel and we struggled to find the right tools for changing a wheel. A man stopped, but was unable to help. He couldn't find anything either. Michelle called her husband Thomas to assist. He came as fast as he could and eventually, after much searching, found the spare wheel underneath the car. It eventually fell onto the road, an impossible situation for a woman to cope with.

The run-down tool kit seemed hopelessly inadequate to me. It was difficult and fiddly for Thomas to use and try as he might he could not get the wheel to let go of the car. Another driver stopped by and the two men tried to help pull it off. No luck, and an hour in freezing temperatures had passed. There's no Automobile Association in France. I felt left out of doing anything to help because I was shaking with shock, cold and despair at not being able to understand anything anyone was saying.

I rang The Professor to tell him what had happened and that we were having difficulties with changing the tires.

He said, "Oh, that happened to me once. It's life. Hope you enjoy the car."

And that was that; no sorry, no offer of help to us, even though he didn't live far away.

Michelle rang the garage which normally serviced the car (we'd stopped in there with my boss before he'd handed over the car). Just as it seemed like the mechanic would have to do an emergency trip out to us, another stiff kick from Thomas finally released the rust's hold on the car and the spare could be put on. He drove my car to Caféolait and parked it outside the church, while his wife drove me there in their car.

I left my car outside the church because I needed to find a garage to fix the tire or replace it, and also to put on the new number plates. At that time, each time a car was sold it had to have new number plates. In the light of the next morning I was disappointed to see lots of gouges and scratches on the car that I had not put there and the interior was filthy and run-down. It was a 2002 Peugeot 307 but looked older. Why did I buy it? Because my boss informed that to try to find a car and cope with the processes on my own would be too difficult and that I was getting a good deal. I'd never had the chance to have a good and relaxed look at it or do a test drive because he'd always been too busy, and it was always full to the gunwales with his stuff. He explained he'd made sure it was always well serviced and the engine did seem to run well.

All well and good, but I'd be selling it. It was a mistake and the whole accident thing traumatized me. It was not right for me; too heavy and big in narrow town streets, too hard for me to park and I'd rather have had something with better inside and outside aesthetics, even if it was a wee Twingo. An automatic would be helpful too. This whole experience had been another financial struggle; the cost of the car was more than double what I got for selling my NZ car, the insurance costs were high, I had to find paid parking as most folks living in an apartment cannot park at home. There were the running costs and the cost of a *Carte Grise* was horrifying. That was the change of ownership papers and each time the car was sold it must have new plates. That rule has since changed.

It was scarcely above zero outside. Snow had fallen and I saw it alongside the train track as I made my way sadly and distraughtly from Bent's apartment. My heart was so chilled by the icy blast I'd experienced that morning from him.

I'd been happy to spend time with him. I was even falling in love with him, and he said he'd loved me quickly and deeply and I was perfect for him, that he'd never been so happy in his life. He certainly seemed genuine. He had previously given me a bracelet of his mother's. It was lovely, of an old-fashioned style with a center stone of something brown and with three strands of pearls around the wrist. I was so touched, but thought it a bit odd that there was a tiny oval ticket attached to it. I couldn't see what was on the ticket as he removed it and handed me the bracelet. He told me his mother had been dead for a year and he was organizing disposal of her personal effects. The ticket was odd but I didn't want to question him regarding something that might have been painful for him. My work colleagues later admired the beautiful bracelet when I wore it to work.

Bent informed me that we were to spend a week in Marrakesh during my Christmas holidays. How splendid, I thought. As he spent a week out of every four in Morocco, popping across The Med was normal for him. This sort of lifestyle and these sorts of experience were completely new to me, like the adventures a woman might have in a novel.

We had arranged for me to stay over at his apartment not far from Richefort, for the first time. We were both looking forward to it; he picked me up from work, I introduced him to the ladies in my office. We spent ages in the freezing temperatures getting his groceries whereas he had previously said we might look at the Christmas lights along the Champs Élysées. That was disappointing, but I supposed that a long weekend at his place did require some practical considerations.

We had some lovely cuddles on the couch in front of TV and he told me many times how lucky he was to find such an angel because he had given up hope; he loved me so much. Wow, I thought. Someone who really wants me; an unconventional person, a person who knew how to stand on his own two feet.

He did his level best to convince me to accept his mother's fur coat. I graciously declined as I explained I am absolutely against animals being killed for their fur.

"But it's a wonderful coat, you'd look fantastic in it, just try it on," he cajoled.

"No," I repeated. "I couldn't accept it."

"Please," he insisted, and began to become agitated. "It's your size."

Oh well, I thought I could at least look at it and imagine what it would be like not to have my cast iron principles. He held it out proudly, explaining it was old but in perfect condition and his mother had worn it many times. It was a perfect fit for me, it really was and in mint condition. I looked fabulous, there was no denying it, and the fur was a sensual pleasure under my fingers. I stood there admiring myself in the mirror; I did a twirl and said I agreed that it was absolutely gorgeous, that I still couldn't accept it because it was real fur. Bent was quite put out but accepted defeat.

We spent more intimate time together in the living room, then moved to the bedroom. Being post-menopausal I had some difficulties in sexual activities but consideration and patience could surmount those with a compatible man, which my time with Nicolas had proved. However, having sex with Bent was the worst such experience I'd ever had. He thought plunging in to giving a woman oral sex was foreplay and got annoyed when I wanted to stop and do something else.

"Don't you take my pleasures away from me," he snapped angrily.

There was no romance, variety or finesse, just a lot of ego regarding his physique. Well, the best part of him stopped above the waist.

Being literally bent, even when aroused, his penis just didn't get on the right trajectory. Sex was completely unsuccessful and painful for me because he just kept assaulting me with the damned thing. He became angry. He was impervious to my distress. No wonder he'd had so many women. Who'd want to try a second time? I did my best to make the effort worth his while but it certainly wasn't worth mine. Hugs? Forget it! It certainly wasn't lovemaking. I'm not even sure it qualified as having sex.

When I wake up in the morning it seems natural to me to want to reach over and kiss and cuddle my man. But when I tried to do that the next morning I was told not to; to never kiss him in the morning because it was disgusting without people brushing teeth first, and that he never ever shows affection in the morning, not before lunch. I tried to encourage a little compromise but this didn't work, so I said things weren't working well. That was death to the relationship; that and my attempt to kiss him. I was so shocked and incredulous. He literally turned his back on me.

"Get yourself organized and catch a train home."

That's all he said. So I made my way to the living room, changed from my pajamas and cried. He came in and said nothing, wouldn't look at me. He relented on making me find a bus to the station but he walked ahead of me several spaces, refused to share the lift with me, and instead preferred to take the stairs.

"What's happening with you?" I asked.

"You obviously wanted everything your way. You don't respect me. I can turn my feelings off. If there's a disease I amputate it."

Incredulous, I said, "So are you saying I'm a disease to be amputated now?"

He didn't reply but I knew he meant yes.

I told him he was being cruel to me and he said I was just being clever with my words. This was a devastating experience for me, and completely out of the blue. I'd spent my life never finding a man who really wanted me, who would stay, who valued me and all the loyalty and affection I can bring. They say it but they don't mean it. I dared to love and trust and hope and within ten hours it was over because I wanted to kiss or cuddle my man before lunch.

Yes, his past had been bad and I had discussed this with the ladies in my office. Bent had spent most of his life as a gangster for a 'Godfather'. He told me his job had been to make up the hit lists and put the contracts out on those people Mister Big wanted out of the way. Bent told me he'd only shot one person and killed him, to rescue a woman, but he'd certainly fired guns at bad guys and wounded them, usually in the knees, and been a bank robber. He told me he had inside knowledge on political assassinations in a country bordering the Mediterranean. The latter story details sounded too incredible to be true but he certainly had a gun. He'd shown it to me.

He was writing a number of books on his experiences and told me that if he published any he was certain to end up with a bullet in the brain. I told him to leave the manuscripts with his lawyer and to arrange for them to be published after his natural death. He showed me a few pages of one of his books on his computer. It was in French, but I could understand it, and in it was sprinkled the name of Mister Big. Fortunately for me, I seem to have forgotten it.

He told me he'd spent years with cocaine, cigarettes and champagne and 500 (yes) 500 women, but gave it all up a long time ago. He'd spent a total of fifteen years in jail in various countries for bank robberies. At his stage of life he had realized what he wanted and it wasn't the past life. He often helped other people now, he said.

I'd had an eerie experience with him when visiting a major shopping center near Richefort to buy my coat. He seemed to personally know so many of the merchants and staff. We stopped for a coffee and I sat there watching a number of men in suits walk up to him, hug, and even kiss his hand. I couldn't help thinking it was too much like watching Michael Corleone at the end of the movie The Godfather Part One.

The last night I saw Bent, before the disastrous bedroom fiasco, he told me he might have to risk a trip to Belgium to collect an expensive watch they were keeping for him that he'd lost in prison there. Going back to Belgium risked being jailed there as he wasn't welcome back in the country, he said. I was unhappy he could be jailed for several months so he told me he'd delay the visit in order for us to spend more time together. His past still affected his present, even in small ways. He'd get very anxious whenever we were in the car and saw any kind of police. He said they'd harass him because of his past.

I'd loved talking with him, and holding him and sharing extraordinary tenderness. He'd told me the guys before him must have been assholes not to want me. Strange, Nicolas had told me the same thing. Later, the ladies at work told me that bedding even five hundred women would have been impossible for Bent, considering his jail time. Perhaps he'd got the word wrong by speaking in English; even so …how much of what he'd said had been the truth?

I didn't think I would ever understand Bent's brutal reaction and cruel comments and blame of me. How could a man not want to be woken with a kiss? Had the cocaine use in the past affected his sanity? He was certainly the worst lover I'd ever experienced; the most boring, unimaginative and selfish, as well as physically incompetent. Technically one could say we hadn't been lovers. Well, clearly I didn't have a happy future there. Did I have one anywhere? I was feeling lonelier than ever; there was no special person to share kindnesses with and Christmas now looked horribly bleak.

It arrived silently in the wee hours, magically, like Father Christmas. No doubt he'd be feeling at home here in Caféolait. The snow. And there was plenty more on the way. Everything horizontal was white, everything vertical was black. The view from the train was beautiful.

The air burned the inside of my nose and ears but it was slightly warmer just after it had snowed. I couldn't explain that. The following days seemed even colder. It was dangerous trying to walk outside. Shoes and boots slid. If someone was walking faster than I it was invariably a guy. They must have had better shoes or balance. I set off in the morning and almost reached the train station when my NZ walking shoes gave out. The soles completely detached, so I missed my train and had to turn around and go home for more footwear. It wasn't fun trying to walk in snow and ice without any soles.

After Bent's bizarre and hurtful behavior I was further disappointed by my belongings not arriving when promised. I'd had to take a day off work. They didn't arrive and no one contacted me. Household goods from New Zealand to Europe usually go by way of the United Kingdom. I had to do a bit of research to find someone in the United Kingdom to handle my enquiry. Apparently the haulage company hadn't loaded my stuff the night before. No one knew why. It was bad timing for me, adding to an already miserable day. These sorts of problems are always possible when moving countries.

At 8.30 on Saturday my mobile rang to say the delivery guys were outside the studio with my stuff. Still in my pajamas, I donned my coat and never went outside the rest of the day. Everything arrived in good condition, except a beloved candle vase on a pedestal. It hadn't been packed in the vertical position and so had broken. It was disappointing but not expensive enough for me to waive the excess and lay a claim. I spent the rest of the day trying to refocus my life away from my short-lived relationship with Bent. I wrote him an email explaining how I felt and that I was hurt and didn't understand his reaction. He didn't reply. How very Nicolas-like.

I did receive the following email the next day:

> *Send me quickly all the details of the car: year, model, kilométrage, puissance fiscale, type. Maybe I can sell it to my partner.*

Hmm, was it his way to make contact again? Was he still trying to be helpful? After some brief exchanges he sent a message:

> *Okay, I bring my friend Monday evening at 6h30 in your place. He will bring his car and take yours if he likes it. Remember to ask that amount I told you to ask for your car. Tell him that you paid that sum of money to get the car OK? He will repair the tire if he takes the car and he will drive it until you bring him the car registration.*

Bent knew I hadn't paid quite that amount of money. Why would he want his partner to pay more? He also thought he might know of a small car I could buy inexpensively so I would have some money in my pocket; we'd talked about that several days ago.

I discussed this with the ladies over lunch at work. They were alarmed. They had all sorts of scary hypotheses; if I was given cash it was probably counterfeit, maybe the two men would take the car keys and drive off, maybe they were trying to steal my money, perhaps the other car was stolen, maybe they would discuss ripping me off in rapid French so I wouldn't understand their dastardly plan. Shit! This sort of thing wasn't really an issue in NZ. In fact, there, cash is considered safer than anything else. I was reminded I was not in NZ.

Bent hadn't answered my heartfelt letter to him and hadn't rung me so I decided not to take the risk, and sent him an email and text to cancel the meeting. I wanted to see him to find out what was going on, but he never called me to enquire why I cancelled and he never turned up on my doorstep. How can one believe anything tender guys say even when their eyes suggest they're speaking the truth?

He may had some feelings for me and hoped I would stick around, but it would have been completely on his terms and I wasn't about to be controlled as I had been in the past, and his moodiness wasn't much fun. There would have been further disappointments for me I'm sure, and I deserved better. It was a shame the white side of him lost out to the black. Time would heal my heart again, but it showed me that I really did want and need some tenderness and companionship from a genuinely nice, stable man. Now there was a big void again.

I was also sad about the financial situation I'd put myself into by buying my boss's car. It had been too expensive for me but I'd felt under pressure not to upset The Professor. To change ownership and buy new plates cost more than three hundred euros. On top of that I had to pay more than another three hundred euros to replace two tires and pay for parking for the car. It was horrifying. I was also advised by a car salesman that the condition of the car was such it might be difficult to sell. I'd had no opportunity to test drive nor see the car properly in daylight. I should have insisted on a lot of things, but when it was my temper-prone boss who held my existence in his hand, it made me more timid.

I needed to get some of the insurance money back but was told that would take weeks. There was little money to buy food to eat for the next month. I still had to pay for train trips to work, personal insurance, contents insurance, tax, rent.

I were also the replacement and translation costs associated with the theft of my wallet. This was way beyond my little salary so I had to sell the car somehow to raise funds. *Merde!* This dream of mine wasn't for the faint-hearted. I seemed to have crammed a lot of misfortune into a short period. I loved France, but not this level of struggle.

Camille, Michelle, Victoria and Claire were helpful. Claire invited me over to her place for dinner Saturday night. She knew I was struggling. I spent a delightful evening watching her serve up a French home-cooked meal, met her husband and their two lovely children. We had fun, spoke two languages and I had some good advice from her. She and her husband had worked wonders on what was a derelict house and garden. It had been transformed into a classy and comfortable home for a family and friends. I loved learning about the lives of 'real' French people.

Camille helped me sort out the car. It now had new registration plates and two new tires and under-cover parking. She and Michelle helped me sell the car by putting it on the Internet in French and fielding responses which I wasn't linguistically competent to do.

I still felt I needed a car. It was difficult to do grocery shopping without one. I could buy only tiny quantities with little choice in a more expensive supermarket. I couldn't take up my bellydancing without one, I couldn't visit anyone outside of Caféolait effectively without one, and I couldn't explore the countryside or develop confidence in making an independent life here without being able to drive.

I had taken all these things for granted in NZ; driving, managing my own affairs. Now I was like an adolescent getting into difficulties and needing mum and dad to help me sort things out and learn. I was dependent, and I didn't like it, but I was lucky to find generous people who helped when they could. I was making big mistakes because I wanted to see the positive in things: prudence, more prudence.

I've stood on the Tasman Glacier in the South Island of New Zealand. I've been snowed into my home on a hill with no electricity/cooking/heating/entertainment for three solid days and nights, but this was in a different category. France, and in particular the Ile de France region, was blasted with an incredibly serious snow dump in 2010. It paralyzed Paris.

There I was in my coat, NZ boots, and scarf and gloves, but no hat. The snowflakes fell thickly and stuck to my clothes and hair. Walking was treacherous. By the time I got back to Caféolait from work, cars were queuing up to be pushed up inclines or guided down slopes. In the end a number of central streets were closed to cars because they couldn't keep on the road. Traffic jams were everywhere. The streets of Caféolait are narrow so it's easy to have a snarl-up. Pedestrians were falling and breaking limbs.

My Auckland street boots couldn't cope with snow up to my mid calves. My feet were wet and freezing but, hey, since I was already like that, what were a few more minutes, so I decided to capture the event digitally. Climate change may make such extreme events more common but I wasn't about to let this one pass. As the day faded the snowflakes continued. The chateau, the grounds, the village, my street were all smothered by snow.

The grounds of the chateau were like a wonderland, stunningly beautiful.

The next day the snow softened and then froze. Walking the streets, pavements and station platforms was like walking on glaciers. The ice cracked beneath me. It was so easy to lose my footing and if I was unfortunate to step in some water, well, walking on the ice then became hellish with wet feet. Several of my colleagues couldn't make it into the office.

My train to work was cancelled; in fact they all were for a time, and I had to stand in the freezing conditions for ninety minutes until a train to work was available. The train station staff, women included, had to pitch in with shovels to chip the concrete-like ice off the edges of the platforms so we could board the trains. I felt sorry for them. It was bloody hard work and the shovels soon became bent out of shape.

Despite the frigid weather conditions I put a lot of effort into trying to get the car in an almost fit state to sell. It had been horribly abused and neglected and was in a filthy state. I thought back to the car I'd had to sell in Auckland. My Toyota was spotless inside, tidy and didn't need any spring-cleaning. That's a simple courtesy when you sell a car to someone.

I had discovered that my Peugeot needed fumigating, stripping, and re-carpeting, as well as shampooing, but that was not an option for me. The carpet in the back was rotting from dampness. Food slops were everywhere. Of course, I never saw any of that in the dark when I collected it. It just goes to show what can happen when someone is so far out of their comfort and knowledge zone, and especially when they cannot communicate in the local lingo; how vulnerable they can be, how non-assertive and passive. I certainly made a mistake buying it.

I ended up washing the damn thing in the snow. I had to

clean it when there was time available; when Claire had time to be at home (I cleaned it at her place) and the fact that we had a truly serious dump of snow that week was an inconvenience. It wasn't fun even though I laughed at the absurdity in the photos we took. It wasn't possible to wash the exterior of the car with water in those conditions because water would freeze. The snow was free and a bit crunchy in texture so it worked fine, though my hands and feet became very painful from the cold. I also had to wash the inside of the car; tepid water in a bowl for that.

A few days later I went back to Claire's place to do the car vacuuming and polish all the interior plastic, after walking for a bit to find a petrol station. That was the only place I could get to buy some car cleaner. Without a car (ha) it was difficult to get around to do anything or buy anything so I just had to walk or not do it.

What, no car? I couldn't face driving the station wagon. Having had an 'upset' with it at night in the countryside and left with huge (for me) bills and shock I had no interest in driving it. A smaller car would enable me to get my confidence back and I would be happier with a clean and tidy car, something I could take pleasure in, instead of looking at with regret and distaste.

Eventually I'd be able to put this mistake behind me but at the moment I was in the middle of it and in the red financially. Getting paid monthly was hard when something major went wrong. I needed to sell the Peugeot to get back into the black. It was a shame to go into Christmas like this but it couldn't be helped.

I decided to join Alain in Brittany for a few days. It would be great to see him again and would be a lot more enjoyable spending the festive season with him and his son. It would be good to be with nice people and have my days warm instead of huddling over my little heater on my own in my studio. I was keen to see what happens in a typical French family at Christmas time.

Christmas coquilles

CHAPTER TEN

Lessons hard learned

My plan was to spend Christmas in Brittany, come back to Caféolait, get my domestic chores done, and consider whether I would go to Paris for New Year's Eve; I heard they had fireworks. Maybe if I could stay awake long enough it might be fun to take my camera and watch them. I started looking forward to having some time off from work.

As Christmas approached, it was time for the staff luncheon at a restaurant. I waited at the bus stop for Claire to collect some of us to travel there together. There I was, standing at the bus stop outside the train station at Caféolait (peaceful place, reasonably affluent) waiting for my lift. It was cold and wet, and here and there were still patches of snow from a week ago. People were starting to collect at the bus shelter across the road. One man took off his coat. I was surprised because it was bitterly cold. He seemed warmly dressed with a beanie. I looked away but moments later looked back. You what?

The guy was virtually naked. His trousers and underpants were around his ankles and he was holding his top up high around his neck so there was this large expanse of nakedness in the middle of the street. He had his dick in his hand and he was pissing into a person's property. I find it pretty disgusting that men find pissing on personal and public property of no consequence. It stinks (consider the subways), but this guy was making a real display. There's no need to take your clothes off to pee. It was a little disturbing to see a big lump of a guy doing that next to the bus stop.

I turned to the old woman at the bus stop next to me and remarked to her. She wasn't fazed, as if she'd seen everything and was past disappointment in humanity. She informed me that Caféolait was one of the better areas, as she pointed out the smashed glass in the shelter.

"There are worse areas," she said to me.

"Surely the naked guy's not right in the head," I remarked.

"Probably too much drink," she calmly explained.

She wasn't happy about the state of the world, but ... well ... there you are. Indeed, one ugly naked man pissing on the lamp post to start the day.

It wasn't quite the start of the day, though. Earlier I had been following my language instruction via the TV. I regularly tried to catch a children's program before work to get me into the French language for the day and pick up on some phrases and vocabulary. I watched either Dora the Explorer, or the Mickey Mouse Kids Club (that was difficult with the accents of Donald and Pluto). Babar the elephant was too difficult for me because they had long conversations and spoke too quickly. Dora was ideal because it's education-based rather than entertainment. She repeated things, asked simple questions and followed a formula. No wonder babies learn; they hear simple things over and over again, and their heads aren't full of adult rubbish.

Saturday was a terrific day. I met Alex at the parking building in the morning. He was an American missionary with a growing family, needing a larger car. We were both relieved we could conduct the exercise in English. He was thorough in his inspection and seemed to know what he was doing. He expected every bit of documentation available to me. In the end, after a test drive, he agreed to buy my car for a discounted price which was reasonable. He was to meet with me the next day, but the snow was too bad, so hopefully I would have the money and he would have the car on Tuesday night. It all worked out in the end. The car was sold, I'd recouped some of my money, though it would be an extremely long time before I would have a car again. I felt so incredibly lucky, but more was ahead.

As I walked back from the meeting, I was accosted by a guy and his colleague with a public address system and a microphone. It seemed I had been chosen to win a prize at the markets.

"Err, how is your French?" he asked.

"Not good, I replied."

This was clearly a signal for him to proceed in asking me a question on famous monuments, in French, of course. I understood sixty percent which was enough for me to reply with the answer in French. Hello, ten euros to spend at the markets, awesome. Hello thermal underwear, top and bottom for an amazing ten euros. Learning French was paying off.

The snow had been falling for fourteen hours so I decided to get reckless and splash out thirty euros at the market on cheap snow boots. They were inexpensive and a bit too small but were better than the running shoes I'd been wearing until now. I was so happy; not a moment too soon as the snow got thicker and thicker. I changed into my new boots and headed off to meet Brad at the train station.

Brad was a fellow couchsurfer who lived in Antwerp, Belgium. He was in Paris for the weekend, and we'd arranged to meet up. Despite our age difference we had a lot in common. We headed back to my studio where we chatted and I made lunch. Then it was time for a hot chocolate at a restaurant, then off to the Chateau de Caféolait. We were a bit early so I decided we'd explore the park in the snow. More good luck; as we were walking, along came two men in a wagon drawn by a draft horse. The driver invited us up for a free ride. Cool; Brad and I were beaming. The horse picked up speed and the slipstream blew the driver's hat off into the snow. His colleague retrieved it and we all laughed like school kids.

Brad enjoyed seeing the inside of the Chateau. More good luck; they decided to give us a rare commentary in English. The young lady who was training to be an archaeologist had a strong French accent and spoke quietly, but I picked up a few new bits of historical info.

The snow was turning into a whiteout as Brad and I and our guide set out to walk in the park. The sun had gone down and night was on us. We walked along the snow-covered road in the dark. It was so beautiful even though it wasn't comfortable. My hands and feet were freezing but I had the clothes to dress appropriately now, to keep my body core temperature at a normal level. The exercise helped too. Brad caught his trains safely back to Paris, and I watched the young ice-skaters enjoying the temporary rink in the snowstorm.

There was no point in stopping doing things just because the weather was awful, because it was like that most days now. I walked down the middle of the snowy street hauling my trundler to the laundromat and back twice. I was an expert now. After lunch I decided to catch a bus to the shopping center.

Yuck, it was now raining with a stiff icy wind that rattled and shook the bus shelter where I huddled for the bus. No bus came ... still no bus came. After forty minutes I still saw no buses or passengers so back home I went. Checking the Internet revealed all buses were cancelled for three days due to the snow. Why couldn't they have put a sign up? On the whole it had been a great weekend, though I cut my finger rather badly on the bread knife. I'd lost my coordination because my hands were frozen, and I was desperate to eat, so I wasn't careful enough. There was lots of blood but I had bandages in the studio now. Things were looking up.

It was time to turn up for my appointment to obtain my *titre de séjour*. I left work and waited for a train to Paris. After that I headed out to the immigration department, on the Metro. I got a bit lost because the town where it was situated has decided to split itself into two names, depending on how schizophrenic it felt about the railway line through the middle. How was I to know that? I expected the same name for the same road to stay in one town. First I picked the wrong direction but an extra walk got me to the other end and the OFII immigration people.

They only spoke French. Good grief, they were handling immigration but no quarter was given to the foreign nationals. It was as well I could hold my own enough to get on side with those I could and make a point with those I couldn't, even though my spoken French was extremely weak.

They were forever expecting me to be Free. That was not my legal name in New Zealand and hadn't been since I was twenty-one. The French do things very differently; a birth name is the most important and stays with a person on all their documentation.

At least I managed a joke with a couple of nurses. There I was with a heavily bandaged finger (from an altercation with my breadknife), then they put a big plaster on another finger; test for diabetes. We laughed about my two bandages and they asked if I would like a third.

"Non merci, ça suffit."

Blood pressure, urine, Xray of chest.

"How old are you?" enquired the doctor.

It should have been obvious from my records.

"Have you ever been sick or had an injury in your life?"

I looked at him incredulously, how stupid.

"At my age, of course I have," I replied.

He asked if there'd been anything serious, so I replied no. He told me I should get an eye checked out. Well I couldn't see the silly wee numbers that small, especially when I pressed my hand very hard to the right eye to test the other one and probably pressed too hard so I took ages to work out what the letters were until my eye recovered. Oops!

The doctor insisted on listening to my heart but didn't notice my heart condition. I have a very loud and distinctive murmur from a defective valve. Weight and height had been checked; they don't admit giants or pygmies? Chest X-ray, Okay. I was told I was supposed to be vaccinated for polio. Done that, I said. He insisted that in NZ you have to do it every ten years.

After a further long wait I was seen for all the paperwork. I had done my homework meticulously because I didn't want any foul-ups. A young guy studied everything in my dossier and then said "*Malheureusement* ..." Oh-oh that wasn't sounding good. Cockup by French staff. They hadn't created a *titre de séjour* with the matching numbers of my visa and they must match. Though it wasn't my fault I was told I must go away and come back another time. That cost me half a day of work plus money travelling on four trains. They said they would contact me in a few weeks and I would have to come back at my expense. I didn't see that one coming.

Thanks to my friend Alain's generosity I was enjoying and learning about a French family Christmas. It was my first Christmas here in France so it was an important milestone. I arrived in Alain's village, 15 kilometers outside the main city of Rennes, and settled in. Alain's friend Pascal, whom I'd met earlier in the year, and his new girlfriend arrived to join us. Alain's daughter whom I'd previously met was there too.

It was Christmas Eve and he'd gone all-out with his catering: aperitifs (including pieces of quiche for me because I don't eat *foie gras* or seafood), Coquilles Saint Jacques, leg of lamb crusted with lemon juice and honey, roasted slices of potato, green salad, cheeses, a chocolate and cream log for dessert, lots of wine, rose champagne to start with. Certainly, with the guys together I knew there'd be a lot of laughing and teasing and maybe some general silliness among them. I managed to cope with the language situation. Sometimes the guys would assist with some English but mostly everything was in French. Christmas presents were exchanged and the night became morning without my awareness of it.

On Christmas Day we collected Alain's son from his mother, and drove deep into Brittany, the Morbihan, to spend the day with Alain's mother and extended family. Along the way we drove near the Forest of Brocéliande. Legend has it this is where King Arthur and his Knights of the Round Table spent much time. Merlin lived there and so did his not-so-nice half-sister Morgan le Fey, as well as the Lady of the Lake. It's an ancient place of legend, druids, and great deeds. I wanted to visit it one day.

Alain's family were incredibly wonderful people. The acceptance and warmth I experienced in just one afternoon and evening with them completely overshadowed my experiences with my own family of a lifetime; sad but true. I wanted to experience a true French family Christmas and I couldn't have had a better experience. Warm hugs and smiles, kisses and laughter were all around. Those who could speak a little English tried to, but most of the time I found I could use the French I knew to be part of things. It was a little easier this time around the social circuit. I met Alain's older sister, his younger brother, his mother Marie and her boyfriend Raymond, partners, children, neighbors.

The food; Alain was rather concerned about me because most of the traditional fare was impossible for me to eat, but it wasn't a problem. I tried some special mushrooms; edible but not to my taste, plus little aperitif biscuits which were yummy. Champagne corks popped to start things off, white wine and then later red wine followed, seafood, bread, and Breton butter, leg of lamb (cooked differently from how we do it in NZ, and anyway the meat was Australian) mixed vegetables and French fries, green salad followed by cheese (I tried some new ones and enjoyed them). Dessert logs of different flavors tempted everyone's over-stuffed tummies but, of course, my favorite log was chocolate. There were amazing dark chocolates too, offered by Raymond. I was moved to tears by the richness of the experience, then Raymond started crying too. This wouldn't happen easily in a NZ family. Nothing was superficial with this French family; the members were all genuinely close.

A few days later I left for Paris and then Caféolait. It had been wonderful to spend time again with Alain and his family. We'd have a lot of laughs but I wasn't used to such an indolent life. Yes, I was on holiday, but it was time to leave lovely Brittany and get back into the rhythm of life in Caféolait before going back to work.

I hadn't been physically alone during the week and that had been a lovely change. I'd experienced a lot of friendliness and helpfulness but there had been no emotional connection from anyone. I didn't know if I'd see Alain again, only if he wanted to I supposed. He seemed more distant, cooler, and said he never came to Paris and certainly never as far as my village. He was too busy, and he told me that anyway, he had teams of friends for any occasion; so different from me but I didn't need a lot of friends. Just a handful would be great, but I would want to feel I loved each and every one of them and that my feelings were returned.

It had grown painfully clear to me that my search of a lifetime, for genuine love was no closer to realization than it had ever been, yet the feeling was becoming so strong. It was a bit how I felt about needing to live in France, part of my life necessities somehow. Living in France didn't seem enough to distract me from the other important need I had for a deep and meaningful emotional connection.

Many women my age find themselves alone, often for the rest of their lives. Some say they would never bother with a man again because they're too much trouble and women have to give up too much of themselves. Others tell themselves they don't need a man but wistfully want one, and then others are desperate and make bad decisions. The general agreement is that there are not enough men available for older women. French people tell me there are more women than men in

France but at my age the options were limited. I needed some personal tenderness in my life, but in the meantime I needed to look out for myself.

I wasn't well. I had to excuse myself from a drinks and nibbles event that a female friend of Alain's was hosting on my last night in Brittany. My head, throat and chest weren't happy. I had a cough and was frequently dizzy. It had gradually developed over the week. The energy just drained out of me. Now I understood why. I wasn't getting enough oxygen.

On the train back to Paris, then Caféolait, it was clear I was now suffering asthma and a build-up of mucus brought on by a week of forced exposure to incessant smoking. I had explained to Alain and his daughter that it's bad for my health, gave me chronic health problems in my childhood and that I now had a heart condition and lungs highly sensitive to cigarette smoke. They were unconcerned and if anything smoked all the more.

Alain hadn't smoked in front of me the previous time I'd stayed with him. He explained he could smoke anytime without being addicted and did it because he liked it and could stop anytime. He chose not to stop during my visit. I hadn't realized I would be subjected to this when I accepted the invitation. Of course, it was even worse when friends arrived. They could have smoked outside or in another room but again chose not to, it was Alain's house, so now breathing was painful and I spent New Year alone, coughing and feeling dreadful.

After sitting in the train from Paris, at the station, not moving for an hour and a half, with no food or drink or toilet access (the toilets are locked automatically while not moving) we got going only to glide so slowly along the track I could have got out and walked. I tried to amuse myself by peering into apartment windows to see what people were doing. Twenty minutes later we came to a complete stop in the darkness of nowhere. I don't know why. We just sat. Being unwell I was desperate to get home. By the time I eventually arrived in Caféolait it was two hours later than expected and nothing was open, so I had no dinner, no breakfast. Not even a cup of tea. I was feeling dejected.

New Year's Eve arrived. What a pathetic figure I was in my dressing gown, wheezing and dragging myself around; no trip to see fireworks in Paris. Maybe it wouldn't have been safe. They'd brought in extra police and posted notices on the TV about thieves. Instead I dragged myself along the street to the laudromat and bought some essential food, a warm jumper, and a pot to boil up some pasta. I sure hoped 2011 had some great stuff ahead for me. Hey, this time last year, who would have thought I'd actually be living in France. Amazing, but it was difficult, too.

Once again, through state error, I had to leave work early and spend money and precious time getting to where dwells the Immigration Department. Again I endured the waiting, and being sent to the wrong office, being told I would have to go back to NZ to get my *titre de séjour*. What? They seemed to have no idea what to do with me. There was no sign of me being offered the "Becoming French orientation sessions". They refused to speak English and I kept repeating I was only there to pick up the sticker, nothing else. My dossier was complete but an officious woman told me there was only one person who could give my card to me and she wasn't available all day. I explained I was told to come that afternoon. So she told me to come back, for the third time, on Monday.

Okay, enough already. I had nothing to lose. My identity sticker was ready, I just needed somebody to give it to me. Why was that impossible?

"It's your fault," I said. "The Immigration Department is in the wrong and I cannot come back again, I cannot spend money like this and I cannot get more time off work, it's impossible."

I made a noisy fuss and stood my ground.

People came out of offices to see what was up. Suddenly one of them grabbed my dossier from somewhere and started rifling through it, backwards and forwards. I endeavored to explain the mistake of immigration staff because, clearly, this guy couldn't see it. OOhh. Right. Sticker in Passport, off I went.

So why was I treated like this with no service at all? Just because they can. What if immigrants don't speak French? My French wasn't adequate for situations like this and it caused me a lot of stress. I would have to come back three months before things expired and let them know if an extension would be required. I hoped so after all this. Why did I need this sticker? Because a visa to work and live in France is not sufficient. You must have official identification and residency, as each French person must. We didn't have this in NZ. We just used our driver license for identification.

Later in the day I went to see the doctor for the second time since arriving in Caféolait. It was getting easier to manage the communication with doctors as I had just enough vocabulary to explain the problem. My strategy was to say as much as possible up front so they had less to say, and that meant less for me not to understand. This worked quite well and I repeated important stuff to check I had understood. It was different to how things were done in NZ. In Caféolait the waiting rooms were old, rundown, spartan, there were no receptionists or busy atmospheres. There were some French magazines and one old toilet usually, and the doctors were never on time. The doctors had exceedingly inadequate signage, just a tiny plaque screwed to the wall. It's illegal for French doctors to advertise. Anglo-Saxon business practices are totally frowned on; doctors aren't there to make money, they're there to serve.

Off to the chemist. This was a little more challenging because they are so systems driven and those systems are different. They don't print out dosage instructions on the bottles or packets so I asked the lady pharmacist to write notes on them for me; telling me once in French was no good. The little boxes generally have Braille on them and standard instructions inside. French doctors don't use medications in a 'creative' way as they do in NZ. One size seemed to fit all, it seemed. I asked the pharmacist if she had any other Kiwi clients. She wasn't aware of any, but she was friendly and helpful and didn't mind my bumbling French at all.

I was now armed with a cough syrup, some short-term steroids/anti-inflammatories, and a nose spray that had the effect that night of totally aggravating my nose bleeds to the extent I had to cover my pillows with towels. I was hopeful that I'd be my old energetic self by the weekend.

Unfortunately, determination wasn't enough. The pain got worse. After taking the steroids prescribed and appreciating the fact they seemed to help the general pain I experienced each day, things became truly unpleasant. The side effects caused general pain and inflammation throughout my body and then did nasty things to my stomach. I went out to keep myself distracted. I stayed in bed to rest. Nothing helped.

I dragged myself out of bed on the Monday and limped along the streets to the train. I was actually sitting in the train to go to work, trying to decide if I was being a fool by going there. In the end the pain decided that I should get off the train and walk in misery back home. Later in the morning I queued at the doctor's. It didn't matter if I had an appointment or not, I still had to wait a minimum of an hour and a half. I was obviously sick and in pain but no one else was going to give up their position in the queue.

I had written a letter to the doctor because he didn't speak English and I needed to explain the complexities of stomach, arthritis, bowel interactions and what products I had used to try to help myself. It was tricky, and being completely alone, with no cups of tea nor a hug or kind word when you are really sick in a foreign country is rather scary. The doctor started talking about blood tests and investigations into the stomach. No way, I had no money. And I still didn't have my *Carte Vitale* health card.

The painkillers prescribed didn't take away all the pain and stiffness but I was completely zonked so I didn't care. I couldn't even raise the energy to turn over in bed. No problem, at least it was a break from the searing, grinding, aching pain everywhere. The doctor explained I'd had a bit of bad luck with my reaction to the anti-inflammatories/steroids. If I needed to, I could take the next day off work, he said.

There came a point where I could no longer look after myself. By Tuesday I was very ill but staying at home wasn't helping. I thought I could go into work late but as I dragged myself out of bed to get dressed I discovered the weakness and pain were too much for me. Going back to the doctor seemed a waste of time as nothing he'd given me had helped, in fact it had made things worse. I began to feel desperate and afraid. I could no longer eat and drink. To take a sip of water resulted in violent vomiting. It takes a lot to make stuff evict my body from either end; this was a disturbing sign. I hadn't been able to sleep and I was becoming shaky and anxious.

I phoned my work colleagues, at the end of my will-power to help myself. They told me I must go to hospital but I had no idea in my fuddled state what to do. They rang the number 15 for me. Sometime later a *pompier* rang me to determine my address and said they'd be on their way in thirty minutes. I scraped some spare knickers, my phone, toothbrush and pajamas into an overnight bag, unlocked my door, and clung to the bed.

Two guys in dark grey uniforms carrying kit bags walked past my studio so I let them know, yes it was me. None of this was easy because I was now in a situation for which I had little vocabulary. They asked me some questions, I tried to explain my problem. I locked up the bedsit while they carried my bag, and then installed myself in a seat in the quaint little red truck ambulance.

I had never been in an ambulance before. I'd always driven myself to hospital, even in emergency situations. It was very cramped. The guys, both young, good-looking and serious, checked my vital signs and asked questions about medicine. I was handed a barf bag. Alas, I needed it but, the vomiting was so violent that I couldn't aim properly. They weren't worried about the pool of yellow stomach acid on the floor. We didn't have far to drive but I couldn't see how we got there or where we were. I was wheel-chaired into emergency and there I was left, in distress, a lot of pain, in the corridor where everyone just ignored me apart from the silliness of asking for my birth name, and went about their cheerful business. Torturous hours went by, maybe only two but it felt much longer.

Eventually I progressed through the questions and pre-admission stuff (including a guy starting to take off my hospital gown without explaining who he was; not a doctor, just an orderly, to being connected to IV, never a pleasant experience and a room was found for me. Nil by mouth for two days, under observation, many blood tests, urine tests, ultrasound of my stomach, x-ray of stomach, scanner of lungs and stomach. I got used to the routine of the nurses and recognized what they were asking me to do even if I didn't understand all the words.

I became distressed when I saw a list of prices on the wall of my room, pointing this out to the registrar but he said not to worry, they weren't the USA. I tried not to worry. There was nothing for me to do each day or night except stare at the walls and ceiling. I was so grateful to have my own little room; I could shut out the sounds of a foreign language all around me, and the noise and light at night.

I was not encouraged to shower despite my request. Having a fever meant I was perspiring so badly I needed one but instead I was handed paper towels and told to use the tap and the liquid soap in the toilet. That was tricky with one arm out of action. It got trickier as the days went by, and each arm developed venous problems due to the IV. Several unsuccessful attempts to open collapsed veins just added to my misery, but I was told there was no choice. I must stay on IV and as soon as one arm became unusable they would switch back to the other one.

The diagnosis from the scan revealed I had a serious lung infection and fever. My doctor had never picked up on it, declaring my lungs fine both visits and, instead had prescribed oral steroids, a complete no-no. His medications created havoc in my stomach and left the door open for the infection to rage. A doctor at the hospital said the regime I had been put on by my doctor should never have happened. My general practitioner had not listened to my concerns, he was cursory in his examination. Friends of mine in NZ tried to ring him and left a message but this was ignored, perhaps because of the language barrier. I'd like to know what was said when the doctors from the hospital rang him. I decided to find another doctor in future; someone less 'nice' but more competent.

As is normal, there was a range of 'service ethic' across the staff. Some chose to ignore my concerns or requests until too late (problems with side effects of one of the antibiotics. I gave up and suffered). Almost no one spoke any English despite medical degrees. I felt so isolated and lost. One bright spot occurred when a different orderly noticed I wasn't eating the roast chicken, or pork, or fish, or plain yoghurt. He went in search of something to tempt me and came back with some *fromage frais* for kids in berry flavors. I was so grateful for his observation and thoughtfulness. Later he asked me if I would like a coffee. Yes, but could I have a cup of tea? Milk and sugar? He'd get right on to it. It's not usual for cups of tea to have milk supplied in France. That cup of tea, when it arrived with a cookie, was so wonderful. I thanked him profusely and he rushed off to get me another one.

"Superb," I said, "You're the best."

The next day I lost my little room and was moved up to level three cardiopulmonary service.

I shared a room with an elderly French lady who was almost impossible to understand, due to her mumbling, and her breathing problems. I introduced myself and for the next day helped subtly where I could. She was a bit rebellious and didn't want to co-operate and use the oxygen, even though she clearly needed it. She would put it down as soon as the nurses left the room, so I told staff she was having 'some problems'. They handled her by allowing no rebellion and no negotiation, by speaking so she couldn't get a word in edgeways, in an unnaturally cheerful way, punctuated frequently by loud *voila*s.

By now I had been incommunicado for many days and was becoming anxious that folks back in NZ might be wondering what had happened to me? There was no way for me to contact them. I gave staff Laura's name and email address, as I had no close friends in France. I couldn't phone from my mobile as it was prepay, and I didn't have enough credits for international. I didn't have my phone charger either. My colleagues kept a phone contact with me each day but that was the extent of their help.

I couldn't sleep so a senior nurse allowed me to use her computer to send Laura a message, and for me to leave a message on my blog. There was a firewall preventing access to Facebook, alas. That would have been better. Leaving a public message helped my anxiety somewhat. It was a small gesture, but a kind and important one by the nurse, so I could let folks know I had a problem but that it was under control.

On my last afternoon in the hospital The Professor stopped by. I'd had no visitors during my entire four-day stay, so it was good to see a known face, and to discuss work while the little old lady read her book.

Getting out of the hospital later that day wasn't easy. The doctor informed me they couldn't help me further but that I would be given Augmentin to continue my recovery at home. Woo-hoo, but no paperwork arrived. I was dressed and ready to go. Several times I asked staff what was happening, but each time they would just disappear. I had no idea what paperwork would be required (very little in fact). Eventually I was on my way out but had to take a number and wait to check out at a cashier's booth.

Oh God, I was presented with a bill for 3,500 euros.

"It's not free you know", I was told. "Can't pay for every Tom, Dick and Harry who gets sick".

In NZ, if you are working, and especially if it's an emergency, you don't get charged anything in a public hospital. This sum was completely beyond my salary to pay. I was asked about my social security number.

"I'm waiting for my card, still," I replied.

This fell on deaf ears. Without that, I must pay the full amount.

"I don't have any money to pay this," I said.

Suddenly pleasant woman stood up and left, and unpleasant woman sat down and glared at me. She explained how much I would pay if I had social security; much less, but still many months of penny-pinching to pay for it. I wasn't well, having just been discharged, and to be hit with this was horrendous. Every month something happened to threaten my financial viability to live. Tears of despair held no 'water' with my interrogator. I was told to speak to social security to establish my situation and come back and pay the bill.

Feeling hopeless and helpless I asked in what direction the center of Caféolait was from the hospital, and set out with my bag to walk all the way home in the wintry cold. Not ideal; I had no money for a taxi.

Parc du Chateau, Rambouillet, Ile de France

CHAPTER ELEVEN

New year, new opportunities

The year 2011 certainly didn't start well but I was feeling better. Not 100% yet, I suspected the lung infection was still lurking inside, but the antibiotics helped and maybe my immune system sorted out the rest, eventually.

After visits again to the social security and the hospital I now had a temporary social security number and *attestation* and had until the end of February to pay 711 euros. I was now investigating yet more insurance in case the unthinkable happened (again) but it was expensive. To do or not to do, that was the question. Imagine if I was in hospital more than four days, horrors. I didn't know how to get settled financially in France. Everything seemed to be enormous outgoings and extremely modest incomings

I was still trying to get out there and meet people, searching for companionship, friends, and hopefully expose myself to the love of my life. Well, so far I had met a few guys who weren't interested in me even though they enjoyed meeting me. I wasn't sure what the issues were. Most of the time it wasn't my diet nor my level of French. In fact, I got by with my smattering of French fairly well. I didn't understand a lot of what they said but enough all the same to hold my own. It was a good exercise for my language acquisition and confidence.

I had now met Damien, a pleasant and interesting man who treated me well. He was gentlemanly enough to drive me all the way home to Caféolait after a meeting; a very long way from his home north of Paris. He picked me up from work and took me to Richefort where we had a lovely chateaubriand steak (well-cooked for me) at a restaurant frequented by those of an artistic and political persuasion, celebrities. We enjoyed ourselves scribbling all over the paper tablecloth. These tablecloths are often to be found in restaurants used by writers and artists. It was fun discussing lovely parts of France to visit, interesting vocabulary, and getting to know each other via a large piece of paper.

We then drove to Paris, along the Champs Élysées, past the Tour Eiffel, around the back of the Arc de Triomphe, past the giant Christmas ferris wheel called La Grande Roue, by the Place de la Concorde.

From there we eventually found a park and stopped into the bar at the four-star luxury hotel Lotti for a hot drink and tiny sweet munchies. The Lotti, located near the Tuilleries Gardens in central Paris, was established by Monieur Lotti and the Duke of Westminster in 1910. My meeting with Damien went well, so we decided to meet up again in the future.

The Professor informed me I must move out of my studio for a bit because he was having some insurance hassles. He'd had a mini disaster at his house a few weeks earlier, so the insurance company was checking he wasn't hiding anything at my place. They were suspicious of his claim. He said everything of mine of any value had to go. I found that distressing. I'd been trying to get settled and was forever waiting for the boss's big stuff to be taken out so I could have the space I paid for. I had to spend my evenings packing up with almost no packing materials. I had no bubble-wrap or paper or cartons and I wasn't given any help from him.

I did my best to wrap my things in my clothes or towels, borrowed a couple of cartons from colleagues and had to arrange to store my smaller items with them. The bigger items, like my TV were put in a van with no protection, by complete strangers who were not professional movers. Then I was expected to hand over my keys so my boss and the insurance company could come in and look at what was left. I wasn't allowed to be present.

I had to go and stay with The Professor's second-in-charge, and his family for a night. I was worried about the risk of damage to my few precious possession while guys uplifted them. I'd then have to get everything back, and connect up my electronics, and unpack my stuff again.

Imagine how I felt; invasion of privacy, moving in and out of the same little studio twice in four months. I really hoped I could have my own life now, and be allowed to settle. I hoped I could have some peace and quiet to get well. If only the boss's life didn't have to affect mine.

Having to move out meant I couldn't meet commitments. I was supposed to teach English in a nearby town to a couple of groups. It was voluntary, but I thought helping out might be good for meeting people. Somehow the opportunity never came along again.

On Thursday Damien picked me up from work and we visited Montmartre in Paris. I was surprised at how small the cathedral was inside. It was nice, but not exceptional, though the view from the hill is probably lovely in daytime and in summer. There was no photography allowed inside, but no matter; it wasn't all that interesting in the church.

The weather was so horribly cold it was unpleasant to be outside, so we didn't linger, but headed for a touristy restaurant on the Place du Tertre where all the artists congregate in summer. It was empty and sad looking in winter, though. My entrecote steak was well done to perfection; the benefit of dealing with tourists, I guess, but the down-side was the profiteroles, touristy and defrosted, not fresh and not worth ordering. Profiteroles, decent ones, were becoming hard to find in French restaurants.

After a pleasant evening at the restaurant Damien kindly drove me all the way home to Caféolait, several hours away. He was gentlemanly and generous, and I managed to keep up a conversation with him for several hours. We had a fair bit in common.

It never ceases to amaze me just what can happen in a day. In just a few hours, life can change markedly and off I go, ending up having to move in a direction I didn't want. Sunday dawned reasonably well; cold, overcast, but with a suggestion that blue sky might appear. Mid-morning Damien and I travelled all the way to Rambouillet. We went for a walk and ended up walking to the Bergerie Nationale, Louis XVI's experimental royal farm. The Merinos weren't making their presence known, but I imagined they were saving their strength for the open day for families, later in the day.

After a long and cold walk we visited the magnificent chateau there. We also walked to the Queen's Dairy and the Shell Cottage where I managed to sneak off a photo before I was told to stop.

Following that, there was time for a walk through the park, looking at the waterfowl, past the gardens and back home in time for me to cook dinner and offer a DVD. All well and good, we enjoyed our day, but the hour got late and it was time for Damien to head home. Out of the blue he asked when I thought I might fall in love with him? What was my time frame? Heh? Being honest, I said I didn't know at this stage, but I greatly enjoyed my time with him and that he was a nice sort of man. It was only the fourth time we had met. We'd had some lovely meetings, such as the day he cooked me chocolate crepes in his apartment, and I thought things were going well, even if he was a little overly enthusiastic at times, a bit pushy. I had mentioned to him at our first meeting that I had had a few bad experiences and that I was taking things carefully and needed him to go slowly.

Clearly I was too slow. I wasn't ready to take things to another level. He seemed like a reasonable and normal sort of guy but I was prudent this time. I had decided not to rush into an emotional entanglement too soon. Damien decided he wasn't prepared to invest anymore time in me if I couldn't guarantee if and when I'd be in love with him. He left. He also left his camera behind, but when I contacted him he refused to come back for it and told me to throw it in the rubbish bin. How odd.

I checked; it wasn't working but it had a lot of holiday photos of another woman on it from back in August. She looked decidedly miserable, and the two photos of Damien didn't seem happy ones either.

I also discovered he had gone to my blog and copied a photo I had taken of him at Chantilly and had posted it as his profile photo on Meetic, the dating site, already. There was no class in that action; using a personal moment we shared to promote himself to other women. I guessed he couldn't have been grieving very long over me. I thought I had a lovely friend, but he wasn't interested enough in me to spend more time with me. Back to the drawing board.

It had been another quiet weekend, but at least there had been no dramas. Camille met up with me on Saturday morning to sort me out with some medical insurance. After the financially disastrous hospital admission episode I couldn't afford to take any risks. Now I was covered (mostly) for the bits the social security didn't cover. It wasn't 100% coverage, but it would avoid impossibly large bills for the next twelve months. This past week I had to see a doctor yet again due to effects of antibiotics, different antibiotics this time. Hopefully, soon I would have less health complications to deal with. The weather was now mostly above zero; the days were lengthening.

Sundays in general were 'teaching myself to cook French dishes' days. With no one to see and nowhere to go I applied myself to making two dishes; a reprise of Quiche Lorraine and an orange cake. Both turned out entirely edible, but I think I was a bit generous with the syrup at the end. The cake was a bit too moist. Maybe orange icing would have been better.

The quiche didn't go tidal on me this time with a smaller pan, but I could still see room for improvement. I thought I might research a meat dish next, but was mindful of not having a lot of basic equipment. It wasn't easy squeezing oranges without an orange squeezer, just my hands and a fork; slow and messy, and inefficient. I'd invited Claire and Camille over for dinner to say thanks for helping me, so I needed to have sussed out the menu well before then.

There was nothing on the 'love' front, though I made plenty of effort on the Internet; time and numbers, I supposed. I was also investigating if there was a possibility of becoming a part-time tour guide in the weekends to cater for English-speaking tourists. I'd had plenty of recent experience doing tours as well as other sorts of tours twenty years ago. I'd also started reviewing some of my dance choreographies; no serious practice, but running things over in my mind. If only I knew I could stay longer, a lot longer, I could plan things. Right now the best I could come up with was to save up for an orange-squeezer.

Another Saint Valentine's Day had passed without a lover to share it with, but I decided to do something with the night anyway. I went to Paris to meet up with Rachid, who was a young couchsurfing ambassador. He was also a Paris tour guide and knew a lot of people socially. He invited me to meet him at a British pub called The Lions, it's a sports bar where couchsurfers meet up, in the second arrondissement. It became jam-packed while we discussed tour guiding, love, and romance, philosophy, politics and following one's dreams. He totally monopolized me, so I never got to meet anyone else. Later we went for a walk through the Parisian streets, past the Louvre, along the Seine and across the Pont des Arts, the lovers' bridge.

There were lovers on the bridge; some were clasping each other in various poses, some were sitting on the ground having a picnic with their duvets for shelter; well, it was cold but clear, and then there were the padlocks, hundreds of them. It is the tradition for lovers to attach a padlock with their names on it to the bridge to symbolize their life-long attachment to each other. All shapes and sizes and even colors were represented, what a surprising sight.

Ah, Paris was beautiful, as always; splendidly lit, tranquil, but with a relaxed purpose. Rachid and I parted company at the metro, by the fountain. Tour guiding didn't seem to be a goer for me right now. Apparently I needed to be self-employed and find my own clients. This would have required research, marketing, time and some other income while I was setting things up. Plus, I'd have need a specialty. My visa also precluded me setting up my own business. Darn.

I was looking for ways I could possibly stay in France, feeling a bit jittery with only a few months left. The possibility of being evicted from the place that mattered most was more than depressing, it was scary. I had nowhere else to go, nowhere else I'd choose to go. Optimism had brought me here; maybe it could find a way for me to stay.

There were no trains running to my home at that hour so I had to wait until 12.30am for a train to Caféolait, which took two hours to get there. Fancy me being out so late by myself on Saint Valentine's Day, but I reminded myself that I didn't have to rush home to kids, husbands, animals, or any other commitments. It was okay for me to do other things with my time, but difficult to break the mindset and habits of a lifetime. I needed practice in living freely and spontaneously.

As an extremely light drinker I wouldn't normally be hanging around in pubs; certainly not two within three days. It was where people congregated so that was sometimes where I needed to be. For me, it was a lengthy and expensive exercise visiting Paris but this one week I'd done it three times, to meet people and maybe establish friendships and contacts.

Saturday dawned somewhat wet. That was disappointing as I had scheduled to go to Paris again, this time to meet Jean-Pierre. Oh well, I strapped on my camera bag, grabbed my brolly and headed off to the train station. This time I was visiting the eleventh arrondissement, Place de la Bastille, a cafe called Indiana. By the time I arrived, the rain was heavy and my brolly was barely coping. It was clear I would not be doing much sight-seeing. Even the rain had made a table reservation; it was coming through the roof and filling any concave surface it could find.

I located Jean-Pierre and we sat down to a hot drink and introductions. He'd lived many years in Manhattan in the US, so spoke English quite well. He'd had an interesting life. Like me, he'd been a teacher and had a daughter as an only child. His daughter was four years older than my Laura. Jean-Pierre was forthcoming and happy to speak at length about his experiences but he seemed so much more 'out of form' than in his Internet photo.

After a while the cafe became uncomfortable so we set out under my tiny umbrella, treading carefully between the puddles, along some of the oldest streets in Paris. I'd been to the Marais before. I enjoyed this part of Paris. As we passed Place Leon Blum by Boulevard Voltaire the decision was made to abandon the walk and have a hot drink at his apartment nearby. This gave me a chance to blow dry my sodden hair and dissipate some of the chill.

It was always a bit of a culture shock when I visited French apartments. They are so small, and usually lacking in amenities New Zealanders would take for granted. I thought back to the modest existence I'd had in NZ. It now seemed wealthy compared to French apartment existence for the average person and my own studio situation. Unless a person can afford a detached house and garden in France, they just can't have the space and amenities most people can have in NZ. The percentage of income spent on housing is frightening. A state house in Otara, Auckland, is more palatial than living in an urban environment in Europe. Jean-Pierre was fortunate he could look out onto some trees and grass from his windows. Despite a pleasant time with him, I could see there wasn't any chemistry, so we parted amicably.

As I sat in the train going home I had time for reflection. I considered myself and where I wanted to live. I was more and more certain that living in Caféolait must come to an end if I was to have a half-way interesting life here. Paris was where I was comfortable. It's a very large city but I felt safer there than in Auckland. There were a few spots in Paris I wouldn't hang out in but generally I was completely at ease there, even when I got lost, which happened often.

Paris was the only place that seemed to have any 'life' to it, for me. I was single. I didn't have friends and family, I was not retired therefore Caféolait had shown me all it could offer and it was much too quiet, too limited. I wondered if I could find a way to live in Paris, horrendously expensive as it was. I'm a city girl who appreciates the beauty, space and tranquility of the countryside, but I needed the facilities and energy that a large city could offer; opportunities, adventures, chance meetings, entertainment, creating a social network.

Then there was me and who I was. I was content with myself. I liked the motivations, dreams and efforts, daily experiences, and hopes that defined me. I had so much to offer, there was a 'potential' aching to get out with the right opportunity. Walking the quiet streets of Caféolait at night, I felt open, enlarged. I couldn't squeeze myself back into the box I used to live in in New Zealand. There was no going back; I didn't fit the space I used to occupy.

There were many moments when I was afraid of my choice to sacrifice all for the hope of realizing my dream; such a dreadful risk. If I couldn't stay in France, it would be an emotional and financial disaster. I couldn't even afford to go home and live in my old house. So instead of feeling like a victim of circumstance, I was asking for something extraordinary to happen. I was ready, I'd work for it, my heart was open, and my soul needed to grow. I was ready for that extraordinary person I needed to meet and love, who'd be worthy of everything I could give.

It was February 22nd 2011. After getting out of bed and putting my hot chocolate on to heat, I switched on my TV to listen to French news while I got myself ready for work. The day before there had been a short story about pilot whales stranding off Stewart Island. Any sort of coverage of New Zealand was rare in France. It usually involved rugby when it happened. I was rather taken aback to hear another story on NZ. This one sent me scrambling to my laptop awash with horror and anxiety. An even more devastating earthquake had hit Christchurch less than six months from the first, and this time devastation was on a horrendous scale. People were crushed under buildings and inside buses, iconic buildings that had survived the earlier earthquake of September 2010 succumbed.

Christchurch would never be the same. So much history had been lost. To me and many others, Christchurch, New Zealand's second-largest city, was the most beautiful. It had preserved much of its colonial British past. It was well designed and justifiably called the Garden City. I was shocked and numb. I was devastated and so sad for what had been lost. Yes, people had lost their lives too, and that was dreadful; it would be unbearable for their friends and families. I was hoping none of the people I knew there were dead or injured.

I tried to discover if my mother was alright but I couldn't contact anyone. In desperation I posted her name and phone number on Facebook in case someone out there could get through, but the phone lines were either down or not working through lack of electricity. My mother was old and lived alone, but my brother was in Christchurch, and my mother was part of a church group so I was hoping it was just a communication problem, not having any news.

I thought of my oldest friend Lorraine. We'd met at high school when I was fifteen. We'd played violin in the school orchestra, her a year ahead of me. We'd hung out at the cinema, sewed ballgowns together, attended music camp together. Social media is a wonderful tool during emergencies. It connects people who might not normally connect and it facilitates community spirit. Lorraine's daughter Kiri was on Facebook, so I could ask her if her Mum was alright. Lorraine and her husband were fine, with just some broken windows.

I didn't know if my second-oldest friend was well. Chrissie and I had met at Teachers College when I was eighteen. She'd been my bridesmaid for my first marriage back in 1976. Distance and circumstances had separated us since but when we had managed to meet it always felt natural, like old times. I hoped she and her husband had minimal side-effects from the earthquake. Lorraine and Chrissie were in a photo from my wedding, somewhere. Photos were especially precious now.

Looking at the before and after photos of specific buildings had me bawling my eyes out. I knew them. Most of them had some significance for me. I'd been born there and lived in Christchurch for more than thirty-five years, and I associated places with events, people, experiences in my life which I would forget if it weren't for their existence to remind me; the buildings where I'd gone to school, met this person, divorced that one, had a romantic date here, held a wedding there.

I couldn't bear the fact that some special historic buildings so precious to such a new country were likely to disappear and be replaced by something not at all representative of British history. Could they bring some masons in and recreate those beautiful monuments to Christchurch's past? I wondered.

People die, disappear, leave, but special buildings are supposed to remain as markers, memory-joggers, part of our collective identity, aren't they? And if they are gone, what do we do about their function? I grieved. To think that young children would never see Christchurch in the special character it had for me and all those who went before was sad. When the past is obliterated how can people understand Christchurch's story?

I was feeling a big loss because I thought Christchurch, as it was, would always be there, with small modifications as time went by. Now all I had were a few photographs. There were so few reminders of my own story for me. I'd forgotten whole chunks of my life and I no longer had many belongings to remind me of past experiences. I wished I'd taken many more photographs of this extraordinarily beautiful city.

Christchurch before the earthquake

It was nerve-wracking waiting for news of my mother and brother somewhere in shattered Christchurch, so I decided to keep myself busy and get out and about. After the usual Saturday domestic regime, I headed off to Paris, camera in hand and with Laura's birthday present to give to Veronique so she could take it to Auckland for me on her forthcoming trip to visit her daughter in Auckland.

Once in Paris I took Line 4 Metro to Odeon, and then started walking toward Musée Cluny. This is the National Museum of the Middle Ages. The complex is opposite the Sorbonne University. The buildings include the northern thermal baths of Lutetia; the only important Gallo-Roman monument surviving in Paris, built in the late first century and used for two hundred years. There were cold and tepid baths as well as hot once upon a time. The other building is the Hotel de Cluny built in the late fifteenth century for the Cluny abbots.

The museum display includes ivories, sculptures, altarpieces, stained glass, choir stalls, archers' shields and manuscripts and, naturally, tapestries. The crowning glory is the magnificent six-piece tapestry called the Lady and the Unicorn. By the time I emerged from the museum it was pouring with rain and I had no brolly. Hugging my camera to protect it from the raindrops I walked, and walked, and walked from the fifth arrondissement to the thirteenth, to Veronique's apartment. I bought some French macarons on the way to give to her. In France there are entire shops devoted to these sweet delights. Why, I had no idea, having never tasted one until now. They have a consistency of cooked meringue filled with a flavored filling; surprisingly tasty little cookie things but I wouldn't describe them as biscuits; well, folks just have to try them.

I shared a meal with Veronique and a Norwegian couple who were couchsurfing with her. They spoke good English and it was a convivial evening, until I had to catch a train to Chartres, getting off at Caféolait. The travel to and from Caféolait certainly was time-consuming. Starting the next day I'd be able to use my expanded Train Pass to go anywhere in the region for a monthly fee of 113 euros. I was ready to explore.

The next day, Sunday, I was taken to lunch at a restaurant in Caféolait by Jean-François . He was a retired dentist of sixty-five years of age, living in a tiny village 30 kilometers from Chartres, in the Centre region. The restaurant seemed to be silver service, though the food was disappointing. However, I was happy to meet someone new and interesting and share a pleasant meal. After Sunday lunch there, we headed off to his place in his little village, where I was really interested in his inherited and collected furniture. There was even an armoire from the time of Louis XIV, and furniture in the style of Napoleon 2.

We talked and danced to music. I had the challenge of holding a conversation completely in French for nine hours. I probably understood 40% at most, but at least I gave it a go. I knew enough to understand when he said he would never, ever marry. He said the happiest day of his life was when he got divorced. That put a bit of a dampener on things for me; not that I needed to get married at this stage in my life, but his attitude was a bit off-putting.

Despite that, Jean-François was good company, very pleasant and educated. The only startling surprise was to be found in the kitchen, lounge, and his office. The kitchen had eyes; sad and tired eyes of taxidermied animals such as a pheasant, and a duck. There were birds in other rooms such as a *poule d'eau*, and in the office, male and female *chevreuils* (small deer) whose heads were mounted on the wall. Gulp! Poor things. JF was a hunter in the forest, as a hobby, though I'd met him at the end of the hunting season. He had a rather energetic hunting dog of a breed I didn't recognize, but Jean-François made certain she didn't bother me.

Jean-François collected me the next weekend and took me

to a big shopping center. He liked shopping. Quite a few French guys do, not necessarily to buy much but to help their women choose clothes. Most kiwi guys hate it. I wondered what causes this cultural difference. He bought me a CD of Etienne Daho I'd wanted for a long time. That was very kind, and we played it later in the day. I had almost nothing in the way of French CDs, partly because I couldn't afford them and partly because I didn't know what I would like. Etienne's been around decades, but I prefer his later stuff. We also managed to fit in a quick drive past an old chateau which is now a private hotel for the well-heeled who arrive for clandestine hookups from Paris via helicopter.

Dinner was some well-cooked (for me) steak and potatoes *dauphinois*, always a good bet, and JF had thoughtfully bought some milk so I could have a cup of tea. We drove to the nearby Chateau de Maintenon, which is famous because Madame de Maintenon was the mistress and secret wife of Louis XIV. There was a chateau in Maintenon in the thirteenth century which went through various owners until it was purchased by the widow Scarron (Françoise d'Aubigné) who received generous financial support from the king. The chateau was extended, and famous landscape gardener le Notre designed the gardens. Françoise became Madame de Maintenon but had no descendants and so the castle went to her niece.

More remodeling occurred in the nineteenth century, and the castle was severely damaged by allied bombing raids in the twentieth. Restoration is fairly recent and took fifteen years. I found it quite beautiful and the artworks were impressive. Naturally Louis XIV (the sun king of Versailles) features prominently. I loved it: the romantic exterior details, the beautiful interiors, the furniture (though some was in poor condition).

The next Sunday, a memorial service was held for the victims of the Christchurch Earthquake, and to support those who survived I travelled to Paris to be part of it. I was here in France, alone, so far away and not part of the Kiwi expats community, yet I had much feeling for Christchurch. After all, I'd been born there. It had been hard being on the other side of the world. There was little news on French media. I'd grab a moment here and there to check the NZ Herald and TV3 news sites for updates, frantically employing Facebook, Twitter and any networks I had, to find my mother.

I still didn't know how she was, where she was, only that the police said she was alive. There was, disappointingly, no news from the Red Cross regarding my mother or brother, despite my giving them detailed descriptions of what I remembered of their bodies, but I had to assume no news was good news. I felt in limbo and invisible.

I have a dysfunctional family, not at all close, though I've always wanted it otherwise from the moment I was born. Alas, some families have love and others don't. Still, they were the only family members (other than Laura) that I had, so I'd tried hard to check on them. It was impossible to phone. Mum didn't seem to be living at her former address, and my brother did not appear in the phone book. Neither of them contacted me. I had sent a care parcel to Mum before the quake but I still didn't know if she had since received it, or if she checked her mail.

So, the only way I could share in the caring and acknowledgement of loss, death and that the city would never be the city I remember, was to go to the service. It was religious, being at Saint Michael's church in Paris. This church is a few rooms in a modern sort of building and typically minimalist. I'm not at all religious but this was all that was on offer, so I just let that bit wash over me and appreciated the intentions. Two observations I had were that I still knew the hymns, virtually by heart, after all these decades of atheism, and secondly, for some reason I found my voice. For the past few decades it has slumbered, unfit, out of tune and condition and not the singing voice I once had, but that day for reasons I don't understand, it soared high over many others with no effort at all, in tune. Where did it come from? Of course, hymns are designed to be singable, but our National Anthem, God Defend New Zealand, has a particularly challenging high note. It was achievable, and I was pleased.

I went to acknowledge my emotional support for all those in Christchurch; struggling with the aftermath which will drag on for years. Those who were homeless, bereaved, who'd lost their incomes, their most precious personal possessions. Where would they find the energy to start over-how would the elderly keep going, would some of those give up because they no longer had the energy and time to build a life all over again? I kept expecting The Professor to arrive, being a fellow New Zealander and coming from Christchurch, like I did, but he didn't.

The service was timed for 12.30pm, same time as the Christchurch one which had taken place the day before. There was a pianist, a priest from the Wellington Cathedral, Rt Hon Simon Upton, NZ Ambassador to France (Rosemary Banks) and the service was presided over by the Rev Philip Mounstephen. Toward the end we each lit a little tea light candle and some of us trotted upstairs for refreshments; a glass of orange juice and a lamington cake, among other traditional kiwi fare.

Next weekend I pottered around the bottom of Jean-François's property. It was wild in this section and fenced to keep JF's dog from hunting everything there. We could see the beginnings of spring; a faint flush of green on some of the trees, the ground covered in nettles, violets, and mini-ranunculi. Along the river and in boggy places were found slightly bigger ranunculi, bulrushes, and iris. On the other side of the stream was a raised railway line. It had been abandoned since World War 2 because the allies bombed the bridges and the line was unprofitable. JF explained there were lots of bomb craters. The locals filled them with rubbish and let them grow over. One of the stone bridges was in original condition.

It was quiet. JF was observant and pointed out any ducks and other birds in the vicinity. A quick flash across a little foot-bridge was caused by two *chevreuils*. They were the first animals I'd seen in a French forest and I barely captured one in a photo.

I had now passed the six-month milestone of my life in France. It had been quite a ride. As I reflected back on my myriad of experiences, there were some I expected, difficulties one could predict, meeting some lovely people, but also rather too many negative experiences; but experiences they were, and it was certainly true that I would never have experienced anything like them if I had stayed in NZ.

My life in NZ had been dismantled. I could never have back what I had there, even if I returned. That had always been a strategy of mine, to make it hard to abandon my dream of France and slink back to NZ when things got tough, and tough they did get. I thought they would be challenging for a long time to come. I was living hand to mouth, with no savings, no security of any kind other than my resilience, which had to expand with each travail that came along. I wanted to grow. I suppose I must have, subtly, but I didn't feel stronger. There were times of despair, the tears and the fear I experienced on train trips or alone in my room.

The language difficulties were the most frustrating and isolating. However, it doesn't take a lot to lift me up, fill me with hope, and discover a flash of joy, a momentary flash of feeling comfortable. I had to create my own brand of faith in this endeavor. What was the basis of this faith? I don't believe in God and I'm not sure about destiny. I didn't know and I didn't need the answer, I could live with ambiguity in this.

I'd had plenty of time to review my single-minded determination to do this and the enormous sacrifices it had cost me, but it didn't matter. It would only matter if I gave in and tried to go back to what I could no longer have. The world had moved on and so had I. My life had changed and so had Laura's. She was an independent woman now, with her own life, and car, and friends. My only regrets were giving up some of my precious possessions, and not being able to share life with Laura. I missed my closest friends and ex-colleagues but of course, they had their own lives. I had been, most of the time, effectively alone in Auckland. I figured I might as well be alone in France where bigger things were possible. NZ had run out of plot lines for me -I needed a new writer.

CHAPTER TWELVE

An unexpected proposition

I wanted to do something romantic for Jean-François. For me, that meant creating an evening with a theme. I wanted to show him that he was special, so I posted an invitation to a special event and set about creating it. This meant I needed to brush up on some of my bellydance choreographies, design a program of dances, check costumes, decide on food, and especially to decorate my studio in a Middle-Eastern Harem theme. This wasn't easy to do with my limited resources, but I had enough to do it.

Jean-François arrived looking fantastic in a suit and tie. He'd made a great effort, and accompanying him was a bottle of champagne, and a bottle of perfume for me to use liberally every day; very unexpected, unnecessary, but thoughtful and kind. We explored my efforts at transforming the studio, then settled into the champagne and nibbles. There were fresh dates and dried figs, hummus and chips and pita, dried mango, sausage nibbles, the ever-scrummy peach-flavored heart lollies. We didn't eat much, we were too busy talking.

It was time for me to perform. I'd turned my bathroom into a changing room and timed the CD I'd burnt, to allow time for costume changes. The program had a variety of styles including veil and fan. I was nervous before Jean-François's arrival, but as soon as I started dancing I felt comfortable. He was a respectful and attentive audience.

The *pièce de résistance* was a choreography I had for teaching women how to dance seductively for their men. I'd conducted several hen parties and workshops in NZ and enjoyed the response from the ladies who seemed to gain so much confidence over the course of two hours of laughing, shrieking, discovering their inner 'goddess', and coming away with something practical to share that was tasteful and fun. I'd never actually performed it for a man before, and never without clothes underneath. Despite teetering around the tiny floorspace of my studio in black high heels, things went well and Jean-François was a good sport, following instructions to the letter. Sans clothes, one could say, it was definitely a successful choreography.

My original plan had been to cook a meal after the show because I can't eat a lot before dancing. As it turned out, we never got around to cooking and eating a meal. We picked at some fruit and discovered that one of my candles was seriously on fire. I'd decorated the candles with old bits of dance jewelry, and had placed them where they wouldn't be knocked over. Perhaps the air movement from my veil made the candle burn unevenly. The result was that the glass decoration caught fire and needed serious dowsing. That large candle-holder hadn't survived the move from NZ very well. Now it was rather black, but I managed to salvage it. There could have been a catastrophe if Jean-François hadn't been observant.

We woke up with the sun streaming through the windows despite the curtains. I looked across my big bed and there was

Jean-François, ready to get on with the day. I started taking some of the decorations down, and showing him some of my personal items, like my old teddy bear with the tummy button that still played Twinkle, twinkle, little star, when I pushed it. How nice it was to share a little part of my life with a nice man.

That night I received a phone call from him. He seemed less at ease than normal and rather insistent.

"Can I ask you a direct question?" he said.

"Oh, course you can," I replied.

"Do you want to come and live with me?" he announced.

"You what?" I spluttered, I was so surprised, as we hadn't known each other long.

"You heard me," he said. "Just think about it. I don't want the answer now. Give it some thought and we'll talk about it on Sunday."

"This is quite a surprise, it's unexpected," I said, "but sure, I'll think about it and we can discuss it on Sunday."

I was shocked and didn't know what to feel. I knew him to be a careful and cautious person, not given to impulse decisions. This was serious, and I needed to calm down and consider the idea carefully because I didn't want to be hasty. I didn't want to spoil a good friendship which had become intimate. I also knew I loved spending time with him, pottering about at his place, sharing debates and meal-making, gardening together. He was a very considerate and gentle lover who always showed me respect. I often felt upset when it was time to head back home on Sundays. What if we could spend every day together; him on his property, me working and then us coming together most evenings and for the weekends? I debated the pros and cons for two days.

On the second day afterwards he popped in unexpectedly to

see me, as he was in the area. I loved it when he did that, and I loved the excitement on his face when he looked at me. After a quick hug and a sentence or two I asked him if he wanted my answer now. I was positive and enthusiastic. He stopped and looked almost angry

"No. I don't want your answer now. We'll discuss it on Sunday, on the weekend."

It seemed a bit abrupt and broke the cozy atmosphere and delight in seeing each other. I resigned myself to being patient, but it wasn't easy. Once I'd made up my mind and gone through the emotional processes I just wanted to get on with things. I was nervous for the rest of the week.

I explained to Victoria what had happened. She thought he must be genuine and keen and mentioned ways I might need to protect myself if things went belly-up. Fair enough; I had all to lose, not him, by changing my life and surroundings again. I was prepared to ease into it gradually so we could become accustomed to the changes, so I'd have time to alert my boss to my change of lodgings. I'd decided that I would live with him but that I'd make the move progressively so if things didn't work out in the first couple of months I would still be able to go back to my studio.

Saturday came and went. Sunday dawned and we sat together in bed eating our breakfasts. That would have been the right time to ask me, but nothing happened. Nothing happened at all. He had asked me a monumental question that would have changed both our lives. It's not the sort of thing a person just forgets to ask. The question was never discussed. This hurt my feelings greatly. He'd thrown a rock in my pond and created such ripples I'd had to look at things deeply, adjust myself emotionally and now it was as if it had never happened. I didn't understand why. For me, it hovered in the air over our relationship. I was sad knowing something like that wasn't important enough to say again, or even discuss.

If he had changed his mind he could have said so, or explained he may have been precipitous but let's see how things pan out, but no, nothing. Maybe he could forget it but I couldn't. There was no closure for me without discussion. I had to readjust my emotions but some things don't fit back in their box and this was one of them. I thought maybe he didn't know how to handle it, so I let it be and just took each day as it came.

Jean-François lent me a very old bike he had in storage. It worked, needed some minor attention, and would be of temporary help until I knew if I could stay longer in France.

There he was, water-blasting it clean, with me testing the brakes and learning that helmets aren't compulsory in France. He was always helpful where practical considerations were concerned. There was still the problem of where to keep it. I had nowhere under cover. Jean-François advised me to chain it to the bars on my windows somehow, and if anyone complained about the visual eyesore to explain that others had space for a bike but I didn't. He bought me a couple of *anti-vols* (locks). That seemed to work well, apart from having my light stolen one night and my lights broken another day. Cycling wasn't so good in the rain and snow because in that case I had to park the wet, dripping, muddy thing next to my bed or in the tiny kitchen area. Still, the bike was useful to get around Caféolait.

I received a lovely message from Laura to celebrate Mother's Day. We were apart but were in each other's thoughts. It was very important for me to have such contact because it was still difficult being completely removed from everything I'd known, and it was hard being strong all the time. I hoped she was feeling positive in her life. I didn't know much about her now, unlike the way things were eight months before. She rarely wrote or contacted me. It seemed there were still plenty of adjustments to make, even now.

I had started working on a European project as part of my job. It was funded by the European Commission and involved many countries throughout Europe, the African continent, Asia and South America. I was always interested in helping the world's citizens become aware of environmental issues and help those prepared to stand up and do something about it.

It was designed to promote mutual learning and collaboration among stakeholders who make use of sustainability sciences. My small role in this project was to assist with providing communications advice and produce materials for training and teaching, as well as my other tasks at the research center.

We were now settled into the new offices. The building itself was centuries old but the interior couldn't have been more modern. We had a multimedia room, an e-learning room, a little kitchen, meeting room and offices for admin, researchers, professors and PhD students to work. I shared a room with two others and we all got on well.

Moving office is never fun but it was finished, and some of the teething problems were being ironed out. I was, however, surprised to receive a message informing me that the water wasn't potable and that's why we had bottled water supplied, at expense. Great. I'd been there six working days and I found that out now. Apparently there was pollution in it which couldn't be eradicated. Luckily I seemed to have survived the tap water, not that there were many of us actually in the building at any given time.

The building had been renovated by the university and partners at a cost of many millions, but most of the time, especially on Wednesdays, there was barely a handful of us working there. Sometimes I was almost alone. Many mothers don't work Wednesdays in France because their children don't have school that day. Most of the offices at the research center were empty much of the time because the professors and PhD students were often elsewhere, and there weren't a lot of classes being held there. It was certainly an oddly luxurious environment to work, in such an isolated spot.

One of the biggest differences in France, for me, was the lack of provision for modesty. If I questioned any French woman about it, she wondered what the heck I was on about and I risked getting the 'prudish Anglo-Saxon' label. After several months in France I decided to have a gynecological checkup. It had been a while and at my age things didn't necessarily work properly and created all sorts of health problems. I located a nice lady doctor in Caféolait. That's where I was introduced to 'The Chair' and French mammograms and ultrasound. That's when I started to learn the new rules.

1. I would never be given a sheet or blanket to cover any of my body
2. If I felt 'exposed' I mustn't mention it
3. I would be expected to walk around topless or naked
4. If having a male doctor look at my female bits there would not be a female nurse in the same room and there would not be a curtain around the bed
5. I might feel completely vulnerable and helpless--too

bad, that was irrelevant

In NZ, when I was having a smear test, I was under a sheet and or blanket, sometimes on my side and it was all very sensitive and modest. In France I was told to take everything off and walk into a room that looked like a torture chamber, where I was confronted by The Chair. Hideous thing! So there I was, without a stitch on, feeling a bit chilled, and sitting in the chair with my legs in those ghastly stirrups, with my knees apart. What a sight! It didn't make the process any more comfortable or efficient than the Kiwi version, but there was no option, and no sympathy. I then had to put my smear sample in the letter box, at my expense, and actually post it to a laboratory. My nose still wrinkles when I contemplate what must be going through the post on any day in France.

If I was having an x-ray or ultrasound of my breasts, I was not given a robe. I had to walk about topless, and it was likely that a guy was going to rub gel all over my boobs and explore them with a sensor, thoroughly. It was me and him in the dark room. Thank goodness I was allowed to clean the gel off by myself. The French are comfortable with bodies. Modesty is not a consideration. I was trying to be cool about this, but it took a little getting used to.

Generally, I found the French health system, though not as comfortable to use as back home in New Zealand, worked well for patients and made specialists' visits affordable. Dental visits, on the other hand, were not well subsidized and could be very expensive for someone with aging teeth, like me. Crowns, veneers or extraction seemed likely in the future. Many people are opting for extraction for financial reasons.

Picturesque Brittany

Binic, Brittany

CHAPTER THIRTEEN

Exploring France

A long weekend of four days is always a wonderful opportunity for the French to get out of the Paris area and into the countryside. Many have family homes in more rural areas which they can escape to, and was the case for Jean-Francois. We were off to Binic, a small seaside town on the northern coast of Brittany. *La Morue en Fete* is a festival celebrating traditional Binic life and seafood. They were expecting anywhere between 20,000 and 40,000 visitors for the weekend.

Brittany seemed greener than Ile de France; at least the trees and fields weren't struggling quite so much with the drought that was tightening its grip on France. Crops traditionally grown here are cauliflowers and artichokes, but there's plenty of cereal too.

Sometimes one can see wildflowers growing optimistically alongside the highways and roads. They are becoming rare as farmers maximize production of crops by using herbicides, so the beautiful meadows painted by Monet and Van Gogh have disappeared. The scatterings that remain comprise meadow plants and small versions of old-fashioned plants that my grandmother used to grow, but which are generally not seen in the wild in NZ; the *coquelicots* (poppies), digitalis, daisies, centranthus, periwinkles and others I recognize, but whose names have long since faded from my childhood memory.

Binic is quaint, picturesque and lively during this weekend. The main thoroughfare is pedestrian-use only and lined with merchants selling local products. The port structure was built by Louis XIV and is tidal. There are harbor doors that open and shut during the tides to allow the boats into the inner harbor. A large expanse of sand provides relaxation for bathers, but the water is cold and the coastline rugged.

Folk dancing at Binic, Brittany

I especially enjoyed the entertainment. The traditional Breton dancing was charming, but I didn't see any of the old traditional tall lace hats Bretonne women used to wear. The musical instruments had a Franco-Celtic sound as one would expect; Celtic bagpipes, flutes, accordions, drums. Brittany is of Celtic heritage, different from the rest of France and the residents are proud of the differences. There's even a Breton black and white flag. Recently there'd been a bit of a resurgence in the old Breton language. Place signs usually have both French and Breton labels.

I met Jean-François's father Marcel, who was ninety years old. He lived several months of the year in the house he built thirty years ago atop a slight ridge near the church bell tower. There was a lovely view of the harbor from Jean-François's bedroom. The house is built on three levels in a typical style. After exploring the center of Binic, we explored the trail from Binic north, which winds around the cliffs. Both of us took frequent photo stops to try to capture some of this wild and beautiful countryside. As is so often the case, we were stymied by sea fog and haze. At other times we contented ourselves by trying to find houses and calvaires representative of Brittany, scattered about in hamlets, villages, or towns like Paimpol.

We set off again to explore the northern section of this part of the coast, in particular Bréhat. The Isle de Bréhat is a large island set among an archipelago on the northern coast of Brittany. It's reached via a ferry which runs between the main island and la Pointe de l'Arcouest, at the extremity of la Côte de Goëlo. The pier, or landing, is made of rose granite, a feature of this landscape and a popular building material for 'bad taste' houses of the end of the nineteenth century.

The boat trip occurred closer to low tide than high tide so we cruised around the outside of the isle rather than going through a picturesque passage through the middle. We were fortunate to see a seal lounging on a group of sharp rocks. The rocks are up thrust in this area. The island has an old Gallo-Roman monastery on it and a sea-powered windmill (neither of which we could visit that day). We had the option of stopping at the island, but I was much too tired to do that and lacked reasonable walking shoes, so we stuck to the boat trip.

Visitors can't escape the plethora of lighthouses of all shapes and sizes on the coast of Brittany and there were heaps in this archipelago. I enjoyed seeing them, feeling the fresh ocean air on my face and looking out toward the English Channel, wondering about all the adventures folks from France and Brittany must have shared via that stretch of water.

Rose granite coast, Brittany

Evenings in Binic were spent listening to whatever free entertainment was provided for the festival. A Celtic group consisting of a violinist, guitarist, drummer, harpist/vocalist provided atmospheric listening, and the harbor was pretty in the evening light. The sun didn't go down properly until after 10pm there, at that time of the year. Saturday night ended with a hiss and a boom as the town set off a fireworks display which we watched from JF's room upstairs; a perfect view.

Regrettably, next day the Breton weather behaved as it often does, with rain, drizzle, and sea fog. It was too wet to visit the forest of Brocéliande. It's a fair drive from Binic using indirect roads, but we decided to at least drive to the area on our way back home. There are many cute little stone villages, but a dearth of toilets, so I learned to pee on the roadside with just the passenger side doors of the car open to give a semblance of privacy.

We arrived at the Chateau de Comper which is now a center dedicated to Arthurian legend. How much of the Arthur story is real and how much is fiction? I read a book in French about that very subject but it didn't really answer the question.

The center was established twenty years ago, behind the ruins of medieval ramparts and a dried moat. At the back of the Chateau is a vast lake. Could it be The Lake containing the Lady of the Lake who loved Arthur, took back the sword Excalibur and ferried the dead Arthur to Avalon? It certainly looked as if it could be.

The ancient oaks had structures of character, the weather was damp, mysterious. The rocks were pink and the stream a noisy tumbling ribbon beside the castle. Yes, you could imagine the Knights of the Round Table having fights and assignations, ladies in elaborate sleeves and headdresses giggling and plotting trysts. I was intrigued by Arthur's genealogy displayed inside the building and a chronology of writings and films through the ages relating to Arthur, Guinevere, Lancelot and Gawain, and Morgan le Fey and her nasty son Mordred.

I hoped one day I could explore the Forest of Brocéliande and its Fountain of Youth, Merlin's Tomb, The Valley of No Return, The Fountain of Barenton and the trees themselves, just thirty kilometers west of Rennes. There are less of them now. In 1990 a terrible fire devastated more than 400 hectares of it. A golden tree (sculptured branches really) was created at the entrance to the Valley of No Return in memory of the ancient forest. Paimpont/Brocéliande reminds me somewhat of the forest of the elves in Tolkien's Middle Earth during the time of the tales in J.R.R Tolkien's The Silmarillion. The geography in that tale is remarkably similar to Brittany

My fifty-sixth birthday dawned cool, but with the possibility of sunshine. Here I was, in France (miracle #1), at Mont Saint Michel (miracle #2) with a lovely French man (miracle #3). What more could a woman want? After driving a short distance down the road (causeway), we parked the car, assembled our cameras, and set off to explore this very historic national monument.

The first thing I noticed was the canon on my right, so old and marking the fortified entrance. This monastery has survived so long despite wars, fires, natural disasters. I felt rather emotional being there. The other thing about this site is that the topography has changed markedly in the past few years, mostly due to human activity. The bay has silted up and vegetation has appeared where it shouldn't. It's increasingly losing its magnificent isolation and becoming united with the mainland instead of being surrounded by sea. This is as a result of the construction of the causeway and parking areas as well as other human land-use.

The bay has the fourth largest tidal range in the world (fourteen meters). The tides carry in silt but would normally also flush it out. Instead, there are now salty paddocks with particular breeds of sheep capable of eating savory grass.

However, a mammoth engineering feat had just been completed which would enable nature to reverse the processes and bring the site eventually close to its original condition. It's an interesting project costing close to 200 million euros, and it's expected that the site will be back to its optimal condition within fifteen years.

Pressing on to Cherbourg, we found a place to eat and kip down. After a couple of glasses of wine I was pretty relaxed. What a great day I'd had; laughs, serious debates, exploring, taking photos, smelling the sea and ancient history in the country I loved. Magic!

We left Cherbourg on Sunday morning, determined to visit some but not all of the Normandy beaches and learn something about this historic area; historic for its contribution to the end of World War II when the allies landed on the beaches and started mopping up the German occupiers. The main beaches are almost seamless and are quite similar, being a vast stretch of sand so we concentrated on two of them, but first, a stop at where it all began, Sainte-Mère-Église (Basse Normandie).

This was one of the first towns liberated on 6 June 1944 as part of Operation Overlord. American parachutists started landing (and being slaughtered) along with special gliders (many of which crashed). There's the famous story of soldier John Steele whose parachute caught on the clock tower and he had to hang wounded while all the action was going on.

The town featured in the movie The Longest Day (1962), portraying itself. The film featured John Wayne, Robert Ryan and Richard Burton and even Sean Connery amongst a star-studded cast.

American Airborne Museum, Sainte-Mère-Église

After photographing the church and a borne that starts Liberty Road, we visited the American Airborne museum. It was impressive and interesting. We watched a short documentary which was moving. I think the most impressive thing about this museum is the personal way it handles a terrible subject. Individuals involved in this event are profiled, their belongings are on display. The soldiers and villagers went through a lot together and formed close bonds. Some soldiers came back to visit the town years later. This place is definitely recommended as a stop-off.

Cruising through the countryside trying to find our way in new territory, we visited two of the main landing sites. I was surprised by the depth of the shell holes and the wildness of the cliffs at Pointe du Hoc. No wonder the soldiers had a tough time knocking out German batteries before the invasion got fully underway.

I loved the metal sculpture at Omaha Beach. It's beautiful

from every direction, whereas the other part of the monument in front of it is a ghastly and ugly thing. We had lunch at Omaha after visiting Pointe du Hoc. After that we felt we'd done all we needed to do concerning these sorts of visits. We didn't have time to visit any war cemeteries. Even if visitors are anti-war, it's worth visiting these beaches and other war sites. They're important and they're surprisingly emotional. Their stories are about real people (not just men, women too); the soldiers and the French villagers.

Omaha Beach, Normandy

My first cat I named Claude, in honor of Claude Monet, the French Impressionist painter. My second to last cat was named Monet, for the same reason. I've always loved the impressionist painters since I was introduced to them; it's just that I can't remember when or the situation. Maybe it was the art class at Teachers College, maybe it was high school, that's more like it;

Renoir, Degas, Monet, the others too, but Monet stood out because he painted his garden and his garden was created as an inspiration for his painting. I'd had cheap prints in my home for years until they all turned blue from the light and I always wanted to see his famed garden.

I did just that. It was a bit of an expedition. The drive to Giverny required a lot of patience in the Easter traffic, and there were the inevitable toll stops requiring payment. Travel sickness was an unwelcome companion too. We stopped off and munched some sandwiches we'd brought, then, somehow managed to find the village of Giverny. It's small, above the Seine west of Paris.

Springtime at Giverny

The lily pond is beautiful, but the trees and humanity have a way of depositing in it, so a boatman was busy skimming. I suspect in Monet's time (the beginning of the twentieth century) there was more admiring and less skimming. At this stage of the season there were no water lilies to admire, but that didn't matter to me. The garden grows right to the edges of the pond and there's color everywhere. The color combinations throughout the complex are amazing. There's little room for weeds to grow, but the business of keeping it all looking tidy and colorful 364 days of the year requires thirty gardeners working at night.

There was the Japanese bridge smothered in tourists having their photos taken on it, the rhododendrons and azaleas, tulips and forget-me-nots, pansies, maples, and peonies. I thoroughly enjoyed my time at this popular tourist spot, but I chose to next visit something less well-known and perhaps more representative of the French countryside, certainly in the Beauce region.

Le Moulin Pelard à Bois de Feugères is on the N10 motorway. It's unusual in that it's a pivot windmill where the whole thing pivots, not just the top section. It's typical of the Beauce region and dates from 1796. Until 1941 it belonged to the Pelard family who had been millers for generations. It was then bequeathed to the local authorities when the family line died out.

It was abandoned for several years before volunteers began renovating in 1976 with the help of gifts and grants. In 1977, before the renovations had been completed, it was destroyed in a violent storm. Fortunately, work resumed immediately and it was completed in September 1990 when the red sails were put in place. The sails are colored red to discourage mold. It's in full working order and is open to the public. Though it has no commercial activity it does mill wheat. The flour is sold in the mill itself. We climbed the stairs which are somewhat unsteady as the whole thing responds to the wind. Standing inside is like being inside a boat with the constant motion. It has an anchor which is used to position it in the best angle to catch the wind.

Le Moulin Pelard à Bois de Feugères

Two of the arms have half sails otherwise the wind would get too strong for it, a bit like the situation for a sailing ship. There's an old-fashioned bell to sound the alarm when the wheat supply is running low, and brakes, too. There remain some of the original timbers from the eighteenth century with some names carved in by those slightly literate in the nineteenth century. The engineering is rather clever for its time, I thought. The wheat box shakes the grains down to the milling stones, one only of which turns, the other remains stationary. The flour comes down into a long vertical box. There's provision for sacks to be lowered to the ground instead of humping them up and down the narrow wooden stairs.

I'm fascinated by Napoleon. Born simply in Corsica, clever with his battle strategies, ends up Emperor, loses an important battle and gets demoted and exiled, escapes and raises an army, gets defeated again and is exiled permanently, his son dies prematurely in exile in Austria. Well, it's all stirring stuff, so I wanted to visit the Chateau de Fontainebleau, a magnificent place set in a magnificent forest; a monument that has survived the ravages of time and history better than Versailles.

The first references to the chateau date back to the twelfth century. Since then, all the great Kings of France have lived there. It's a residence that has been cherished and inhabited for eight centuries.

Napoleon contributed much to Fontainebleau. There's a museum in his honor which has interesting exhibits such as his clothing, army bed, weapons, and a rather horrid contraption for dealing with constipation while on campaign. There was his magnificent throne room. JF and I visited Fontainebleau on a day when they were having an exhibition dedicated to his ill-fated son the King of Rome; amazing to see the young son's clothes, bassinet, and paintings. I also loved the emblems Napoleon chose to decorate his interiors and furniture; bees and eagles and the big N.

During my time in France I've been intrigued to see how the countryside changes week by week. In New Zealand the seasonal changes are more muted, especially in the North Island. With so many evergreen plants and trees, the seasons there are less marked, and with so many farms devoted to sheep and cows, the fields always look the same.

Here in France, in particular Ile de France, the countryside reflects the growing seasons more spectacularly. The crops seem to literally spring up before one's eyes, desperately, it seems, to get all their growing done before the long dark freeze returns.

My first delight was seeing a field of flowering colza for the first time. Colza is rapeseed or Canola. There are kilometers of it throughout France, interspersed with barley and wheat. Colza looks like a brassica flower, yellow, and simple on a multi-floretted stem. After flowering the fields become awfully sad looking as the yellow fades to a greenish blue, then mid-green and finally a dried-out beige before it's harvested. By that stage it's up to my waist and the flowers have turned into long bean-like seed pods on a stem. This crop flowers long before the barley produces its grain heads with its spikey fringes.

There were fields and fields of barley and wheat. They made a welcome patchwork with the colza. Right now they were very pale and scorched looking like the wheat fields, and much of it was being harvested into bales.

From time to time I'd see pretty dots of red along the sides of the roads. These were *coquelicots* (Papaver rhoeas) poppies. They are becoming rare from the use of herbicides on fields to intensify production of food crops. They're no longer welcome because they don't have a market value. Imagine if Monet had been alive today; he'd never have been able to paint his countrysides in all their natural splendor. Sadly, it's his paintings that will outlast these charming and cheerful plants. I would have to wait two years for the opportunity of seeing a large field of them in flower.

Coquelicots

As the poppies are flowering so do the lilacs in French gardens, and beside the roads where properties have been abandoned. Oh, the joy of seeing this beautiful old-fashioned plant still being appreciated. Street sellers sell bunches of it and it smells heavenly, a reminder of my grandmother who always tried to have a jug of lilac branches in front of the fireplace in late spring.

Daisies and gentians flower in wilder parts of the countryside. They may be simple flowers, but on mass they certainly gladden the heart and feed the bees. I couldn't resist getting in among them. There were plenty of garden foxgloves about but I enjoyed seeking out the tiny wild ones that would pop up in fields and along the sides of the roads where the weed killer hadn't destroyed everything. It was a joy to see some biodiversity in the landscape.

Sometimes there were tiny gentians scattered amongst them but I really had to get down on my stomach to discover and appreciate their tiny perfection.

One weekend Jean-François and I drove toward Paris, then out to visit one of the seventeenth century's greatest achievements, the Chateau Vaux le Vicomte, a truly amazing place with a chilling story behind it. It was never a fortified chateau or a royal residence. Instead it was an extravagant undertaking from the gifted and charming Fouquet who aimed too high and fell so low.

Vaux le Vicomte

It's a sad story of a talented, rich man, a patron of the arts who was set up by a spiteful Louis XIV and Fouquet's jealous and malicious colleague Colbert. He was arrested by the musketeer d'Artagnan on trumped-up charges, falsely convicted, and thrown in a distant prison for the rest of his life. It was a high price to pay for wealth, talent and good taste. Louis later used ideas in the architecture of Vaux as inspiration for Versailles, even hiring the same talented architect, painter and gardener whose legacies remain at Vaux.

It was my first 14th July, Fête Nationale in France, and I was going back to Binic in Brittany with Jean-Claude to watch the fireworks over the water at the little port. Incredibly, the long weekend traffic was flowing smoothly with no problems as we made our way there, taking the toll routes which are generally safer roads to use.

The fireworks weren't due to start until 11pm so we spent part of the afternoon and evening taking more photos of the port, visiting a little art gallery and scouting for a vantage spot for the evening's brief entertainment. There was the sea-wall, lighthouse, and entrance to the little Port, which had been ordered by Colbert, the dastardly minister who plotted with Louis XIV to get rid of the shining Fouquet. Colbert ordered a number of major public works and coastal fortifications in his time because France was incessantly at war in that era and Binic profited from that.

It wasn't evident in the countryside that it was France's National Day; it seemed to be business as usual with nothing special happening. It would be a different story if I had been in Paris, of course. The military services had been practicing during the week to get the parade just right down the Champs Elysée. After a late dinner, JF and I found a spot to stand overlooking the entrance to the port and waited until 11pm.

It seemed as if the whole of Binic and more besides was there. The town switched off the street lights and the crowd gave an "Ahhhhhhh!" Canned music began but I wondered why ColdPlay was chosen to accompany the *feux d'artifice* as they whizzed, popped, banged and boomed. As fireworks shows go, it wasn't impressive or creative or particularly interesting and not choreographed to the music at all, but I imagined it's expensive for a town to have to provide this. The crowd clapped appreciatively at the end. I hoped the silly youths on the beach didn't suffer any lasting damage as they shot fireworks at each other. Stupidity knows no geographical bounds.

The people wound their way around the path up the cliffs, heading home. I stopped several times to look out over the Bay of Saint Brieuc at the other little towns twinkling away in the dark distance. Two of them clearly had fireworks displays going long after ours was finished. The atmosphere around France must have been rather thick for a short time that night with thousands of public events revolving around burning gunpowder. How odd that politics in England (Guy Fawkes) and its former colonies, and politics in France, have created such scenes of air pollution now.

Fireworks displays are less numerous in NZ than they once were. When I was a child everyone celebrated Guy Fawkes' attempts to blow up the British Parliament, by buying fireworks and letting them off at home as a family event. There weren't public displays. Times changed. People became more irresponsible, and there were deaths, too many fires, maimings of idiots and cruelty to animals occurring, so opportunities to celebrate at home became legally limited. Now, many families just don't bother because it's like lighting a match to one's wallet. It's expensive to buy fireworks and they seem less magical now than they did in the 1960s when I was a child.

These days there are limited public displays which people must often pay to see, and queue for forever. Many people probably spend their fireworks night in front of their computer.

Once Laura was too old to warrant spending hard-earned money in setting things on fire and risking danger, I did the computer thing too, but here I was, in France, with fine, mild weather having a change and enjoying it. It was nice to share it with someone; that can be said for any public event. After our late night we had to be up fairly promptly to head northwest for a boat trip around the Seven Islands. I started downing the anti-seasick pills.

Jean-François had organized for us to explore more of the Breton coast, in particular the Rose Granite coast from Trestraou to Ploumanc'h, which is only ten kilometers long but includes a "custom officer's path" along the cliffs, offering great views. JF had included a boat trip to the Seven Isles (five islands plus two big rocks) to see the gannet colony.

First we stopped off at the quaint coastal village of Ploumanac'h. There are two sea mills from the fourteenth century in the harbor, and Gustave Eiffel built a granite house there around the same time he was building the Eiffel Tower. Another item of note is the oratory of Saint Guirec, on the beach. The story goes that young women who were hoping to marry would come there with a hair pin and insert it into the nose of the statue of the saint. If it stayed in, they'd marry; if it didn't, well, they were out of luck. It's thought the current statue was preceded by one in wood which was quickly worn out by ardent women with pins. The current statue is much the worse for wear, too. Clearly there must be a lot of hopeful women out there.

Oratory of Saint-Guirec, Brittany

After steak and chips and lashings of anti-seasickness pills, I felt fortified enough to take the boat out into the English Channel. The sea was fairly calm and the boat comfortable, but I kept the medication going as travel sickness is a 'given' with me. We stopped off at the gannet colony where between 14,000 and 20,000 couples nest (there's a big discrepancy between what one piece of publicity says and another regarding the population).

We could smell them before we could see them. There they were, white blobs stuck to the almost vertical rocks or wheeling in the air. There, too, were black shags. I would have liked to see some of the rather rare puffins, but this day there was no sign of them, only a lone gannet on the lowest rocks. He was there because he was sick, and it was unlikely that he'd survive much longer, away from the colony and his mate.

After admiring the colony and watching the younger birds skimming in curiosity over our boat, we went farther to see some seals. When the person doing the commentary talks about phoques (seals) he's not using a rude word, but it certainly sounds like it when the French say it. It was hard for me to keep a straight face. The boat disgorged its passengers onto the only island where visitors are permitted as these islands are a nature reserve. I always like visiting Brittany. There's some magic in the place, and the forests and sea remind me of New Zealand.

Jean-François and I made our way to the Arc de Triomphe at the Place de l'Etoile where so many main boulevards in Paris meet. There are no lanes circling it; it's basically a free-for-all and seems rather dangerous. Pedestrians access the Arc and the other side via a pedestrian subway, very handy.

This day the old military guys were having a remembrance. A band with sousaphones was there, young army guys, and lots of tourists. There was the eternal flame marking the tomb of the Unknown Soldier. The road circling the Arc was then stopped for traffic for a bit, then everything took off again, including an ancient Parisian bus in green livery.

Walking back up the other side of the Champs Élysées, we

came across buskers, famous restaurants and shops, and a guy due to get married who had a novel way of raising funds for his wedding. He was asking for one euro donations. In return, one was given a condom (capote). Amused, Jean-François donated a euro, received his condom in return, and proceeded to wander up the Champs Élysées, waving it about in his hand, as he tried to explain the sights to me. I thought that was rather interesting. No one batted an eyelid. As we were nearing Jean-François's home we chanced upon a 'herd' of balloons coming in to land. It was a beautiful sight, over the fields of barley and wheat as the daylight faded. One was large and low and the folks aboard all wanted to wave to me. I returned the courtesy and had fun capturing the sight on my camera. I'd like to fly in a Mongolfier one day -serene, peaceful, beautiful and romantic.

One of the hardest things to deal with in France was my lack of creative outlets, and inability to pursue my previous leisure activities. I was someone who had always been active, in and outside of work, with multiple interests.

In my youth I was busy with ballet, music, singing lessons with contralto Anthea Moller, violin lessons (I could have done without the sexual harassment though), theatre performances, modeling, and acting in musicals, and as a member of the Elmwood Players. Later, I took up piano lessons, guitar lessons from Phil Garland (a well-known folk singer at the time), had a pedigree breeding stud for cavies and competed with them in shows too, knitting, jazz ballet, crochet and embroidery, Beginner Japanese, model-making of spaceships (non-fiction and fiction) as well as other forms of transport.

Much later in life I was a keen member of Toastmasters International (ranked second in NZ for impromptu speaking 2007), was a film extra and kept fit by studying salsa and French jive (Le Bop), as well as belly-dancing. The latter led to costume design and performing Danse du Ventre/Raks Sharqi as a solo artist. All through my life I had been an avid reader, cinema-goer, pet guardian and, most of all, gardener.

Sadly, the move to France had put paid to almost everything I'd enjoyed in my personal life. If it wasn't for a lack of money (almost always), it was a lack of opportunities. My collection of books was so small now, and I tended to have to read stuff in French as a last resort, so I couldn't enjoy reading as I once did. My books had been sold or given away, and I couldn't afford many new ones via Amazon. I tried to register for violin lessons (after nearly 40 years of not playing) but the classes were all full.

There were no belly-dance teachers within forty-seven kilometers, and I had no car, so lessons of any kind went in the too hard basket. I did send some enquiries out further afield, and a few weeks later a bellydance teacher unknown to me asked me if I'd like to take over her classes while she was heavily pregnant. In return for that, she would give me private lessons and a solo spot in her next concert. I accepted; that's a cool challenge, I thought. So I practiced small combinations, planned the music and the lesson formats. It meant walking through Caféolait to the fitness center, squeezing past the treadmills and sweaty men, and setting up the resident stereo.

The ladies were mostly beginners with a couple of them a little more coordinated. I thought they enjoyed their lessons; in fact I had them doing things they'd never tried before, such as veil dances, but as soon as she had her baby the dance teacher contacted me and said she was coming straight back after only a few weeks. I reminded her about my lessons. She took a while getting back to me and suggested two dates with short notice. I wrote back and accepted the dates, but she never replied to my text or email messages. I'd been used.

Living with an uncertain future in a studio apartment meant I had no garden. This was a difficult thing to deal with. I had my window boxes and my herb garden, which was lovely, but I yearned for a garden to design, work in, to leave the planet in a more beautiful state than when I found it.

I missed having pets, too. For most of my life there had always been animals; frogs, mice, birds but especially black and white cats. I'd worried about what to do about my last cat as I was contemplating leaving New Zealand, but he developed cat AIDS and died unpleasantly despite Laura and I trying to rescue him from a sad, slow and lonely death. At one stage of my life I'd had a pedigree cavy stud. My lovely little cavies had been a delight for me and won me a few ribbons in shows, but a change in job and accommodation in the past had meant I could no longer keep them.

My lack of outlets needed to find a solution. Sitting around in a one-room apartment was not enough for my happiness, intellect and mental health. Action was required; it wasn't any good brooding and complaining too long.

I helped out in Jean-François's garden. It was a different experience from what I'd had before in my life. He found it unacceptable for a woman to have to do heavy digging or anything physically demanding. He dug out all the old soil, mixed it with compost he'd made, fertilized and raked, so that all I had to do was plant the plants, move some others and top up with any compost required. I enjoyed helping him choose the plants even though climate restrictions (the big freeze) were more limiting in Europe. We discussed, compromised, agreed.

I didn't find myself doing all the hard work while my partner did his own thing. He would ask my opinion on plants, but he never did anything I suggested that would have physically changed his flower beds or radically changed his ideas on what he put in them. I suggested several times to have a vegetable garden. He knew I wanted and needed one, but he was always adamant, no. His reasoning was it would be too much work, and the foxes might piss on it and give him rabies. I gave up.

Marcel Proust Museum, Illiers-Combray

CHAPTER FOURTEEN

The cradle of my family

It can take between five and six hours of fast driving to get between Jean-François's home and Rochefort in the Charente-Maritime area, Atlantic Coast of France. Prepared for change-able weather predicted, I settled in to the journey, watching the changing countryside.

In Ile de France and also the Centre regions there are a lot of cereal crops being grown, but as we got farther south this gave way somewhat to cattle, maize and sunflowers. Ah those *tournesols* (sunflowers). They make incredible impressions on the landscape, and it was so unfortunate that we were arriving about three weeks too early to see them in full bloom. They're grown for their oil. It's used in the commercial production of crisps and oil for cooking.

The countryside also included, along the way, great files of *eoliens* (wind turbines) marching along waving their arms like white skeletons or benign Martian machine; and then there were the cooling towers of Chinon nuclear power station. As we headed south, the architecture changed, too. Here the houses have orange-tiled roofs and lighter colored cladding. It's less massive and more Mediterranean.

I was here in the Poitou-Charente region to meet members of my French family whom I'd never met, distant cousins. It had taken years to finally be able to arrange a meetup. We were headed to Rochefort for the night, but stopped off at Brouage, which is further south. It's a medieval town with ramparts, which was once bounded by the sea but, like so many towns like this, the coastline has changed over the centuries and silt and vegetation have replaced water.

The town was key for defense in the region with all the struggles against the British and French nobles with powerful aspirations. Visitors can still see the ancient walls as well as the old graffiti carved by residents and tourists. This is the village where Samuel Champlain, the founder of Quebec in 1608, was born. The connection with the village and Quebec is celebrated in the stained-glass windows of the town church.

I was particularly interested in discovering examples of buildings my ancestors would have known around 1800-1840, such as the old Marine hospital and other key buildings. This city has changed a lot over the centuries. It's no longer representative of its important past; La Rochelle has surpassed it.

La Corderie Royale at Rochefort has a fascinating history. Located alongside the Charente River it was a navy arsenal created by Louis XIV to supply and build his warships to protect his empire, to conquer the new worlds, and bring back exotic goodies. It manufactured rope for rigging ships, both military and merchant. The process was laborious and required precision and a very long building.

Other buildings on site included a forge, powder store, foundry, and dry-docks for boat repairs. Five hundred ships and boats were constructed here until it closed in 1927. Rope-making for the navy ground to a halt around 1867 as new technologies rendered it obsolete.

The Corderie was mostly destroyed by a deliberate fire set by the departing Germans in 1944; a tragedy. Admiral Dupont worked to have funds established to rebuild it. Work commenced in 1988 and since 1986 it has housed a museum and maritime training center.

Corderie Royale

We followed up this visit by exploring the replica of the frigate Hermione, the ship on which the Marquis de La Fayette embarked in 1780, to bring help and support to the American insurgents during the War of Independence in the American colony. He seems to have fancied himself as a French version of George Washington, hero for freedom. He harried the British and became a lifelong friend of Washington. La Fayette commanded the troops at the Battle of Yorktown and spent his life (76 years) in and out of political roles, years spent in an Austrian prison, saw Louis XVI succumb to the guillotine,

Napoleon come and go and a new style of French government put in place.

His boat, the original of which was built at the arsenal, was being lovingly recreated with only essential nods to modern technology. We all had to wear hard hats because the ceilings were so low. All through the tour I heard 'bonk .... bonk ... bonk' as visitors hit their heads unexpectedly.

Jean-François and I spent the evening with Alain and Annick at their home not far from Rochefort. I was so tired and it was difficult to concentrate on what the native French speakers were saying at times, so opportunities for me to participate were very limited. Dinner didn't start until 10pm but was beautifully presented. Alain is a distant French cousin. It was a really treasured moment to meet him. He was regularly in contact with relations I'd never met in NZ and France, and Annick seemed to have an excellent knowledge of her husband's genealogy too; lovely, friendly and welcoming people. Tomorrow we'd be spending a special day with them and with another of my French cousins.

The story of my family and the establishment of New Zealand's only French settlement began in 1840 on the banks of the Charente River, Rochefort, France. Joseph and Madeleine Libeau and their children would have stood on the deck of the Comte de Paris watching the preparations for casting off. They would have seen the old naval buildings and the Corderie Royale and hoped the voyage of at least three months wouldn't be a nightmare, but it didn't start well.

Before they reached the open sea of the Atlantic, the pilot stupidly beached the boat on purpose, to get home, thinking the next high tide would refloat the boat, but it didn't. The passengers and crew had to take everything off. A woman drowned herself in despair. Two weeks later they finally left France, arriving in Akaroa in August 1840 only to discover that the South Island of New Zealand was now British. Along the way their family had increased by another child.

Joseph had two wives: his French one (who died as a result of a later childbirth), then an English one who ended up in a mental institution. Eighteen children in total were born and seventeen survived. Oddly enough, I'm descended from both wives; Julie from his first wife, was my maternal grandmother's grandmother, and Josephine, from his second wife, was my maternal grandfather's grandmother.

Joseph and his first wife were both gardeners. This passion for growing things runs strong through my lineage and is my most passionate interest. The two pioneers did well in creating a successful new life for themselves at the end of the earth, taking on market gardening, brick-making, wine-making, and dairying.

I'd known all my life I had French ancestry, but that heritage was never very evident in my childhood. Still, there was a tug on my heart, even a subtle one, which saw me study French for five years at High School, one year at Canterbury University, three years at Teacher's College and then initiate a program of including French language into my teaching class at Tawhai School in Wellington. The parents were so pleased with the results that the inspectorate allowed my French lessons to continue the following year, then my interest in France languished for many years while I changed careers and partners. It took off again as the twentieth century drew to a close and was at fever pitch from 2008 onward.

My tiny immediate family has never provided emotional support for me, so my heart has crossed the oceans of the world in search of other family who might be interested in me. For almost five years I'd been sending out emails to the Libeau Society and French family members in France, to little avail. In the past month I received encouraging definitive responses from Alain. He organized that I meet up with our mutual cousin Gilles, and also Michel, yet another cousin living in the Charente area.

June 18 is the day I spent exploring the birthplace of Joseph Libeau, and the neighboring countryside. It was also the day I spent with my two cousins Alain and Gilles, along with Peter Tremewan, the New Zealand author of a well-published authoritative book on the French at Akaroa. What an amazing serendipity that we would all end up in the area on the same weekend.

In a two-car convoy we travelled north toward Nantes; Jean-François and I with Alain and Annick, Gilles and his wife Micheline with Peter Tremewan and his wife Christine. The countryside changed to viticulture (Muscadet) as we approached the tiny village of L'Elaudiere - birthplace of Joseph Libeau. We had no idea which ramshackle building he lived in as a child, maybe his home was now just a pile of rubble, or maybe it was one of those still standing.

We looked through the gate at the only mansion and large garden in the village. Perhaps he tended the garden there? The main thing I noted was the excitement we three cousins felt to be together ... there. My cousins are descended from one of Joseph's daughters who returned with another French couple to France. She stayed in France, and it's through her that I am related to these cousins. The French members are small in number, but the Kiwi members of the family number in the thousands. I feel very proud of my very direct lineage to one of the founding families of Akaroa, a settlement established ten years before the English established Christchurch.

On Sunday we departed La Rochelle with its three towers and colorful port. We collected the car and drove toward Ile de Madame to meet up with Alain, Gilles, and our other cousin, Michel. This area at the mouth of the Charente gave us a view of the channel leading to open water; the channel the Comte de Paris took and was stranded on. We tried to identify the exact location, but it wasn't certain.

There's a low causeway, accessible at low tide, to the Ile which is topped by a fort. We inched our cars along the rocky road, then drove along the coastline looking at the intriguing fishing cabins installed at the tide-line. Some are large enough to sleep in if need be.

There's an aquafarm and attached restaurant on the Ile. We made for that. Gilles had brought flags of NZ and France for fun. Working my way through the lunch courses and wines (plenty of that over this trip) and listening to all the French language swirling around me (much of which I couldn't understand) I felt like a tiny part of an important story.

As we were checking out, a French guy overhead that at least one of us was a Kiwi and started up a conversation.

"Hey, New Zealander, you are far. I like the All Blacks. Good team, good player Richie McCaw. What's the thing they do before the start of the match?"

"That's the haka," I replied, hoping I wouldn't have to demonstrate this Maori war dance in public, for a third time in France.

He and his friend were knowledgeable about some of the All Black Greats, so thank goodness I could name-drop a few players from the past, even though I don't like the sport. It was a very warm exchange between strangers. It's a shame the French know NZ rugby players, but not about their country's original foray into the South Pacific. The French government gave up on NZ, which was their first choice for a base in the South Pacific, and moved on to the Marquesas and Tahiti.

Jean-François and I had to leave, which was a bit sad. Everyone except me was retired and their time was free to do what they choose, but I still had to work, and the trip back to Paris was a long one. There were lots of hugs and *bises*, then an uneventful return journey.

Fishing cabin, Ile de Madame

CHAPTER FIFTEEN

Reunion

Almost a year after leaving Laura in Auckland, we met again. I'd refinanced my home mortgage in Auckland so I could buy plane tickets to get her to France. It was important to show her my new life and spend precious time with her. It was exciting planning what we might do, but I was fighting mounting anxiety and panic attacks from another direction.

The constant harassment from The Professor was taking its toll. The put downs, sarcasm, veiled threats, the neglect, lack of direction, aggressive behavior from him in public and in private, meant I was scared all the time. He knew my existence in France was dependent on his providing me work. My complete vulnerability played into his hands. I wasn't the only one to suffer maltreatment and his temper tantrums. All the staff had witnessed and suffered varying amounts but my situation was the most precarious. I was helpless to do anything about it. His wife was a powerful person at the university for most of that time, so he was invulnerable, politically protected. He was also my landlord, and that wasn't a cheerful experience.

One day he'd appeared on my doorstep, very early before work, demanding money. He said he hadn't organized himself to get money for an overseas trip he had to make later that day so he wanted me to provide it. The rent wasn't due for two weeks, I hadn't been paid recently, and I tried to explain that, but he insisted that I go find an automatic teller machine and withdraw as much money as possible. I felt I had no choice. It was always like that.

The daily stress built to such a level I admitted myself to the emergency department at Caféolait hospital, in desperation. Jean-François came with me because I couldn't think straight, or stop shaking and crying. I was put on anti-anxiolytics and antidepressants. They weren't entirely successful because the cause remained the same--my situation at work. Colleagues sympathized but no one could do anything. Despite not being in good shape, I only missed two days of work. I was too scared to miss more; I didn't want to create an excuse to get rid of me, or to let my colleagues down, so I endured, but the physical symptoms were bad, and I couldn't get on with things as I wanted to. Jean-François understood the type of character my boss was, having seen him in action briefly at the airport on a previous occasion, so he tried to help out in a practical way. He took me out to the airport to pick up Laura.

Despite my fear, exhaustion, and shaking, it was so good to see her walk into the terminal. I hugged her, as I had so many times in the past, and felt safer just by her presence. I was determined to distract myself from what was going on with my body, so we could have a good time together. This wasn't all that successful. There were days when all I wanted to do was walk around and around my bedsit to get rid of some the adrenalin surging inside me, and Laura was exhausted from the jetlag. We shared my big bed and got out and about when we could; slurping chocolate ice-creams while walking past the

Paris Plages, taking a Paris Walking Tour, hopping aboard the Batobus cruising along the Seine. We took a lot of photos and made memories. There's Laura in one photo with a baguette in her hand, another gazing over the Seine, yet another in a sea of blown bubbles at Azay-le-Rideau.

I was realistic enough to realize life had moved on, my daughter was an adult, I wasn't part of her daily life anymore, so there was now a part of her I couldn't know, understand, and relate to. Perhaps it was the same for her; seeing her Mum in a completely different context for which she had no real background. We'd lost something, but the best remained.

"Some people didn't approve of what you did Mum," she confided one day. "They didn't think it right that you walked away and left me."

"You were virtually an adult. I was younger than you when I left home, and I didn't have any support from either of my parents. One of us leaving was going to happen sometime and I didn't know what else I could do to have a future. Such an opportunity to change my life wouldn't have come again, and I couldn't get work in New Zealand, you remember."

"I think you did the right thing, but it was really hard for me for the first few months. You'd always been there in my life everyday", she explained. "I couldn't help feeling sad."

One of the iconic places to go in Paris, after dark, is the famous Moulin Rouge, the cabaret made famous by post-impressionist painter Henri Toulouse Lautrec (the short guy). Henri, a friend to Van Gogh and Oscar Wilde, used to hang out in Montmartre and paint the dancers and prostitutes, amongst other subjects. He drew a series of posters for the cabaret, and thus earned himself a permanent seat there, as well as a place to display his art.

His painting career lasted less than twenty years and ended due to alcoholism and syphilis in his 36th year but his style is synonymous with the famous cabaret where the cancan was created. I was determined that Laura and I would experience the magic of this place.

I'd reserved dinner and a show for Laura and me in advance. Guest can choose their menu online according to taste and price. I'd also reserved a hotel room in the middle of Pigalle; Villa Royale, which was in a *Belle Epoque* style in keeping with our Montmartre experiences.

Travelling by train and metro we were delighted to discover that our hotel was just across from the metro station, and that our room had been upgraded to a view of the Sacre Coeur cathedral. Our bathroom was spacious and the receptionist very helpful. As we went up in the lift, artworks scrolled down the side. Each room has an individual name. Ours was Claude Debussy, located on the sixth floor.

Laura was still suffering the effects of jetlag. Tired with constant headaches, it was difficult for her to relax and admire the city, but it didn't stop the guys in La Pigalle from jumping out at her, offering to marry her (or do other things). Slightly amusing, I think it also unnerved her a bit, at least initially. I explained that this is the red light district of Paris, so it's to be expected. Sex shops seemed to out-number any other kind.

Too tired to drink our half-bottles of wine, we got ourselves into our evening clothes and makeup, just as the sky turned ominously dark and the wind picked up. Soon the curtains were lashing themselves about and we had to shut ourselves out from the view of the rain pelting down. It was fortunate I'd thought to bring my umbrella, and I knew it wasn't all that far to walk to the cabaret. We completely underestimated what would happen and we could never have imagined it anyway.

By the time we'd tottered downstairs in our high heels and best party clothes, the weather had turned unbelievably bad. No sensible person was walking on the streets. In fact you could barely make out the footpaths because the downpours were so heavy and fast that the storm-water system couldn't cope after five minutes, and the streets flooded. Each intersection with a side road or alleyway became a major ford. With only one umbrella between us I hugged Laura as close as she could breathe. We had to walk without delay because we needed to collect the tickets for the performance and get into the queue. A walk of five paces saw anyone soaked to the skin. We had to walk a few hundred meters.

The shop keepers and their customers were sheltering in shop doorways, gazing in amazement at the amount of water falling, and then in amusement as we two stomped by, up to our ankles, evening shoes completely drowned. There came a moment when we reached some traffic lights, and had to step off the pavement to cross. I had a bad feeling about it, and the unusual sense of anticipation I was receiving from a couple of smirking spectators did nothing to dispel it.

We stepped onto the crossing and up to our knees in raging water, dresses flowing in the torrent, leggings inundated, hair drenched, and shoes underwater. A shriek of laughter went up at our plight and we had to laugh, too. It was the most amazing downpour we had ever seen.

We were having some unexpected experiences, but it was highly unpleasant standing in a queue, waiting to be let into the Moulin Rouge, in such a cold and soaked state. The cloakroom and its fee was compulsory. I handed over two soaked jackets from me and one from Laura, plus our umbrella. The cloak-room ladies looked at us as if we'd survived a major natural disaster.

We forgot about being wet and cold as we soaked up the atmosphere, the food and the extraordinary entertainment of the evening for three hours. The topless Doris girls are lovely to watch and nothing is sleazy. The choreographies and costumes are outstanding, the variety acts like the ventriloquist, the little ponies, the acrobats and clowns are first rate. Everything is highly professional. It's expensive, so most of the patrons are tourists or business people with sizeable expense accounts, but it was worth the months of scrimping. It turned out to be the high point of Laura's trip. For a moment the two of us could lose ourselves in one of the world's special spectacles and do it together. Afterwards, damp coats retrieved, we walked down drier streets, past the grins of various men, back to our hotel room and fell into bed. We were looking forward to going up the Eiffel Tower the next day.

It wasn't to be. Laura became unexpectedly ill and the next morning was spent trying to find a doctor in Pigalle who could see us at short notice. We did find one and then it was challeng-ing for me to do the explanations in French and the translations for Laura in English. We obtained some effective medicine but it was clear we'd have to go straight home. A terrible shame but nothing else for it. We consoled ourselves with the fact we had a spare day up our sleeves the following week.

A couple of days later, we spent two days exploring four selected chateaux in the Loire Valley. We started with Cheverny, a small chateau well-furnished and maintained. The Cheverny estate has belonged to the Hurault family for more than six centuries. This is unusual, in that most changed hands or were destroyed during historical events. The architect's father was chancellor (Justice Minister) to French kings Henri III and Henri IV. The present Château de Cheverny is an original jewel among the more famous monuments that stretch along the Loire Valley and is built in the purest Louis XIII classical style.

Chateau de Chambord

Laura and I, with Jean-François's help, visited the grandiose Chambord and the delicate Azay-le-Rideau, as well as Chenonceau chateau straddling the Cher River. Four major chateaux was enough, on top of what we'd already visited. Time was running out.

For her final day in France, Jean-François and I took Laura back to Paris, to a couple of iconic landmarks, and to stroll around parts we hadn't visited before. On our earlier visits to Paris it hadn't been possible to go up the Eiffel Tour because the queues were ridiculously long. It's best to arrive at 9am.

Unfortunately we had to arrive later. Never mind, we snacked between the grand old lady's legs and let fate take its course.

There are always plenty of security personnel present here; police and the army. Laura was absolutely chuffed when two armed soldiers agreed to have their photo taken with her. I explained it was for French-NZ relations. Well, a similar line had worked with President Clinton last year. We still couldn't spare an hour and a half standing in a queue, so we abandoned going up the tower and found an alternative instead.

We walked across the bridge to the Palais de Chaillot/Trocadero, but it started to pour. We decided to head to the Champs Élysées and the Arc de Triomphe. None of us had been to the top, and I was determined that Laura get a view of Paris from on high. This climb isn't for the unfit. It's up a narrow staircase and it's wise to let the vigorous youths pass, and go on ahead. This gives the lactic acid in your muscles a bit of time to disperse before you have to do it all over again, and again. That said, the 360 degree view from the top is great, not as high as the Tour Eiffel or Tour Montparnasse but it's still lovely to see all the boulevards radiating out from this central point. Visitors need to pay an entrance fee of course, but this monument by Napoleon is well restored and worth doing.

The next day I had the sad task of seeing Laura off on the Eurostar, bound for London and then back to New Zealand. I didn't know when we would see each other again. Her life was changing rapidly and mine was so completely different to what we'd shared together last year. My future had still to unfold and reveal any sort of stability. For my daughter and me it was the end of an era but not the end. I sincerely hoped she could find a way to visit me again one day, for much longer. I wanted to take her to the south of France one day, and hoped it wouldn't be too many years until we shared our time together again.

Azay-le-Rideau, Loire Valley

Fountain at Versailles

CHAPTER SIXTEEN

Into nature

A beautiful sunny autumn morning dawned for the start of the hunting season. I'd agreed to come along with Jean-François, his son Vincent and his girlfriend. I was wearing old clothes, added to that Jean-François's oldest hunting jacket and a hi-viz vest, topped off with my new hunting boots, and I was armed with my camera. The men were armed with rifles. Around their waists were cartridge belts. Around their necks were dog 'peepers' to whistle to the dog and electrical dog controllers which emit a small electric charge if the dog doesn't do what it's told. This is important for the dog's own safety.

I was impressed to see that Jean-François followed good safety procedures with the vests. He also walked along with the barrel of his rifle open. This way he couldn't accidently fire at someone or himself if he tripped. I was told to keep one or two meters behind Jean-François in case he had to turn and fire suddenly.

Baika, Jean-François's hunting dog, also followed safety procedures. She wore two collars when on the hunt. One, a hi-viz collar with something like a little mini cow-bell. In this way Jean-François could hear where she was in the undergrowth.

266 · INTO NATURE

The other collar had an electrical device attached which emitted small electric shocks activated by the handler by remote control.

There was a section of woods where one side dropped steeply to the road. It was dangerous for man and dog. If she didn't respond to voice commands she would receive a zap.

Baika was six years old and exercised her hunting instinct every day, hunting on JF's property for rabbits, mice, ducks and anything else she could smell.

The hunt wasn't organized. It was just the two men and two women with cameras plus the dog. We set out down the road and walked about two hundred meters before leaving the road and plunging into the woods. After a couple of minutes we emerged onto farmland. Hunters get a lot of exercise on the hunt. I found the hunting boots an absolute necessity as I trudged along up and down sloping fields, wading through dense brambles and dead branches in woods, climbing steep banks under old railway bridges.

At one point Jean-François asked me to carry his rifle while he helped Vincent look for a shot bird down a slope. Jeepers. It was heavy, but not too heavy, and I carried it barrel open with the cartridges showing, for safety. From time to time we came across other hunters. Some had dogs and some didn't, but none of them had safety precautions in place like JF and Vincent. One guy seemed to want to pose for me with his dead pheasant sticking out of his jacket. Hunting jackets have a big pocket in the back for kills. The dog finds the prey and helps the hunter flush it out. The hunter fires and may or may not hit the target. When the animal goes down, the dog is supposed to find it and allow the hunter to retrieve it.

All morning I heard 'sniper' fire reverberating around the

slopes. Those guns are loud close up. The men had double-barreled rifles and cartridge belts around their waists. I didn't feel unsafe; it simply sounded a bit like very loud car backfires though I knew it was the sound of death for something.

The adrenaline surging through Jean-François when a bird flew up from trees was palpable. I was surprised to see that the birds struggled to gain altitude quickly. They seemed like people who have fallen from a great height into deep water and must battle their way desperately to the surface and life. Though it only took seconds, it seemed such a long time, watching the pheasants trying to get high enough into the air, but with a double-barreled rifle the hunter has the advantage if the first shot misses. Vincent was quite successful. He bagged two pheasants, a cock, and a hen. I was so focused on the plight of the birds each time, I forgot to take a photo.

Jean-François didn't hit anything, which was normal for him. He told me his pleasure came from watching his dog work. She would run along with her nose to the ground. If she smelt something interesting, she'd stop and look. Her nose would cast around for what was there and where it was. In woods she would bound about like a gamboling lamb in the undergrowth, directed by peeps and shouts from JF and Vincent. At regular intervals JF or Vincent would let out a 'whoop' which the other would repeat in the distance. This enabled them to know where each was for tactical and safety reasons. Other hunters seemed rather lax in that.

It was somewhat difficult to enjoy nature. For starters, I had to keep up with the hunters, so I couldn't slow down or stop to look around and soak up the scenery. Also, the countryside wasn't that interesting. For the most part it looked empty (smart critters would have gone on vacation to a city). The woods were not all that beautiful or full of interesting plants and insects, birds or animals. I was used to New Zealand forests, woods, rivers, lakes and mountains and fields, which seem rather more dense and interesting with their variety of living things. We did see a small deer dash past us, but the men needed a special cartridge to bring it down, and it was too close to the road; not fair for the animal or motorists, so the men let it go.

Jean-François pointed out where small deer had been sleeping. He seemed able to smell where certain types of animal had passed by. That was rather impressive. Near a clearing he said the bad smell would be a dead animal somewhere close by. I couldn't smell much, but was happy to move on.

We doubled back and headed toward the creek at the back of Jean-François's place looking for duck, trudging through nettles and brambles, trying not to trip over parts of the disused railway line. The train hasn't used it since the tracks were bombed during WWII. It's overgrown with weeds and saplings but is easy for hunters to use. Vincent shot an unlucky duck at the water's edge. Baika was told to jump into the creek and retrieve it. She had some problems handing it over, so Vincent had to lean down and pull it up, and wrap it in a plastic bag, and shove it into his jacket. The duck didn't look pretty after that, covered in mud.

Even in the fields and woods there was litter, so unsightly. I can't understand why someone would want to light a fire and leave cans and plastic rubbish bags, full and bottles lying around in nature. When Jean-François was president of the local hunt club he organized the hunters to do a massive cleanup of the local countryside. They even removed old rusting cars; their contribution to the environment I suppose. Hunters pay fees to hunt. Part of this goes to the landowners. Sometimes the hunters try to protect disappearing ecosystems. Each year they do a wildlife census to determine populations of species. This year one bird species and hares were on the 'not to be hunted' list.

We walked back to Jean-François's place and had a BBQ lunch of *brochettes* made the night before. These are metal skewers with diced vegetables and assorted meat, in this case, pork, beef and lamb interspersed with pieces of green peppers and onions. In addition, there were fries, fruit and ice-creams. What an indulgence. It was a merry dining table with four adults and four children. The children had stayed back at the house while we hunted.

Vincent explained it wasn't the killing he enjoyed; it was the childhood memories of the countryside as he re-encountered the sights and smells of his childhood. Each to his own means of nostalgia, I guess. For me, memories of my childhood would need to involve my Grandmother and my pets, and they've been dead for years. I find the creatures in nature more beautiful when they're alive and not panicked. I don't want to possess them. I eat meat, yes. I'm glad I don't have to kill it. It was interesting to go on the hunt and see what it's all about, but I didn't need to do it again.

On another occasion I accompanied the local hunters on their annual animal census. This census is important to determine what species can be hunted in the forthcoming season and how many animals of each species can be taken. Some animals and birds remain on the not-to-be-hunted list because they have become endangered, such as *La Perdrix Grise,* a small grouse-like bird that is the emblem of La Beauce. The motorways, grain harvesters, weed killers, and birds of prey are taking a terrible toll on this bird population.

The census required a lot of standing around in freezing fog while various guys divided up and started patrolling parcels of land. Maps were spread out on vehicles, bread and cheese and wine were scoffed down in farm sheds. I was almost the only female, but it was more the language barrier that made me feel so isolated. Jean-François was there, but the guys weren't interested in speaking to me, and he was busy catching up on news and gossip.

All was not lost. I learnt how to officially count animals, counting only the animals that ran past me on my right, between me and the next person counting on my right. I counted two hares and saw several others and some *chevreuils* in the distance, but the lack of animals to count made things tedious and gloomy. Human beings had destroyed the habitats and there were few critters to hunt. The French Hunt was on the way out.

Jean-François with his hunting dog, Baika

CHAPTER SEVENTEEN

Further afield

The year was flying by and I had opportunities to see other parts of the world; firstly Barcelona in Spain, then Budapest in Hungary. I only had 24 hours in the later to attend a one-day conference on intergenerational fairness. Budapest is the capital of Hungary. As the largest city of Hungary, it's the country's principal political, cultural, commercial, industrial, and transportation center. Budapest became a single city occupying both banks of the river Danube with a unification on 17 November 1873 of west-bank Buda and Óbuda with east-bank Pest.

Flying over Europe was quite a novel experience. I was so used to flying over water, the Pacific Ocean to be exact, or desert (Australia) that the idea of powering across countries without geographic borders was amazing to me. I felt quite comfortable exploring European cities alone. Budapest felt safe and livable. It wasn't possible for me to do much in just a few hours though. I had approximately five hours to explore and have dinner. Naturally I started with The Danube, the mighty river flowing through this part of Europe. For size, it's impressive, but the majority of buildings alongside it aren't. It can't possibly compare with Paris, and it's less intensely built-up.

There are, after all, less than two million people there. Not long after my trip to Hungary I was in the United States of America. The day started auspiciously. The New Zealand All Blacks rugby team narrowly won the Rugby World Cup 2011 over France as I boarded my plane for Chicago, IL. I was part of a small delegation from the University who were visiting a college in Michigan IL to develop a partner relationship between our two institutions. I'd never been to the American Mid-West before, so I was curious about the whole experience. The flight between Paris Charles de Gaulle Airport and O'Hare Airport in Chicago takes about nine hours; more than long enough in economy class seats which seem to get tinier by the year, even though many passengers are getting bigger.

As we flew over the Great Lakes of Huron and Michigan I was struck by the strangeness of these enormous lakes from the air. They're not oceans, but I had expected they might behave a little bit like seas due to their vast size; apparently not this day. There were no boats on the lakes; that seemed strange to me. The water didn't seem to move; rather it seemed frozen, except for fine rivulets which caught the light. Surely they weren't iced up yet with the day's temperature of 19 degrees Celsius. Of course they weren't, but they gave an eerie impression of emptiness and other-worldliness. From the air, the land in Michigan is divided into large rectangles, intersected by very long roads and highways.

The college is small and consists only of students studying for an undergraduate degree so it's not a university which would offer Masters and PhD programs too. The town where the college is situated isn't affluent, and in fact we were informed that the state of Michigan was struggling a lot in these dark financial times. The campus itself is extensive and beautiful, full of charming buildings, woods, deer and the ubiquitous squirrels in black, brown and grey coats. They were everywhere, not tame but also not timid. It was so cute when they sat up on their hind legs, balancing on their bushy tails to nibble nuts and student leftovers.

Deer could also be seen from our accommodation in the Manor which is used for visitor accommodation and conferences. It's beautifully decorated with antique furniture and china. It was a delight to eat breakfast there each day off the lovely china, and look out over the fields, and woods, and equestrian center. We'd arrived in the lead-up to Halloween so many of the doorways and houses were decorated with pumpkins, and witches, ghouls and cobwebs; lots of fun.

My third day at the college, I was in the middle of an important meeting between our two organizations when I suddenly suffered a major nosebleed. A trip to the ladies' toilet cleaned most of the blood off my face, but it just wouldn't stop, like a tap left on. The provost kindly drove me to a family clinic in the town while the others continued with the meeting.

On arrival I was asked about the problem, (fairly obvious with a gusher and tissues everywhere). Okay, then I was asked if I'd be likely to come back for any future treatment. Well, no. Sorry, they told me, they couldn't treat me and I'd have to find somewhere else to take me. The provost then had to drive me to the emergency department at a hospital in a neighboring town. This was dangerous in my opinion.

The hospital was appalled when I told then the attitude at the town clinic. I must give the hospital staff their due, they were very friendly, relaxed, tried not to keep me waiting too long (waiting is necessary of course) and enjoyed having someone different to deal with. Well, it turned out I was the first international patient they'd had. Life must be rather quiet there I suppose.

Entering my contact details was an incompatible mission as the data fields are totally US-centric and the staff there can't read a French identity paper. We all laughed about it and were all confident I'd receive the bill. I never did.

The doctor came and had a look and said he could see the damage. He guessed it might be caused by allergies to the environment and/or too hot and dry air. Aha! Apparently many people develop asthma after living in Michigan State. Oh. Treatment consisted of cauterization. No problem, but he did it to the nostril that wasn't gushing. I asked him why he wasn't doing the offending nostril. He said he couldn't see any damage in that one so he wasn't about to cauterize blindly. That was rather unsettling, so I asked how come the bleeding had been mostly from the left. He surmised that the blood must have risen to the back of the nose, over and around to the other nostril. I felt skeptical and said I supposed I'd just have to trust him. The doctor suggested I take antihistamines and put Vaseline inside my nostrils to try to keep them moist. The treatment worked. The doctor was right after all.

Advice to those suffering nosebleeds; don't lie down, and do not lean back, or the blood will run down your throat. Mine was so bad it poured in both directions and the blood clots had me gagging, so lean forward and pinch the nose.

Eventually I would visit the college three times over two years. It was always a pleasure to work with such friendly and professional people.

Jean-François took me on a five-day cruise of the Greek Islands. I'd never been on a cruise before. He was skeptical about whether he'd like it, but we both enjoyed arriving in new places, having excursions and meals organized for us. The only down-side for me was that it was all in French. To be in France is to be at the gateway to all of Europe. I couldn't help thinking that with a bit more job security and a little more money I'd be off exploring so many interesting and historic places, getting first-hand experience of different cultures, but at least, with JF's help, I was doing things other Kiwis only dream of.

I still couldn't do anything about getting a car. Months ago I'd gone into the sous-prefecture with all the documentation re-quired to convert my NZ driver's license to a French one. I went armed with additional proof that this process was, indeed, ap-proved by the French Government. Okay, my documentation was all in order, and I was told that I'd have to stop driving on the expiry date of my old visa. Well, how long was it going to take to get the new license? She shrugged and said she had no idea, that every country was different.

I had no choice. I reached the expiry of my visa, my renewed *titre de séjour* kicked in, but there was no sign of anything re-lating to the driver's license, so I waited more. I couldn't drive, I couldn't even practice driving. Two months later I went in and explained the situation was getting critical. There was then a lot of 'kerfuffling' in the background as if they couldn't find my dossier (that would have been a complete disaster as one must have applied for a license exchange within one year of arriving in France).

Finally the woman came back to the counter and said there was a problem, signal for twisting guts and a hot flush to arrive. I was told that the woman responsible for my dossier had left to have a baby and she hadn't been replaced by management. They were a bit over-worked so nothing had been done. And that's a real weakness in France; people don't do things if it's not written into their contract, teamwork doesn't seem to exist, so unfortunate people like me are just conveniently ignored, no matter how it screws up their lives. Nobody cared, no one was accountable, and no one took any initiative.

Oh, and by the way, this other woman had decided that my impeccable documentation was now no longer complete. I needed a translation of my license.

"No problem," I said, smiling. "This international license supplies the translation." Alas, she refused to accept it. For goodness sake, how much translation is required of my name, a date, and a few random letters of the alphabet? Because that's all there was.

No, I must find an officially approved translator, spend money, get it sent to me, come back and get this woman to give me a 'note from the teacher' to say my real license was on its way. My disguised anger should have choked me. Instead I had to be gracious and grateful. After emailing translators and getting no reply, I decided to go to the NZ Embassy in Paris and organize it all there. I should have the translation in a week (having paid sixty euros). The one thing I was grateful for is that NZ and France have an agreement to exchange licenses, so I didn't have to spend thousands of euros and a lot of stress doing French theory and practical tests in France. I'd been driving for nearly forty years.

I went back to the sous-prefecture in Caféolait because I now had an expensive translation for my NZ driver license. Surely now I'd get my French one? Nope. First I was told I didn't need the translation (incorrect) then was told nothing had still been done about it. Three women crowded around a computer trying to work out which date they should go by; the date on my visa or the date stamp on my first *titre de séjour*. They didn't know the answer and still couldn't fathom the translated driver's license. I didn't leave until they gave me a paper saying I could drive for six months, while they tried to work out what to do. I was left standing for an hour and a half, with no explanations while they disappeared and fluffed around. French folks standing in the queue glanced sympathetically, and world-wearily at me as I passed.

In France, Christmas trees get wrapped in a net, for customers, to make it easier to transport them; a great idea because the needles are rather sharp and painful. I weighted the bottom of Jean-François's tree container with his collection of fossilized sea urchins that he'd collected on rambles in the woods and fields over the years; that was certainly different! We bought new fiber optic lights, and some extra baubles to go along with what he already had. After a few hours I'd finished decorating it, the fire was on, and as darkness deepened, the pretty little lights twinkled and cast a romantic aura over the room as JF and I sat back to admire everything.

Being Christmas, I sent out my usual Christmas newsletter from myself, with a contribution from Laura, to various friends and special contacts. Most responded with either a brief hello or a longer, newsier update or article of their own; fantastic, I felt a little more reconnected. People I enjoyed in the past I still enjoyed. The miles mattered little in that regard. Some friends were off on their own adventures elsewhere in the world, enduring jobs they didn't like, reviewing what they wanted to do next year, having grandchildren, looking after aging parents.

My ex-husband got engaged, folks dropped out of the conventional 'stream' of things. I hadn't heard yet from my friends

278 · FURTHER AFIELD

back in Christchurch who were still suffering multiple major earthquakes more than fifteen months after the devastating second one.

I received a call from Alain in Brittany. Contact from him was extremely rare, so it was lovely to hear from him and know he was thinking of me and even discussing me with his friend Pascal whom I'd met the previous year. That Christmas I'd spent with Alain's family. His Mum still asked after me. They're lovely people and Alain will always be a good friend in my heart for introducing me to the beauty of Brittany, and all the laughs we shared.

My second Christmas would be spent with someone special and intimate in my life, Jean-François, who had added so much color and richness to this year for me. It was quiet. His daughter and her son were there for a few days so it was a French family Christmas, but without a lot of people. It was easier to converse like that and a rest was welcome but it was still difficult to feel included because of the language obstacle.

At Christmas Eve in Jean-François's house one shared presents around midnight. If the kids were asleep, they were woken up to unwrap what Father Christmas had delivered. Right now the tree lights were twinkling, the fire was crackling and flaming. JF and I swapped presents. We ate roast lamb for dinner, cooked completely differently to what we'd do in NZ, having had a delicious roast pork with sauce accompanied by a superb Pinot Gris for lunch. La Belle France.

I was sitting up in bed munching warmed *pain au chocolat* washed down with a cup of tea for my breakfast. The duvet was pulled up, the house was warm with the fire dancing in the grate. Outside there was a spectacle in progress.

Overnight it had started to snow. The temperature dropped steeply and, although the snow was predicted, the exact amount of snowfall could never be known in advance. It was so quiet other than JF moving around the house. Baika the dog had completely changed her behavior and now preferred to be confined to the warm kitchen instead of exploring JF's extensive property.

I was discovering more about the behavior of snowflakes (*flocons*). As I watched, there was a dance going on. It was as if there were several large gangs of snowflakes clashing and intersecting in their struggles to gain space to land. They were crossing paths; it was a melee, but suddenly all changed; now they were a school of fish swimming obliquely, all synchronized. This lasted perhaps a minute until it all changed again and the *flocons* agreed to fall vertically down, all at the same speed, all the same size. Snowflake sizes changed all the time. Sometimes they were small, fine and fast; little sprinters in a hurry to hit the ground. Other times they were larger and fluffier and fell like feathers until they caressed their compatriots who had already landed.

I especially loved it when the branches of trees became so overloaded with snow that they tipped big quantities off. It cascaded to the ground and suddenly, ploof! It was like an ice fire sending crystal smoke into the air. So beautiful. Yes, it was a fascinating spectacle, until I opened the door, in my pajamas.

The intense cold struck immediately, but I wasn't as shocked as I expected so I lingered, taking some photos, running to the end of the property and taking more photos. As adrenaline took me farther and farther from the house, I realized that perhaps it really was too cold to be doing this. Those minus degrees found a way in under my skin, and it was painful to be out in it without protection. So, a few last photos and I was racing the dog to get back into the house. She arrived just after me and literally leaped for her basket in the kitchen. Her momentum sent it and her sliding across the room. It was so comical, and JF asked her if she'd had the courtesy to change her paws before coming inside with her snow.

Over at Caféolait, the park looked beautiful. There were few animals to be seen. The domestic ones (sheep, pigs and chickens) were now all indoors. The geese, ducks, and other water-loving birds were doing it tough. The lakes were all frozen over, so the birds went for walks on them or huddled in a cold group, all species sharing their warmth. I couldn't work out why the middle of a solid snowy lake was better than the land for a snooze. It must have been pretty miserable in those conditions, and I didn't know what they could find to eat.

The Louvre, Paris

CHAPTER EIGHTEEN

On the move

U2 have a song where the lyrics go--"stuck in a moment and you can't get out of it." That seemed apt for me right now. I wondered if I'd come down with that winter blues malady some folks got in France during the long European winters. I had no energy, felt demotivated and rather depressed on top of the background anxiety I always felt. I was wondering what on earth my future could possibly be and the effort required to survive here.

Things weren't so bad. I had the basics of life though little else. I was getting used to life in France, more and more each week. I had my wonderful friend Jean-François, and I was still employed, but there had been a lot of tension and stress at work. Days, weeks, and months like that can get tough. Everything in my life seemed so temporary. I felt worn down. I was impatient to move myself forward somehow, but had no resources to do so. I'd had plenty of time recently to reflect on just how tough this determination to realize my dream had become and the constant sacrifice required to keep it alive.

I'd been asking myself what I really wanted, now that I was in France. I'd given up on trying to get a ten year visa in the distant future. For me it wasn't good enough. I'd decided to hang in there, employment-wise, for seven years; that was a little over five more years away. Once I'd been working here continuously for five years I could start the application process toward full citizenship. That process can take two years so my struggles to stay in France would have to continue for another five years minimum.

Once I was a French citizen I could stay as of right, regardless of how my employment status might change. It would also make it easier for me to get work, even temporary work because I'd have the right to be there, as much as the British. I could start my own business. I could have dual citizenship, free to move between France and NZ whenever I wanted, on business or for personal reasons. That way I could still enjoy my beloved France but also spend time with my daughter Laura as I got older. That could become quite important for both her and me. This is what the Charter of the Rights and Responsibilities of a French Citizen has to say:

> *You wish to become a French citizen. It is an important decision that you must not take lightly. Becoming French is not an easy administrative task. Acquiring French nationality is a decision that will affect you, and after you, it will affect your descendants.*

From now on, all naturalization candidates must sign this document, as well as passing the assimilation interview that finalized their demand for citizenship. The rules on French language competency had toughened up too. I would have to pass the TFI to prove I had the equivalent of a fifteen-year-old French student, a daunting challenge.

I had a long way to go to make that happen. Somehow I had

to find a way to live above the subsistence level I was on now. I didn't know the answer to that. I wanted a charming little French house with a garden I could design and tend myself, before I got too old and stiff. I didn't need a lot, but I did want that, and enough money to travel to and from the ends of the earth every other year.

I was happy that after six months of hassle visiting the sous-prefecture many times in Caféolait, waiting in queues only to be told they were too under-staffed to process my application for a driver's license, that someone went on maternity leave so nothing was done, that they didn't know which date they should pay attention to, my visa or my *titre de séjour*, the letter arrived. I sprinted in the next day and finished the process. *Voila*, I now had a genuine French driver's license. At last I was allowed to drive a car. To get it I had to surrender my NZ license but I now had the documentation; I just needed the car.

Hours were spent trawling the French second-hand car websites. Jean-François took me on the rounds of concessionaires. It was clear my budget was pretty hopeless. They couldn't suggest anything. Back to the Internet I went, and we found three possible cars I could afford.

We rang each owner and arranged to visit. One was sold just before we arrived, another was in perfect state, but slightly expensive and a little large for my current state of confidence. The third was the smallest car I'd ever driven, but I felt at ease with it. The bodywork was rather knocked about and paint was scratched and missing, but the price was good for me. I had to wait a month while the owner got a *contrôle technique* (warrant of fitness), had repairs from that done, and buried his mother in Turkey. At last I could be independent, as much as the cost of petrol allowed. The effort to find better accommodation was quite another matter.

It was time to take a bigger step and launch myself onto the road of greater independence and comfort. After nearly two years of living in a dark, damp, poorly maintained room, I needed to create my own environment, to have pieces of my own furniture about me, to be able to look around and feel that I was home. I knew I was about to change my life again, and it was with a mixture of hope and apprehension that I committed to the process.

The long, long search on the Internet began. After many weeks I knew the market prices, the vocabulary of *locataire* and *proprietaire, bail* and *rez de chaussee, residence de standing* and *rangements.* My budget was limited, and it appeared that I wouldn't be able to stay in Caféolait. Caféolait was charming, affluent, conservative, and expensive. I cast my net much farther afield, and it had to be south because north took me closer to Paris and that meant rents were too expensive.

I just wanted a one bedroom apartment in better nick than my studio, with parking and, if possible, a terrace or balcony, or even a garden; something bigger, brighter. Eventually I found an apartment in, of all places, Caféolait. While more expensive than my studio, it was just affordable. The rule in France is that you can't pay more than a third of your income, after social security payments, on rent.

Jean-François and I visited it with the real estate agent. First requirement; seduce the agent and get her onside as I was a foreigner and not to be trusted in France. JF and I were well presented. He rolled up in his BMW and I commented in an intelligent and friendly manner where needed, but let JF do most of the talking as he'd needed to get me the appointment.

The apartment had potential despite the horrid rainbow colors of paint in each room. The agent agreed it would be good to do a refurbish (at my expense, of course). She liked us and Jean-François dropped off a dossier proving I was a sound person. The agent later showed it to the owner, who dithered. She had in mind a couple in their forties who earned 100,000 euros per year. The agent tried to explain that no couple earning that amount would be looking for a flat like hers; impossible.

The other complication for me was French attitudes and laws regarding tenants. Tenants are viewed with suspicion and renting to them is an enormous risk for landlords. Tenants, even if they are French, they may need to get another person to act as financial guarantor, no matter who they are or what their background is. Prospective tenants must supply a copy of their official identification, a copy of their work contract, bills from suppliers, and demands from the tax department.

As a foreigner with no fixed job, no job security, I wasn't popular. Without Jean-François making the phone calls and 'selling' me, I wouldn't even have got inspections. The landlord of the Caféolait apartment was old and had been sick for a bit. The apartment had been vacant for a year because whenever any agent proposed a tenant she always said no. We were warned to expect resistance.

Jean-François and I went into overdrive to try to convince the owner to rent to me. The dossier was enlarged with documents indicating I was involved in influential projects, that I was a landlord in NZ. The dossier included photos of me and my boss, photos of me with key French persons or a Mayor in the US. The whole thing was invasive, intrusive, an insult, and humiliating to have all the details of my life on display like that.

"If the old lady doesn't accept you as a tenant, I'm chucking it in with her. I've had enough of her prevaricating. She's done this to every agent in Caféolait, and it's still vacant after a year," said the agent.

In the end after waiting, waiting, losing opportunities for other flats, Jean-François rang her but even his reasoning and charm couldn't make any headway.

Start all over again. All my evenings were spent researching, my weekends and some week-nights were spent visiting. I had to be single-minded. Jean-François was the chauffeur and dossier-maker. More simpering to agents and landlords who viewed me initially with suspicion because, France being so socialist, no one is allowed not to have a roof over his or her head. Therefore, if a tenant stops paying the rent, the landlord finds it very difficult to get rid of them and certainly not in winter. For a landlord to get redress or kick them out, it can take up to three years. Yes, folks squatting for three years with impunity. All the while the landlord must pay all the expenses of the property.

So, here was me, a foreigner with no permanent work, why risk that? I hadn't expected it all to be so hard. No wonder I had never heard from any agent when I'd tried to flat hunt by myself. Having JF to facilitate made all the difference.

In the midst of this The Professor said he would renew my contract another year and give me a small pay increase. That made a difference. I needed an official letter to say I would be hired again, and I needed confirmation of my new salary, none of which was all that simple, but I got there. I still couldn't afford Caféolait, but looking further afield I thought I might just find something suitable if I could win the agent and landlord over. The other thing I was struggling with was what was (not) supplied by landlords.

It was one thing to think I'd found something I wanted to

live in, but quite another to get through the process of moving with minimal hassle. I didn't accomplish the later. Some of the subsequent difficulties were predictable. Others were much worse than I could have imagined.

I found an apartment in a town called Ellernon. This town is even smaller than Caféolait, and until a few months ago I'd known nothing about it. The town was one of the locations which I had visited most often in my search for somewhere to live because it has a train station that can connect to a line to Paris, and I could also get to work from there. It was a little more affordable but required money and time for travelling to and from work. In a way that wasn't such a bad thing. Sometimes it's good to leave the workplace well behind at the end of the day, travel through the French countryside and arrive home in a completely different environment.

The apartment had two small bedrooms and a big balcony and was full of light. I found it on the Internet and needed to deal directly with the owner so no agency fees were involved. Jean-François helped with the details and my dossier was accepted immediately. I had only to wait until the apartment was available, but for a while at least I would have to pay rent for two apartments, as I was required to give my boss two months' notice. This was quite a financial stretch for me, but it was normal in France. Other 'normal' things in France were more challenging, and this was where this Kiwi found the cultural differences tough.

For starters, the apartment had no storage, not one cupboard or shelf anywhere. How do people manage with nothing like that at all? This was standard here. There were usually no built-in wardrobes, vanities, medicine cabinets, kitchen cupboards, or linen cupboards in hallways.

The three consequences of this are as follows:
1. Renters must buy all of this themselves and install it, on top of the expense of moving
2. Everything installed reduces the habitable space so what may have looked workable becomes cramped and uncomfortable
3. When renters move on, they must either leave it all there for the lucky landlord or next tenant, or remove it, and hope it will fit exactly into their next place (unlikely), or try to find a buyer at a time when they're up to their ears in shifting.

This meant I had to consider everything. I had to ensure I budgeted for each of these items on top of trying to find money for essential things like a bed, a table and chairs, a fridge, an electric jug. I had to research on the Internet what was available and how to order it, all in a foreign language. This was quite a challenge for me. I ordered some curtains which had not arrived a month later, some bed linen I ordered was only partially correct but the vacuum cleaner and fridge I ordered via the internet arrived perfectly and functioned very well. Small successes such as these proved important as the rest of the process was arduous and stressful.

I couldn't afford to hire a man with a van to move everything at once (expensive in France) so many trips by car after work and in the weekends were the norm. In the meantime Jean-François put his handyman skills to good use and built some little shelves in the entranceway for me to arrange my DVDs. He used the materials from an old vanity to build something under the sink in the bathroom and built some open shelves and somewhere to hang my coat and put my muddy boots in the hot water cylinder cupboard. Fortunately I'd had the chance to mention to the owner that I was disappointed not to see any storage in the kitchen, and so was told two cupboards and a small bench top would be installed. I was grateful to have that small amount, but there was no work space on the small bench in the kitchen so JF made a little shelf to lift my microwave, to give room for plates underneath.

Speaking of kitchens, it is usual to discover there is just a sink. That constitutes a kitchen in a flat in France. This was a severe culture shock for this Kiwi. In NZ renters can expect an oven and cooktop, kitchen cupboards above and underneath some sort of work bench. They may or may not have a dishwasher but they can at least put food and plates somewhere, and cook a meal. In France tenants need to supply their own kitchen, they only rent the space. The landlords want to maximize the rent from habitable space so they rent out empty rooms. If they don't supply something they are then not liable to maintain it, so there are no light fittings or cooking facilities or appliances.

In some contracts, if tenants in France make a hole in a wall to hang a picture or for any other reason, they may be charged ten euros per hole. My rental contract said nothing about this but it was constantly in my mind when I thought of what I need to do to create a home for myself. Absolutely nothing about this moving experience had been like all my previous ones. The smallest arrangements were fraught with uncertainty and unwelcome surprises. One aspect of my move was particularly grueling.

I needed to order some furniture. Normally this would be rather exciting and a great creative exercise. I was interested to discover what's available in France, how one orders, what are the sizes. I discovered that when one orders furniture it's not automatically delivered and it's not in a state immediately usable. In my price range (that of most French people who don't have much money) it's all flat-pack. Purchasers have to put it together themselves. I can do a small table or desk, but that's it. I gave away all my tools when I left NZ. All I had was a measuring tape and a hammer I bought. Putting together free-standing bookshelves with glass doors, free-standing wardrobes, a bed, table, even chairs, was beyond me so I had to pay to have it all delivered flat-pack, and to have guys assemble it. That made me nervous, and rightly so, because customers can't be sure what they'll end up with. Two guys arrived to unload the van and one was left behind to assemble all the furniture. That in itself was ridiculous; it was also dangerous.

He started in the bedroom, always good practice to get the bedroom sorted first, and I thought that after a while I could head off to Caféolait and collect more of my belongings because today was my moving day. He had difficulties working out things from the instruction booklet, and trying to construct an armoire single-handed was much too heavy for one man. There was a crash right in front of me. He was on his hands and knees with his hands on his head looking in horror at the splintered base of my armoire.

It wasn't a hopeless case, but it was damaged and so was he, on his arm where the base had fallen. He refused my ministrations and stoically tried to carry on, hiding his wound and the splintered section of the armoire under the next layer of construction, but one of the doors to the armoire couldn't function because the wood was bowed.

There were pieces missing from a handle on the chest of drawers and one drawer was too tight for a female to open and close. The bedside cabinet door wouldn't open or close because the key couldn't open it. The bed couldn't be erected because one side had been mysteriously broken. There was no piece of furniture in my bedroom which could function correctly and some was unusable.

The two glass-fronted display/library units I ordered for the living room seemed to have problems with doors not lining up, and the back panel was so thin it was like paper. Most of the chairs rocked markedly on the floor as none of the legs seemed in sync with each other. The side buffet had doors that didn't hang on too well. The only piece of furniture I had bought that was in a decent state to function was my dining table. Everything else had defects or pieces missing. It was a nightmare trying to sort out my belongings as I didn't have anywhere to put them away. Moving was delayed. I had to wait two days to have each piece unpacked and discover parts missing or damaged. This being the French summer, I would have to wait until sometime in September to have things corrected.

What really upset me were the gouges in my bedroom wall. A brand new wall was already marked, and I hadn't slept a night there yet. Marks from packing materials smudged the other wall. There was nothing I could do about either, but it did spoil what should have been an exciting experience. Jean-François and I had to go to their main distribution warehouse to speak to the foreman there and go through every set of assembly instructions to identify each defective or missing part. Luckily for me, JF is a very competent handyman, or I'd have been sunk. One and a half hours of our time was spent doing this.

Days later when the guys from France Telecom came to give me a phone/Internet/TV connection they found they couldn't give me any TV service. Maybe the trouble was the decoder,

I'd have to look into it myself (even though I'd had to pay for the installation that was incomplete). Gritting my teeth, I took off with Jean-François for a few days at his father's place in Brittany.

I would have a lovely place eventually, but the persistence and expense required to move myself forward in any way was exhausting and disappointing. So far this year I had found a car and a home; not so bad. Though I'd visited my new home frequently, I still hadn't lived there. I looked around at the completely new environment. I was starting over again but it would take time for it to feel like me. Once I slept there and had some hotplates for cooking that would help me bond with my new home. I was looking forward to that and to exploring my new town.

It had been a tough week. It started Monday morning when my boss told me, plus a colleague who has only recently joined the research center, that our jobs were at risk. The boss had enemies. If shit hit fan, we'd be the most vulnerable, the first to go, we were told. Was this done in a thoughtful way with consideration? Not at all, standing in the print room where anyone could come in. The financial crisis was only part of the reason, but this was a catastrophic thing to say to me because I was not an EU citizen and not young. I had everything to lose, more than anyone else at work.

I'd recently taken out a bank loan in order to be able to buy basic furniture for my apartment. I didn't own so much as a bed or a tin opener prior to my move out of the depressing old studio. So, knowing that my contract had been renewed for another year, I'd made a commitment to France. With no job I would not able to stay in France. I'd lose my home, my only

FOLLOW MY HEART · 293

friend, this country, my dream, my income, my existence. I didn't even know how I'd even get back to NZ. How would I find the money to bring my bits and bobs back? There'd be no car, no home I could afford to live in, no job and probably no unemployment benefit for months; this was not a prospect that aided sleep, so I wasn't sleeping well.

Even after I eventually moved into my new home things still weren't resolved with the furniture. Four months after I ordered it, I had a head board and the sides and foot of my bed lying around. My dresser still missed a functioning drawer. My bedside table had no way of closing the door properly because the first guy broke the key, and the second guy put the door on the wrong side. My wardrobe door was still buckled and needed replacing. From time to time I received a letter in the mail to tell me a screw had arrived. I might get a separate one telling me a hinge had arrived; a few weeks later I might be told a nail had arrived. Wow!

On a rare occasion a guy might arrive to install something but, wouldn't you know it, he didn't have the right screwdriver, so he'd leave. He was the official installer. I paid a lot of money to have my furniture put together but not one guy had been able to do his job, and they didn't care. There was no accountability because they were contracted. But when it all goes wrong I, or often Jean-François, had to make the endless phone calls, visit distribution centers to identify types of screws, be around when the installer visited (and then abruptly left having done nothing). This was France. The service ethic doesn't apply. If a customer buys anything they often take a risk. The customer is always wrong, in France. Eight months later I finally had everything sorted after multiple interventions by Jean-François.

I was still waiting for my new *titre de séjour*, my legal enti-
tlement to live and work in France. The application had been
done months ago. I waited with my temporary one. That was
about to expire with no sign of the legal/real one. Jean-François
had made enquiries months earlier only to be told the department of immigration was having a restructure. It was all a mess,
nothing could be done during the frequent and lengthy school
holidays, someone was on holiday. No one was following my
case.

A woman at the prefecture knew I was in the system and
advised me to come back two weeks before my temporary paper was due to expire. I did. So what, I was told by someone
else to go away and I'd have to wait until it expired, in case by
chance the 'real' one arrived. Hell, that would make me illegal.
Worse, without a valid *titre de séjour* I wouldn't get paid, and
the wheels of the University were slow and inflexible, even
when I did get it. I went away empty-handed, having been told
they'd try to put my file near the top for priority consideration.
Of course, they never did.

The *fonctionaires* who worked in the public sector didn't
seem to care. Their careers are protected. They have a job for
life. The trick is to find one that might be sympathetic to one's
predicament.

Individuals cannot argue with them; it's not in one's interest
to upset them. A huge proportion of the French workforce are
civil servants. They move piles of paper (on a good day). President Nicolas Sarkozy tried to reduce the number by attrition
but there was a hue and cry. There are so many of them with
vested interests they can bring the country to its knees. President Hollande was actually adding more public servants to the
public debt, as they tended to vote socialist. There are some

nice *fonctionaires*, of course, somewhere, but I usually didn't see them.

My *Carte Vitale* (health card) hadn't been functioning for months. I received conflicting information from doctors and pharmacists. One pharmacist told me it had been cancelled. I thought this might be because of moving to a different region. It was all so complicated here. I took time off work to go to the main center and investigate it. I was told it was in hand and that I'd receive a letter in fifteen days telling me to go to a pharmacy to reactivate my card. I'd been waiting two months. Without it I paid full price, with no reimbursements for doctors and pharmacy visits, even though I was paying for this in my taxes.

More time off work was required, and another visit to the prefecture to be told that people on a salary had to prove they are employed each year, to have their cards renewed. Jean-François had never heard of this. No one had told me this, they just cut off my card. My previous visit had not told me that either even though I'd brought pay slips that time. The woman had said they weren't necessary.

I would have to come back yet again with various proofs that I was working, to get it all going again, yet the tax department was very efficient and knew I was working. The government departments seemed to have no integration at all. This can all do a person's head in when they come from a simpler, better organized country, like New Zealand. It was also scary because these departments can make life in France impossible for one, or miserable at best. Appreciating this came slowly to me - it was really difficult to accept this way of doing things. Just because that's the way it is doesn't make it any good, but it's France and I wasn't yet French.

There were some great things about France. I wanted to become a French citizen, but I hoped I could survive, literally survive, long enough. In the meantime, it wasn't a lot of fun right now. I was scared about my future or lack of; never knowing where I could live in the world from one day to the next, if I would work again in my life, how I would spend old age, if I would lose my only friend in France. Would I be reduced to absolutely nothing again? How would I pick myself up and carry on again if that happened? How would I live knowing I gave it everything and still lost it all, with no hope of getting any of it back?

These worries, along with a stressful work situation probably provoked the significant chronic pain I had now; 'frozen shoulder' and tendonitis in both shoulders. These are extremely painful and long-lasting problems. I really needed that health card, and somewhere along the way I'd aged, arthritis was now my constant companion. With all that, my attempts to retake dance classes and violin classes at Ellernon were terminated after only six and ten weeks. I couldn't physically carry on with them. I felt demoralized, isolated and scared of what was going to happen to me next, but I hadn't lost my vision, nor my determination, nor my sense of humor. I'd hang in there for all I was worth and fight for what I wanted. I was just a little tired.

CHAPTER NINETEEN

What lies ahead

Four Christmases had come and gone in France. I had an apartment and a car. I was still working at the university but now I was teaching English to French students.

I'd resigned from my position at the research center after enduring three years of torment and harassment from The Professor. Perhaps he thought that giving me an opportunity to come to France gave him the right to treat me like a battered dog; perhaps he thought that my being completely dependent on him for my legal existence in France gave him license to demean, humiliate, put me down, and threaten to throw and break mugs at my feet, throw temper tantrums at everyone and conduct other scandalous and unprofessional behavior.

"You're an idiot," he said to me, one day, in front of my colleagues ... "Take what I say seriously... Take this job seriously... Get serious ... I'll renew your contract on the condition you don't do anything of a communications nature with partners ... I'm not a recruitment agency ... Go work in a pub in London."

This person had been protected from the consequences of his worst excesses. For three years I received no effective help from anyone I confided in, and I confided rarely as it was just too dangerous to make a fuss; my existence in France depended on my boss renewing my contract.

The anxiety was enormous and affected my health. Close colleagues felt uncomfortable having someone in their room being dished out so much stress, I think they wished I wasn't there as an illustration of what everyone feared. Well, at least they weren't being harassed and abused to the extent I was. I was the most vulnerable and so the easiest target, though not the first.

There are times one must endure and hope to survive for something better. Nothing lasts, everything changes eventually, I told myself, but it was so hard to work in an environment where everyone was fearful because an unkempt, middle aged man was screaming at someone. My abilities were scarcely used and definitely not appreciated. The dread of seeing his car in the driveway! The dread of being alone in the office when he came in. I once asked why he treated me so badly.

He allowed a smirk to play around the corners of his mouth and said, "Because I enjoy it."

I plucked up courage and tried to contact the medical service for personnel at the university. They took two weeks to reply, then they gave me an appointment sometime later. Just before the day of the appointment they cancelled it. Eventually they came back and arranged another appointment, but again they cancelled it just before the visit. After that it took them over a month to get back to me so I gave up after three months of trying to talk to a service that was supposed to be there for the good of employees. I had no confidence in them, and worried about things being on my record and being held against me.

One of my colleagues must have said something to The Professor because he became more strategic in his harassment. He switched to getting me alone where he had no witnesses.

One day he stood at my desk, knowing no-one else was around, and harangued me, performed character assassinations on me, and complained about my colleagues for an incredible five hours non-stop. He did the same thing for nine hours on my last flight to the US. On my return from that trip; a week trapped with him, I was found by colleagues, vomiting into the toilet at the research center. I pretended I must have picked up some sort of bug. Jean-François had to come and take me home.

The Professor, who always thought rules never applied to him, suddenly started doing performance appraisals. Each employee was entitled to have a colleague present but it seemed I alone wasn't. At the last moment mine were told to leave the room. I was left with no emotional support at all, just because he could.

Nowhere and no one felt safe for me. In desperation I took a risk and explained the situation to the human resources department.

"That research lab is the only one to have so many problems," he said. "You're not to repeat anything of this conversation and to tell no one you were at this meeting."

No help arrived for me and the situation did not improve.

Earlier in the year there had been a mass defection from the research center. Ten teaching staff decided they had had enough. They all had other jobs at the university and all were EU citizens, so they were in a much better situation. My efforts to find another job had been in operation for nearly three years. In the previous six months I'd sent out sixty job applications in France to no avail, even when I had assistance to write letters in French. The problem was my nationality, age, my Anglo-Saxon career full of changes, and I wasn't bilingual. There were three million people unemployed in France. Naturally French, then European Union citizens, always took priority, and I was blocked from teaching in French schools because I wasn't French and hasn't sat a competitive exam (in French) to teach English.

My closest colleague couldn't stand seeing what was happening to me anymore, especially as my contract wasn't to be renewed past February the next year due to politics (undoubtedly) and lack of money (only slightly true). She spoke to someone very senior. A miracle occurred. After trying once again to find a job elsewhere, I was eventually given the opportunity I needed to escape.

I was so grateful and relieved I could end the torment and stay in France a bit longer, but I discovered the salary for the new position was totally insufficient to live on as a single person. My rent was half my take home pay and taxes still had to come out of the rest. I lived simply but I'd had to borrow money to buy furniture and bedding last year when I finally escaped from living in the dark, dank studio I rented from The Professor. I would have to find money from somewhere else just to eat.

The denouement wasn't straight forward. After I resigned in the middle of the usual long French summer holidays The Professor asked if I would do a short job for him, helping a foreign student to settle into her semester at the university. Being the holidays, there was no opportunity to work on a smooth handover. I'd been responsible, in practical terms, for keeping that teaching partnership operating. I figured I could survive him a few more days in order to help out in a really difficult situation, where there would otherwise be no transition.

The project had been one where I felt I'd made a positive difference in my job, a project that was essentially mine, and where others with whom I came into contact did seem to appreciate me. I didn't want the project falling apart for the partner organization that had paid a lot of money to the university for the program. I decided to help a partner organization, keep some reputation for the university, and earn some pocket money, which I desperately needed, to pay forthcoming taxes. It was a naïve decision.

It was just as well I did help out as the university welcome didn't provide correct and basic services for an Anglophone international student on an exchange program, right when she needed it. She was twice in tears because of unfeeling staff behavior and lack of basic facilities. I had to take her home with me for two days, feed her, let her shower, supply Internet to contact her parents, even let her sleep with me in my bed, but in the end I was told by the university that I wouldn't be paid for the sixty hours I'd worked. They told me my boss had hired me illegally, that since I already had a new 'full-time' contract I couldn't have a second job.

Of course, The Professor would have known about that, as director of a university research center. He'd worked in France more than twenty years. A close colleague told me she had known I wouldn't get paid, but had said nothing to me during the three weeks while I worked, as it wasn't her place to say something. Several of my colleagues would have known I'd never be paid. Being a foreigner I had no idea what rules were in play. The Professor, standing in the corridor at work, insisted he'd find a way to pay me what I was owed, and the expenses I incurred, eventually, but he lied; it was just a piece of cinema for him. Just when I thought the bad times were behind me the shadow had followed me. Well, now I really was finished there. I left behind a bunch of colleagues, many of them very pleasant (excluding a small number in senior positions who knew what was going on for years and did nothing to protect me or others who had suffered). That's the way of it; workplace bullying makes everyone put their heads in the sand and feel relieved that at least it's not them in the firing line.

Almost no one seemed to care about my problems or my leaving. There were no farewell drinks such as everyone else leaving enjoyed; I simply faded away as if I never existed. When I made enquiries months later about the payment, The Professor told me to talk to his assistant. Michelle never responded to any of my requests for clarification. Three years as her colleague meant nothing.

An 'anonymous person' clearly au fait with the exact research center (even identifying it) that I had worked for left a message on my blog, obviously designed to intimidate me:

> *Have you read your teaching contract? Putting any student info in the public domain (which your blog is) is illegal. You are already set up for a defamation filing given your allégations of mistreatment re: *****. For all your high drama woes and complaining, not to mention ingrained narcissism ... Legal advice? In short, it's going to cost a lot to battle likely deportation.*

I was frightened because I didn't want to be accused of anything, even falsely, which might put my future citizenship at risk. Jean-François was angry and said he'd help me fight this cowardly person, if necessary. We both knew who it was. It was the same person who had written nasty, spiteful comments via my book website, months earlier; an inveterate harasser. Meanwhile I was doing my best to be the most effective English teacher, despite the conditions. This university was in a dilapidated state. My classrooms didn't have internet access, most had no facilities to watch a video, no effective blackout curtains which functioned, usually just a blackboard and a stub of chalk. The buildings were run-down; the toilets were filthy and often without toilet paper or functioning hand driers. Much of the time there was no service for photocopying material for students to use because management couldn't afford paper. I spent food money on paper and ink cartridges just for the privilege of having my job.

The university was in serious debt and needed an emergency bailout from the government, just to survive a bit longer; to pay staff and keep the doors open. This situation hadn't been helped by past government policies but the real killer, I was told, had been the total mismanagement and funneling of funds into the private sector by a previous president. Protest meetings were held by staff and students. The current president started an online petition to save the university.

None of this helped me feel safe in my situation. I had a one-year contract which could be renewed only once. Would the university be able to renew it? I was getting very good feedback and reviews about my teaching from my students but that counted for nothing with the administration. In France I was simply a contractor who was hired, then disposed of whether I was terrific or not.

I continued to send out speculative letters to Kiwi companies in Europe, even a kiwi-friendly British environmentalist running a foundation. I'd sent out hundreds of job applications but nothing had ever gone so far as an interview stage. I joined

304 · WHAT LIES AHEAD

expatriate groups in Paris but nothing I did helped me find employment. I offered to volunteer my services to my local town, but despite an initial enthusiastic reception by the Mayor my offer went nowhere

"Doesn't surprise me," said Jean-François. "You might stir things up."

"I could make a positive difference," I insisted. "I could translate their website, produce tourist materials in English, run tours in English for tourists, set up an orientation program for non-French new residents. Other towns provide that."

"Obviously they don't think they need it," he said.

Gloomily I resolved to pay a personal visit to the *Maire* in case my email had gone astray. The mayor said she was still interested but that she wouldn't launch anything with the local elections taking place in a couple of months, I'd need to wait. Happily, in the meantime, she invited me to the Annual General Meeting of the *Association d'Ellernon Patrimoine et Alentours* and introduced me as someone interested in helping out with English language materials for this heritage group. I was grateful to have her support, and keen to meet new people and contribute to my town.

I was lucky to still have Jean-François in my life, I reminded myself, but it wasn't all plain sailing. May Day is normally a day when people remind each other how much their relationship matters but last year JF had used the day to dump me.

"Got any plans for next weekend? What time should I arrive?" I asked

He looked down and shifted in his seat. His head shot defiantly up, but he still didn't look at me.

"Actually, I need time to think next weekend. On my own."

"Time to think about what?" I replied.

"I don't think I want to continue with this. I want someone I can have sex with whenever I want, as often as I want and however I want. You have problems. Sex is limited to once or twice a weekend. It's not what I want and need, I'm sorry."

The fabric of the universe seemed to split under me, and for the next few hours I was in a tragic state. There had been no warning that he didn't want me as his girlfriend any more. Didn't all my other qualities count for much?

"Look, you can phone me if you need help with anything, I'm still here. There's still hope but I can't promise, and I won't say I won't look for someone else in the meantime. I won't lie about that."

"I don't want a handyman, a person to solve problems, a person I only speak to on the phone. I want to share feelings, experiences, my life," I tearily replied.

He was moved by my reaction, my broken heart. In fact, for the next few hours he showed me more tenderness than I had seen before from him, as I cried and we discussed. I described, he listened and tried to soften the blow.

He held me and wiped my tears and found it hard to leave me, following me home in his car to make sure I got there safely, coming up to my apartment and giving me a hug.

"I think you've probably shown me the deepest love of any woman I've known. I do have a lot of feelings for you or we wouldn't still be together this long," he said. "You never know."

"You really are a fool to let me go," I said, as I prepared to shut my apartment door on yet another relationship.

"Maybe I am," he replied, then headed out of the building.

He rang me every day to see if I was okay. The following weekend he took me for a drive in the country to give me a break from my apartment but it was hugely sad for me to then go back home, alone at the end of the day. I told myself I had not found what I was looking for in France.

Vaux de Cernay, Vallée de Chevreuse

Gradually he allowed me back into his life as before. He found excuses to see me. He insisted on taking me shopping to buy me a pair of jeans, and eventually things were back as they were, with me spending weekends at his place but my heart had learnt something it couldn't forget, He never apologized or explained why he had changed his mind and wanted me back. When I pointed out one day that I didn't know where I stood anymore he looked very uncomfortable and shook his head dismissively.

"It doesn't matter, that's all done."

"Well, it mattered to me, I was devastated you know."

"Yes I know," he replied.

He wouldn't explain. Instead he opened up his tender side to me and I learnt to forgive.

He's a truly lovely man who tries to do many things to please and help me but he'd rather not change our arrangements. He doesn't spend time with me at my home. He has stayed overnight only two nights at my place in more than three years. That's how he wants things to be, preferring that I stay at his place. He has his 'bubble' as he calls it. I come into this bubble of the life he likes, where he potters around doing handyman things and chopping down trees with his chainsaws, but that bubble is not mine. His independent life is perfect for him as it is, he has his life just as he wants it, and I can understand that. He's nearly ten years older than me and I often wonder how people our age can really meld two separate lives together.

This year I've arranged to see my daughter. Refinancing the mortgage, yet again, on my old home in Auckland freed up a few euros to buy her flight tickets and arrange a little trip for the two of us, to finally explore the south of France together for a week. I'm going to fulfil that promise I made to the two of us so many years ago. We won't have the dreamed of Ferrari but we'll be travelling along the Cote d'Azur and the Italian Riviera by train and bus with the wind in our hair and our sunglasses strapped on. It will be the first decent holiday we'll have ever spent together. We'll make lifetime memories and books of photographs to keep.

I don't know if I will survive in France long enough to apply to be naturalized or even if the French government will agree to it. Even if they do and I achieve my dream there will be no livable old-age pension for me one day. It's a very disturbing prospect and I hadn't thought about that in my decision to change countries. Retirement is becoming a serious concern for expats who live in several countries throughout their careers. I decided to seek advice from a bilingual immigration and work lawyer in Paris, to see what my options for staying in France were but all he could tell me was that I'm free to take any salaried job I can get that pays one and a half times the minimum wage. So far, all my efforts to find work, the hundreds of hours spent in applying for jobs, filling in online forms since November 2010, when I realized the awfulness of the job situation I found myself in, had resulted in a big fat zero. I felt somewhat gloomy about my prospects.

The state of things at work being what they were, I didn't know if I could keep my apartment much longer. I'd been told that my bankrupt employer would be cutting staff (teaching staff) by twenty percent. An administrator told me I should look for something else now, in case of the worst. I needed a miracle.

One arrived, saying my contract would be renewed for the final year. I'm grateful that the university has done that for me and other contracted staff at risk. That sort of contract will not be available to me ever again, anywhere in France. There'll be yet another unpleasant *titre de séjour* process to go through this year. It looks as if Jean-François and I can stay together and enjoy each other's company, and I can keep my connection with France a little longer, but there's no certainty past the next year.

Jean-François tries to help out by letting me take home left-over food and items from his fridge, to help my budget. Sometimes he pays for a hairdresser to cover my grey hairs with a warm reddish-brown, or buys me some clothes, because he knows I can't do it for myself. I know he cares about me, I know he'd be there in an emergency, to help me survive. Things between us are probably closer than ever.

"If I was in your situation, I'd be pretty anxious, too," he told me. "But, believe me when I say, I won't let you fall. I'm here. These past three years mean something."

It's comforting, and we're good together, but I need some security and I want the opportunity to create my own environment; to buy a little house, have a cat, create a garden and decorate my home before I'm too old to do it. It isn't looking likely right now. Jean-François says I will have to be realistic and accept I cannot have the life I wanted in France but I still keep dreaming.

Having said that, there's something special and vulnerable inside his self-sufficiency, and lately he's been letting me see it.

As I arrived at his home recently, I just burst out laughing. He had made a sign on a pole that said Kiwi's Land. It was planted in an empty piece of land near his house. I thought it was pretty romantic in its way, because despite for years telling me he would never have a conventional garden (bare earth), and especially not a vegie garden (too much work and too risky if a fox pissed on the vegies), he had decided that one day, after he'd had the land tidied and levelled, I could have some of it for myself. I'd be able to choose all my favorite flowers and vegetables. I could have a real garden at his place one day, and if I became unemployed I could live with him until I could find a solution to my residency issues, if I could find a permanent salaried job somewhere; the holy grail.

I was touched by this, as he's such an independent person (I am too). It's a very sweet gesture with a message that he sees me in his life in the future. I'm doing all I can not to wreck his independence or mine (at our age it's rather important to both of us).

As I drive through the French countryside or wander the streets of my town I look around and say to myself, "If the French administration hassles and my employment and retirement worries disappeared, I could be very content in this fascinating country".

I've found peace in my soul for the first time in my life. It's linked to being in France, but my heart will break if I have to leave, and my head will always ask the question; was it worth it? Has my persistence simply been a case of stubborn recklessness? There are still so many obstacles to achieving my goal and the risks for my future are serious. I can gain no perspective by trying to imagine the future. Adventures are, I suppose, by their nature, dangerous.

I'm still searching for my place in the world and I'm ready to take on whatever opportunities it offers. Perhaps it's ahead in the road still to come, a bitter-sweet journey toward hope again.

THE END

ABOUT THE AUTHOR

Frances Lawson is a direct descendent of the Libeau family, one of the original French families who left Rochefort, France in 1840 to found a colony in Akaroa, New Zealand. She remains passionate about her French origins and would like to become a French citizen.

A past contributor to *New Zealand Geographic* she is author of the popular blog *To the Ends of the Earth*. When she's not writing she's teaching English, taking photographs, gardening or adding to her bucket list.

htttp://www.followmyheart.co

Author photograph courtesy of Jean-François

ABOUT NEW ZEALAND
Aotearoa

New Zealand is a country located in the Southwestern Pacific Ocean. It consists of two main land masses and numerous smaller islands. During its long isolation of 80 million years, it has developed unique and intriguing flora and fauna.

Before the arrival of the first people in 1250–1300 AD, The Polynesian Maori, it was a land of forests filled with birdsong. The only mammal being a thumb-sized bat. The arrival of humans spelt the beginning of the extinctions of many amazing animals, and the introduction of more mundane ones.

Europeans arrived and accelerated the process. New Zealand became a British colony in 1840 via the Treaty of Waitangi and became self-governing in 1856. New Zealanders, who refer to themselves as kiwis (in honor of the flightless nocturnal bird that is the emblem of the country), fought in both World Wars and many others since. The country is a member of the British Commonwealth, and as such the head of state is Queen Elizabeth II, whose representative in NZ is the Governor General. It has a parliament with elected representatives headed by the Prime Minister.

The largest city is Auckland in the North Island, considered the economic engine of the country. The second largest city is Christchurch, known as the Garden City, in the South Island. Wellington, located at the bottom of the North Island, is the political capital.

New Zealand is very multicultural with its three official languages being English, Maori and sign language. Its people are known for their innovation, adaptability and willingness to solve their own problems. They enjoy an indoor-outdoor life with an agreeable climate and spectacular natural beauty.

Kiwis are fiercely independent, notably in their decision to become a nuclear-free country in 1985. Women gained the right to vote there in 1893, and a well-organized social welfare system was in place by the 1930s.

There are 4.5 million inhabitants. Though a small nation, it punches above its weight in sport, science, education, literature and the film industry, and the production of agricultural products. The list of its world-renowned high achievers is remarkable.

The economy is modern and market-driven, having gone through several restructurings. Seventy-five percent of energy sources are renewables. Agriculture, tourism and the film industry are important to New Zealand but there are also a number of very successful technology companies too.

So what are you waiting for ... come and visit.

http://www.newzealand.com

Printed in Great Britain
by Amazon